Marriage, Divorce and Remarriage

MW01224426

Hong Kong University Press thanks Xu Bing for writing the Press's name in his Square Word Calligraphy for the covers of its books. For further information, see p. iv.

The contributors to this volume are:

Cecilia Lai-Wan CHAN

Grace Mi-Har CHAN

Anita Yuk-Lin FOK

Shirley Suet-Lin HUNG

Winnie Wai-Ming KUNG

Roger Wai-Hong KWAN

LAM Chiu Wan

LAM Wai Man

Natalie Kin-Wai LAW

Timothy Yuk-Ki LEUNG

Laurene Lai-Ping MAN

Monica Lai-Tuen NG

Lianne Yau-Yee TAI

Julia Lai Po-Wah TAO

WONG Lai-Cheung

Ivan Yau-Tat YU

YEUNG Ka-Ching

Katherine Pui-Ha YOUNG

Marriage, Divorce and Remarriage

Professional Practice in the Hong Kong Cultural Context

Edited by

Katherine P.H. Young and Anita Y.L. Fok

香港大學出版社
HONG KONG UNIVERSITY PRESS

Hong Kong University Press
14/F Hing Wai Centre
7 Tin Wan Praya Road
Aberdeen
Hong Kong

ISBN 962 209 741 3

British Library Cataloguing-in-Publication Data

Secure On-line Ordering
http://www.hkupress.org

Printed and bound by Liang Yu Printing Factory Limited, Hong Kong, China.

Hong Kong University Press is honoured that Xu Bing, whose art
explores the complex themes of language across cultures, has
written the Press's name in his Square Word Calligraphy. This signals
our commitment to cross-cultural thinking and the distinctive
nature of our English-language books published in China.

"At first glance, Square Word Calligraphy appears to be nothing
more unusual than Chinese characters, but in fact it is a new way
of rendering English words in the format of a square so they
resemble Chinese characters. Chinese viewers expect to be able to
read Square Word Calligraphy but cannot. Western viewers,
however are surprised to find they can read it. Delight erupts when
meaning is unexpectedly revealed."

— Britta Erickson, *The Art of Xu Bing*

Contents

Foreword

The impact of globalisation in recent years, and its consequent increases in population and labour mobility, longer working hours, unstable employment patterns and diversified lifestyles, has posed formidable challenges to the stability and solidarity of family life in Hong Kong. In this process, we have seen traditional family values steadily and rapidly undermined by seemingly irreversible trends of rising divorces rates, family violence and declining marriage rates and fertility. Family problems have become distressingly familiar, but policy and professional intervention to support families can vary significantly from country to country, mainly due to the differences in cultural traditions and the socio-economic situation. Over the last decade, there has been an increasing recognition of the importance of culturally sensitive and evidence-based family social work practice. At the same time, there has been a growing concern to support marriages and minimise the social costs of divorce.

Katherine Young is known for her work on the theory, practice and research of family social work. Even after retirement, she has remained ardently committed to championing the development of evidence-based and culturally sensitive family social work practice in Hong Kong. This was clearly evident at the Symposium on Chinese Culture and Social Work Practice organised by the Department of Social Work and Social Administration at the University of Hong Kong. At the Symposium,

Mrs Young and a number of prominent academics, supervisors and practitioners in the field made a series of presentations focusing on innovations in family intervention and clinical practice. Now, with Anita Fok, she has edited a small collection of clinical and research work reflecting current professional practice and concerns of the new millennium in Hong Kong, and published them in this book. The articles clearly show that family issues have become more complex. The question of how social workers can strengthen families and marriages, and empower families to face a changing environment, has become a matter of foremost concern. With rising divorce rates, Hong Kong is inevitably moving towards a "divorce culture", in which "marriage is an option, marriage is contingent on the partners meeting each other's needs, and divorce is a gateway to a new life". Yet marriage and happy family life is still considered the foremost "social resource to be prized and protected". Based on a systemic perspective, the contributors acknowledge and respect the family's strengths, culture and ability to make decisions that are appropriate for the family. Facing a wide array of dilemmas and tensions involved in family intervention, practitioners have to review their expectations and aspirations regarding how to strengthen or reinstate a marriage culture in Hong Kong. As advocated by the editors, therapeutic intervention is seen as a value-guided process of exploring and constructing meanings for life experiences. Practitioners should have a clear perception of their own values and beliefs, so that they can avoid the danger of imposing their views and meanings on their clients during the intervention process. Through this "discovery" process of searching for meaning, people can achieve personal growth and rebuild the self.

It is clear that this publication will stimulate further dialogue and reflection in the field, so that a more consolidated practice in marital work can emerge. I am convinced that this book will be a milestone in knowledge-building in the field of family practice in Hong Kong and Chinese society. Indeed, this book will become a benchmark reference work for the further exploration into the concepts, meanings and practice of marriage counselling and divorce mediation. More importantly, the views and findings can re-examine our beliefs, aspirations and culture of marriage and family in Hong Kong as well as in other Chinese communities.

Joe Leung
Head
Department of Social Work and Social Administration
The University of Hong Kong
September 2004

Preface

The idea for this book emerged from the Symposium on Chinese Culture and Social Work Practice held at the University of Hong Kong. During the Symposium, it became clear that a great deal of innovative clinical work and interesting small research studies were being carried out, which could be collected and shared, to arouse further questioning and enquiry. Our hope was to create a debate among practising professionals working in marriage counselling and divorce mediation, and with students in training who could be stimulated to find out more.

Many areas of concentration were proposed. It was eventually decided that this publication should focus on marriage, divorce and remarriage. It seems likely that, in the years to come, adult fulfillment is likely to be found in varying ways: for some through marriage, some through divorce, some through remarriage, and some through the single state. Each of these has its own potentials, tensions, and prospects for growth and development; each offers different though viable lifestyles through which people can develop in adulthood.

Encouraging Dialogue and Debate

While we hope that this collection will create a dialogue over clinical practice in marital work, it is also an attempt to encourage debate on expectations and attitudes towards marriage. Can we, as citizens living in Hong Kong, contribute in a small way to shaping the future aspirations of marriage in our community? In Great Britain, a Department of Marriage and Relationship Support was inaugurated in 1999 to help and support couples to enable them to enter and maintain stable long-term relationships. From the legal perspective, there was a move for the repeal of part of the *Family Law Act 1996*, because it was felt that it did not meet government objectives of saving marriages or helping divorcing couples to resolve problems with a minimum of acrimony (www.hmso.gov.uk/ acts/acts1996 and www.dca.gov.uk/). In the United States, a Marriage Movement has been initiated to strengthen marriage. This is a grassroots movement of citizens coming together "to help more men and women achieve a caring collaborative and committed bond, rooted in equal regard between spouses". Their goal is to renew a marriage culture in the United States (www.marriagemovement.org, Institute for American Values 2000).

Do we have a marriage culture in Hong Kong? Hackstaff (1999) defines marriage culture as a cluster of beliefs, symbols and practices that reinforce marriage and deter divorce. The key beliefs of a marriage culture are that marriage is given, marriage is forever, and divorce is the last resort; whereas, in a divorce culture, the beliefs are that marriage is an option, marriage is contingent on the partners meeting each other's needs, and divorce is a gateway to a new life. Though this way of thinking polarizes the discussion, it serves to highlight the dichotomies that confront us. Analysts of marriage and divorce cultures in America (Hackstaff 1999; Whitehead 1997) consider that some parts of the therapeutic community in the United States have fortified the belief that divorce provides opportunities for freedom and new beginnings, as some of the propositions they present are very attractive. They use a self-oriented vocabulary of free choice, self-expression and individual rights popularized by the human potential movement. Bellah *et al.* started a lively debate when they published their book *Habits of the Heart* (1996, 77) in which they stated that, when individualism is upheld as an end in itself, the criteria for decisions change as "utility" replaces "duty", self-expression unseats responsibility, and "being good" becomes "feeling good".

On the other hand , working on a marriage is demanding in the way it exposes our vulnerabilities, requires us to call on inner resources and skills we are not sure we have, with our efforts leading to uncertain outcomes. When inevitable tensions and conflicts arise in the course of daily life, couples need to be sustained by their emotional bonds and relational ethics attuned to the needs of each other, with values and beliefs emphasizing commitment, mutuality and interdependency derived through close and continuing relationships. Sometimes, personal idiosyncrasies and personal needs, as well as fluctuating relational dynamics, make this marital work even more difficult. A cultural climate that values family living can bolster and offer that extra support to work through such pressures. There is also a need to address gender differences in expectations, attitudes and behaviour that influence close relationships. That men's and women's experiences in marriage and in relationships are not similar is well documented, and these experiences are further affected by changing social, economic, educational and political trends within each society. Marriage partners, apart from their own propensities and personal perspectives, have also to take account of other stakeholders, the young and the old.

In her in-depth review of divorce in the United States, Barbara Whitehead debated the cost of marriage and the cost of divorce, and came to the conclusion that "marriage is a social resource to be prized and protected" (Whitehead 1997, 191). This conclusion, coming from a country that has possibly been the most adventurous in experimentation in marriage and intimate relationships, is one we could well ponder as we explore our own position.

Marriage in Hong Kong

In a study on Contemporary Hong Kong Families in Transition commissioned by the Hong Kong Women's Foundation, the section on marital satisfaction reported that, of the 422 husbands and wives who responded, 68.2% considered their marriages to be satisfactory to very satisfactory, 24.2% fairly satisfactory, and 7.6% unsatisfactory. As regards marital stability, 4.5% frequently considered divorce (Law *et al.*, 1995). Although it could be that the people who responded to the study were those who found family and married life rewarding, such statistics seem to indicate that, at present, a marriage culture rather than a divorce culture is subscribed to by couples in Hong Kong.

Upholding a Marriage Culture in Hong Kong?

It could well be asked whether this is an appropriate time to review our attitudes, expectations, aspirations, practices and policies regarding marriage in Hong Kong, or to examine what we would like the future trends to move towards. In those countries where large numbers of marriages end in divorce, organizations such as the Marriage and Relationship Support Department in Great Britain and the Marriage Movement in the United States are, in a way, proactive thrusts to reinstate a marriage culture. It has also been suggested that a divorce culture could be a transitory phase to enable greater equality and collaboration to emerge in marriage (Cancian 1987, 201). At a more pessimistic level, Pinsof (2002), referring to the fifty-five percent of marriages in America ending in divorce in 1985, draws attention to the scenario that, in Western civilization, divorce has replaced death as the most common end to marriage. Instead of following this trend, can we in Hong Kong avoid entering this phase altogether, and rather strive to maintain the marriage culture we still possess?

Over the last few generations, we have moved a long way from the traditional patriarchal marriage to the conjugal marriage, subscribed to by many in contemporary Hong Kong. Legal changes have reaffirmed and strengthened these social changes. The very definition of the institution of the Chinese marriage has changed for the better. Love and support are now upheld as inherent components in marriage, which recognizes the emotional bond of the marital pair. There is now greater tolerance of diversity in family forms and an increasing acceptance of variations in the nature of the marital relationship, and a broader acceptance that marriage can be many things to many people. These improvements are, however, double-edged. When affection fades or ceases to exist, the relationship becomes vulnerable. With many different family structures and partnership arrangements, the lives of the children become more uncertain. Conventional marriage, at least, offers some sort of model to work towards or against. Do we still wish to uphold a marriage culture built on affection, sacrifice and kinship bonds? Can we shape our family system with its emphasis on continuity and commitment, built on reciprocity and responsibility, so that it continues to contribute to stability and security while also flexibly tuning in to the changing demands of contemporary living?

As society changes, marriage will change. Our concerns would be to tune into this process of change and to influence the pace and the direction of change. By raising debate, we join other movements — the feminist movement, the marriage movement, the gay movement — to add our voice in civic discourse of the way forward in the new millennium.

Katherine P.H. Young and Anita Y.L. Fok

References

Bellah R.N., Madsen R., Sullivan W.M., Swidler A., Tipton S.M. (1996). *Habits of the heart: Individualism and commitment in American life.* Berkley: University of California Press.

Cancian F. (1987). *Love in America: Gender and self-development.* Cambridge: Cambridge University Press.

Hackstaff K.B. (1999). *Marriage in a divorce culture.* Philadelphia, PA: Temple University Press.

Law C.K., Chan L.W.C., Young K., Ko L.P.C., Wong Y.C., Mehrani T., Cheng K.C., Li W.L. (1995). *Contemporary Hong Kong families in transition.* Hong Kong Women's Foundation and Department of Social Work and Social Administration, University of Hong Kong, Monograph Series No. 21.

Pinsof W.M. (2002). The death of "Till death us do part": The transformation of pair bonding in the 20th century. *Family Process.* Vol. 41(2) summer, 135–57.

Whitehead B.D. (1997). *The divorce culture.* New York: Alfred A.Knopf.

Acknowledgements

This publication would not have been possible without the impetus provided by the Symposium on Chinese Culture and Social Work Practice organized by the Department of Social Work and Social Administration at the University of Hong Kong in November 2001. The idea of reflection at the beginning of a millennium and a sharing of experiences among front-line social workers came from the creative mind of Cecilia Chan. The following presenters and chairpersons gave their expertise and time most liberally: Cecilia L.W. Chan, Edward K.L. Chan, Amy Y. M. Chow, Anita Y.L. Fok, Fung Pak Yan, Cecilia S.F. Kwan, Eliza Y.W. Lam, Joe C.B. Leung, Justina Leung, Timothy Y.K. Leung, Anna Mak, Laurene L.P. Man, Sandra K.M. Tsang, Shirley K.Y. Tsang, Susan S.Y. So, and Yeung Ka Ching, Their participation ensured that the discussion and debate was enjoyable and memorable for so many of us.

In the aftermath of the Symposium, through networking we reached out to colleagues practising and researching in the field of marital work, who have joined together to produce this publication. The process of collecting and analysing clinical and research material, refining and revising the manuscript has been long and arduous, although this also offered a delightful opportunity for reconnection and for rethinking issues of deep concern to many of us, even though mainly through email exchanges. We thank the contributors for their flexibility and openness to suggestions, and their gracious response in making amendments and additions to their chapters.

Publication of a multi-authored collection is a collaborative endeavour between the authors, the editors, and the publisher. We thank Dennis Cheung, Managing Editor of Hong Kong University Press, for his meticulous care in guiding us through each step of the publication process and for his encouragement and support.

It is, however, the couples and the clients, in or out of marriage, who by sharing their experiences and dilemmas give meaning to what goes on in intimate relationships. We are deeply indebted to them for their generosity in sharing their personal stories. By adding their voices they immeasurably enrich any debate on the nature and trends of marriage in our society.

Contributors

Chan, Cecilia Lai-Wan — Professor, Department of Social Work & Social Administration; Director, Center for Behavioral Health, University of Hong Kong

Chan, Grace Mi-Har — Social Work Supervisor, Family Service, Caritas, Hong Kong

Fok, Anita Yuk-Lin — Honorary Assistant Professor, Department of Social Work and Social Administration, University of Hong Kong; Family & Marital Therapist, Clinical Supervisor, City Oasis Counselling Center

Hung, Shirley Suet-Lin — Head, Department of Social Sciences, Caritas Francis Hsu College

Kung, Winnie Wai-Ming — Associate Professor, Graduate School of Social Services, Fordham University, New York

Kwan, Roger Wai-Hong — Lecturer in Social Work, Division of Social Studies, City University of Hong Kong.

Lam Chiu Wan — Lecturer, Department of Social Work & Social Administration, University of Hong Kong

Lam Wai Man — Assistant Professor, Department of Social Sciences, University of Macau

Law, Natalie Kin-Wai — Counsellor in Private Practice, Hong Kong

Leung, Timothy Yuk-Ki — Professional Consultant, Department of Social Work, Chinese University of Hong Kong

Man, Laurene Lai-Ping — Family Therapist, Laurene Man Counselling Service, 904 Printing House, 6 Duddell Street, Hong Kong

Ng, Monica Lai-Tuen — Heep Hong Society, Hong Kong

Tai, Lianne Yau-Yee — Field Instructor, Department of Social Work & Social Administration, University of Hong Kong

Tao, Julia Lai Po-Wah — Associate Professor, Department of Public and Social Administration; Director of Governance in Asian Research Center, City University of Hong Kong

Wong Lai-Cheung, Supervisor, Chai Wan Baptist Church Social Service, Hong Kong

Yu, Ivan Yau-Tat — Social Worker in Youth Service, Hong Kong Family Welfare Society

Yeung Ka-Ching — Assistant Professor, Department of Social Work & Social Administration, University of Hong Kong

Young, Katherine Pui-Ha — Honorary Associate Professor, Department of Social Work and Social Administration, University of Hong Kong

1

Rethinking Marriage

KATHERINE P.H. YOUNG

Social Changes and Marital Changes

Social scientists analyzing marriage and inequality in Chinese society point out that, from the classical period on, continuities in marriage customs and practices have been remarkable (Ocko 1991). In China, there were few significant changes in marital conventions until the *Marriage Law of the People's Republic of China of 1950*. It declared marriage to be based on free choice, monogamy and equal rights; prohibited bigamy, concubines, child betrothal, interference with the remarriage of widows; and included provisions for divorce (Meijer 1971). Hong Kong followed with the *Marriage Reform Ordinance* in 1971, restricting marriage to one husband and one wife, and formally abolishing the practice of concubinage. In 1972, no-fault divorce was instituted. After centuries of little change, the last few decades have been remarkable for the tremendous changes in expectations, attitudes, and the very ideology of marriage.

It could be said that, during these years, the ideal of the companionate marriage was established as the norm in Hong Kong. The promulgation of the *Marriage Law of the People's Republic of China of 1950* followed by the Hong Kong *Marriage Reform Ordinance* in 1971 provided a legal framework that encouraged the transition from the traditional to the conjugal marriage. At the same time, the modern industrialization of Hong Kong and its accompanying lifestyle contributed to the development of conjugalism (Wong Fai Ming 1972). Consequently, by the 1990s, studies on young people's attitudes to marriage reflected expectations of the sharing of love, care, mutual help, support, encouragement and companionship in intimate relationships (Yeung and Kwong 1998).

Yet, Hong Kong's demographic trends from the 1980s reflect greater marital and family instability, mounting divorce rates and increasing numbers of single-parent families, marriage at a later age, and later child bearing. These cannot be ascribed merely to higher expectations in marriage. The last few decades were a period of accelerated socio-economic-political change, policies such as equal opportunities in education and employment affecting not only our social structures but also leading to changes in the social expectations and position of women. At the same time, changes in the perception of marriage occurring in Western societies have been felt in our society. Alternative lifestyles have been increasingly accepted, based on short-term, performance-based and contingency commitments. In addition, the opening up of China during these years, and the increased communication with the Mainland, not only at the commercial but also at the personal levels, has introduced further ambiguities into the marital equation. It would be true to say that anyone involved in marital work in present-day Hong Kong is likely to be involved in extraordinary situations which variously could involve an intermix of traditional and modern concepts and of imported ideas and indigenous attitudes. As we begin the new millennium, these trends call for a review of our perceptions of marriage and its place in society, and a reassessment of the ability of marriage and the family bond to serve as the relational context of adult living.

Common Philosophical and Theoretical Perspectives

The articles in this collection offer the means to rethink marriage, through examining the various processes by which husbands and wives cope with the stresses and strains and changing life circumstances that affect their relationships yet find the strength to work through the trauma and pain of these difficult experiences.

For a small collection, the topics cover a wide range. As standardized guidelines for all to follow could be inhibiting, it was left to each author to develop the discussion in a manner most appropriate to his or her experience and thinking. Although there was no prior agreement on a common approach in presentation or in the theoretical and philosophic stance to be adopted, it should be noted that four common trends run through and link the clinical and research chapters. First, the discussions reflect a conceptual stance that we live in interaction within a number of systems. Second, we construct meanings of what happens in our lives from our personal experiences, shaped by beliefs and values that underpin our cultural legacy. Third, counselling or therapy is a process of exploration of meaning, of a search for alternatives and new meanings to determine what is important and significant to each of us. Fourth, self-realization and self-growth come from meaningful relationships with others.

Potential for Therapeutic Work from Systemic and Cultural Perspectives

The authors share a systemic perspective, that human beings are part of many systems, from biological to family to societal systems, which reciprocally affect each other, so that what happens in one system has implications for the others. The chapters also reflect and share the perspective that human beings make meaning of what happens to them. The meaning they make of these experiences is derived from the cultural heritage developed from the family and societal context in which they live. Cultural beliefs and values determine how we define our experiences. This systemic and culturally assigned stance offers both assessment and therapeutic possibilities. It allows the counsellor/therapist, together with the client/couple, to explore the many systemic and cultural implications of what they have to deal with. It allows intervention at various points of the systems and consideration of alternative cultural constructions of meaning to increase life choices for the person to move forward towards growth.

Therapeutic Work and Research Orientation

Whether the therapeutic work involves family-of-origin exploration, working with survivors in the aftermath of childhood sexual abuse, tackling the intrinsic dilemma of extramarital affairs, or empowerment work with divorced women, the therapeutic process itself is one of facilitating an exploration of constructive as well as disruptive experiences. This exploration enables clients and couples to gain access to what is significant for them, to search for and create shifts in meaning so that they can better understand themselves and respond to the demands and dilemmas confronting them. The approach is subtle and can perhaps be described by a phrase graphically used by two of the authors "順水推舟" (to push the boat along the current). The current is life circumstances and cultural imperatives, now and from the past, which move the boat/client along the course. The counsellor eases the momentum of the boat so that the client is enabled to steer in the direction of choices available to him or her.

The research studies also reflect the processes by which men and women give meaning to their experiences, in or out of spousal relationships. The chapters on research reflect the growing trends and interest in the uncoupling process and the aftermath of marital separation. They recount the struggles of men and women as they strive to define and understand the meaning and implications of marital separation and their striving towards recovery and reconnections. The reconnections could be through remarriage, cohabitation, or single life with or without a regular partner. As in many aspects of marriage, gender makes a difference. The importance of and respect for gender differences are addressed in various chapters.

This collection is presented by marriage counsellors or researchers, out of professional interest, generally in association with colleagues sharing similar interests. None of them has been funded by their employing organizations. Thus, limitations of time and a shortage of support personnel have allowed the evaluation of only small caseloads and samples. Putting pen to paper has not been easy for busy professionals with heavy and demanding workloads. Our hope is that the sharing of ongoing endeavours in exploration and experimentation can lead to a further quest for understanding and development in these areas of interest and concern.

Overview of the Chapters

Clinical and Research Presentations

Our lives and our stories start with our family of origin. Spouses bring to a marriage their own unique early experiences of growing up, their own dreams and struggles, their vulnerabilities and their strengths, and their formulations of what it means to live in a family. In "Discovering the Spouse's Other-ness through Family-of-Origin Explorations and Reinventing Partnerships in Marriage", Laurene Man and Natalie Law worked with a couple to review and reconnect with their past, to discover and accept their own idiosyncrasies and those of the spouse. This chapter emphasizes that marriage is very much the intermeshing of the needs and propensities of the self and of the other, within a close and caring partnership. In the intimate sharing of daily life, some of our propensities could be complementary, meeting affiliate needs and reinforcing the sense of togetherness; some have to be adjusted and negotiated; some have to be tolerated and endured by each other in the context of the emotional bond; some could continue to be irritating and conflictual. This balancing of the self and the other within the relationship is an ongoing process, shifting and adjusting in response to changing life circumstances in the couple as well as in society. The fluid nature of this adjustment process enables the discovery of new and different qualities in the partner at various points of the couple's life course together. While this may introduce elements of friction, it also adds excitement and interest to the relationship and could reduce tedium and over-familiarity in the long run. The search into the past with this low-key approach is itself innovative and, as shown, does lead to change.

On the subject of traumatic childhood experiences, Grace Chan examines "Long-Term After-effects of Childhood Sexual Abuse on Married Life: Implications for Practice". She emphasizes the significance of establishing a sense of safety and security in working with survivors who have experienced repeated betrayals of trust in their upbringing. Using a distinctive approach in counselling, she has evolved a method that takes into account the impact of these after-effects. She draws our attention to the effects of childhood sexual abuse on the married partners of the survivors. The partners are also affected by their spouse's traumatic past, and their responses can contribute greatly to the healing and recovery process. However, involving the partner in the therapeutic process is a delicate matter and requires careful assessment of risks and preparation, which Grace Chan discusses with many case examples. Her chapter has much to offer those engaged in marital work, as she helps us appreciate the importance of tuning in and respecting the subtleties and nuances underlying the privacy of spousal living. A particular aspect of her article which should be highlighted is her careful work in preparing a husband to deal with flashbacks during sex, so that he becomes the resource *in situ* to reassure his spouse that she is safe and supported in the current context of their marriage.

What if the loss of trust arises in the marriage from the marital partner? In "Tackling the Intrinsic Dilemma in Marital Infidelity", Anita Fok suggests that the essential dilemma in decision-making lies with the partner involved in the affair working through relational issues in conjunction with the other spouse. In Hong Kong, it is generally the other spouse who seeks help, whereas the partner in the affair avoids engagement in counselling. From her clinical experience, Anita Fok proposes an approach in couple work which focuses primarily on the partner engaged in the affair, at specific phases of the counselling process, and supportive work with the other spouse keeping pace, in a combination of individual and couple work. Selecting a case example of a husband in an affair, she takes him through a personal reflection in an overall review of what he would like to obtain from his life journey. Through these deliberations, he generally reaches an impasse, what Anita calls a "blank" of what to do next, which is accepted and respected. To shift from this, a marital review is suggested, and this is conducted in a fair, neutral, non-coercive manner, the ground rules negotiated with all partners concerned. If this revisiting of the marriage generates relational commitment, the final phase dwells on marriage rebuilding with farewell rituals and recommitment pledges. As marriage counsellors, how often have we in counselling come across this "blank" and not known how to continue? It is from her extensive clinical experience that the author identifies this aspect as part of the process of working through difficult choices of the affair dilemma. Though we all deal with marriage reviews in couple work, the review process proposed in this chapter has many innovative techniques built in which address personal and inner struggles as well as interpersonal and interactional struggles.

The Chinese holistic approach to healing postulates that we forgive not just for the sake of the other but for ourselves, as forgiving frees us from bitterness and liberates energy for growth and transformation. How does this philosophical stance interface with psychotherapeutic propositions, and Christian or other religious beliefs? Wong Lai Cheung, in "Forgiveness in Marriage", addresses these issues in the context of intimate relationships in which hurt can be mutually escalating and interactional. In the course of everyday life, disagreements, abrasive behaviours, being put down, and not being listened to can lead to negative effects in close relationships. Lai Cheung discusses these irritants as well as chronic and serious transgressions devastating and destructive to the relationship. She crystallizes her clinical experiences by presenting various phases of working through hurt and pain in forgiveness work. According to her, the crux of forgiveness work is the sense of freedom from letting go of resentment and anger. Relationships then can be rebuilt, not by suppressing but by assimilating the experience as part of the past, to free energies to relating differently in the future.

In "Reaching the 'Point of No Return': Tracking the Pathway to

Making the Decision to Divorce", Anita Fok takes us through the processes by which a number of wives come to the painful realization that their marriages are no longer retrievable. Anita suggests that uncoupling is a process of disenchantment, punctuated by a series of significant events that call for a re-appraisal of the meaning of the relationship. This evaluation of events in the context of the marital experience may lead the spouses to conclude that there has been a violation of self-identity, of core beliefs and values, of life themes of paramount importance. If this is so, it gives rise to a sense of need for a reconstruction of the self and the rebuilding of a sustaining worldview, outside the relationship. Anita proposes a form of divorce decision therapy to enable spouses in this frame of mind to review their relationships systematically from their experience at the historical level of the marriage, the interactive level, and at the personal internal process level. This highlights for them their own values, needs, expectations, conflicts in the decision-making process and their own priorities. If the client then chooses to reconsider and to save the marriage, the counselling would shift to marital work. If the client is firm about the decision to divorce, then uncoupling counselling or mediation may be appropriate.

For divorced women in a Chinese society, their sense and experience is very much that of a boat without any moorings, adrift in the tide of life. Recovery is thus a case of re-establishing a sense of self and in finding moorings and directions for steering. In "Rediscovery of the 'Self': Culturally Sensitive Intervention for Chinese Divorced Women", Cecilia Chan, Shirley Hung and Winnie Kung have adopted a body-mind-spirit approach, based on holistic health concepts from Chinese medicine, to design and conduct empowerment groups for divorced women. These groups promote the re-establishment of a sense of self and the reformulation of the meaning of life in the context of life outside marriage. Through experiential exercises and various group processes, and through re-evaluating aspects of the Chinese culture that help or hinder healthy living, the divorced wives are empowered to let go of their pain and anger. They are also encouraged to redefine for themselves alternative meanings of what has happened to them, to free their energies for possibilities in the future. This empowerment approach highlights how a reconstruction of meaning can lead to a reconstruction of life experiences.

Whereas the previous two chapters examine the pain and trauma of divorce for women, the next chapter presents the other side of the picture: the stress, the sense of loss and of failure experienced by their counterparts, the husbands. Suggesting that the husbands' needs may be overlooked as they tend to present a strong posture hiding their vulnerability, in "Ambivalent Exit and Ambiguous Entry: Ten Hong Kong Men's Perceptions of Spousal Relationships In and Out of Marriage", Roger Kwan examines the perspectives of divorced fathers on remarriage. To what extent are they affected by the experience of the divorce process, or by their explanation of the marital breakdown, or by the nature of their post-divorce involvement with their children and ex-wives? An interesting finding is that the divorced men in the sample showed themselves to be active fathers with a high regard for the welfare of their children, which influenced their decisions regarding their own future and that of their children. This could be due to the cultural expectation that they meet their obligations to ensure family lineage, or that they wished to maintain the affectionate bond that they had with their children before divorce, or that this particular sample showed a bias. Whatever the reason or combination of reasons, it was clear that time, effort and resources were invested in preserving the father-child relationship following divorce. This is a feature at variance with practices in some cultures in which many children grow up fatherless. This raises another important issue for debate: What sort of ethos is needed in Hong Kong, to actively promote continuing and dynamic father-child connections following parental divorce?

Just as the chapter on divorced fathers draws attention to the importance of children in maintaining the divorced spouses' post-separation relationship, children are also found to be important in shaping the remarriage relationship of their parents. In "The Making of a Second Spring: The Experiences of Remarried Persons in Hong Kong", Lianne Tai describes how children take on various roles within the self-spouse-child triangle characteristic of many second marriages. This chapter discusses the emotional change and redefinition that spouses in their second marriages make of their experiences, which enable them to build resiliency, take constructive action to learn from the past, adapt to challenges, hence to grow and mature. Lianne points out that these endeavours would be greatly facilitated if social support were available and if there could be some revision of cultural perspectives unsympathetic to the remarried state. She suggests that, for stepfamilies and second marriages, what is reflected in the "eyes of others" can help or hinder efforts to establish a viable lifestyle. This contribution draws our attention to a need in our society for a rethinking and revision of the labels and negative attitudes that are displayed towards remarriage. The imagery that remains vivid from this account is that of Mrs Koo sitting in her kitchen, writing in her diary, reading the newspaper, listening to music, smoking a cigarette, drinking some beer ... reflecting that "the kitchen is my place".

This scenario suggests simple and sustaining possibilities for recharging and developing resiliency in the course of everyday life.

In "Gender Considerations in Couple Work: Reflections from Social Workers Involved in Marital Counselling", Timothy Leung, Monica Ng, Yeung Ka Ching and Ivan Yau address the widespread difficulty of reaching out to husbands to elicit their engagement in marital work. Observing that men seem to have a higher tolerance for relationship problems, the social workers in focus groups raised a number of creative suggestions to encourage couples to attend counselling and marriage enrichment groups together and find ways and means to maintain their participation. Some of these approaches may sound somewhat like going the extra mile to "give face" to the men while curbing the women's "pursuing" tendencies. Given the patriarchal legacy that Hong Kong retains, this awareness and tuning into gender differences may be essential in working with marriages at this time in our society. Nevertheless, further revision and reinterpretation of the concept of face in the context of the interpersonal system as embodied in the triad of face, favour, and fate (面子, 人情, 命運) would contribute importantly to a re-examination of another facet of cultural traditions which continue to influence behaviour and beliefs among Chinese people. This could lead to a deeper understanding of the Chinese sense of self as shaped and reshaped by interactions with and reflections from others (Chan 2001; Jia 2001). Drawing from research and clinical findings, local and overseas, and from the accumulated experiences of the social workers who have contributed to this study, the authors query the effectiveness of communication training which promotes mainly talking skills to help couples make changes towards more satisfactory relationships. They draw our attention to the prospect that promoting positive interaction and care-giving in order to facilitate validation and affirmation between the spouses is more likely to contribute to marital cohesion and well-being.

The Societal and Cultural Context

Whatever goes on in marriages, such as the endeavours of spouses to explore, re-evaluate, redefine or restructure their own identity or their relationships, has to be appreciated in the context of our societal and cultural circumstances. Whereas the early chapters are clinical and research oriented, the final two chapters provide conceptual overviews. The discussion on the changing nature and ideology of marriage reviews the marital and family forms evolving over time from various migrations from China and considers the challenges confronting Hong Kong into the future. The final chapter, which develops many of the themes introduced here, critically examines traditional values for their contemporary relevance as the philosophical underpinnings of our cultural heritage.

In the "The Changing Nature and Ideology of Marriage in Hong Kong", Lam Chiu Wan, Lam Wai-Man, and Timothy Leung take us through a carefully documented review of diverse marriage and family patterns, as well as legislative reforms in Hong Kong, which reflect changing socio-economic circumstances and values since World War II. They propose a framework of three principles for debating expectations of marriage as we contemplate the possible challenges into the next millennium, suggesting that any discourse on the future of marriage should take into consideration the principles of "continuity" reflecting historical trends; "feasibility" in serving essential functions of socialization and care-giving; and value choice, indicating what as a society we consider to be "valuable" in contributing to living a good life. The authors offer much food for thought in inviting us to study the concept of "critical familism" based on equal regard, commitment, communication and mutuality to ponder moral and political issues related to marriage. They advocate Hong Kong develop a family policy that respects family resiliency and recognizes the growing diversity in family forms as well as paradigm shifts in perceptions and expectations of marriage.

In "Reconstruction of Traditional Values for Culturally Sensitive Practice", Julia Tao engages in a dialogue with each of the authors. By bringing in some of the cultural dimensions that underlie what goes on in marriage and families in Hong Kong, she draws our attention to the subtle interplay of traditional attitudes and modern concepts involved in so much marital work in Hong Kong. In the process, she examines the importance of striving for a balance in reconciling intimacy, forgiveness and harmony critical for achieving and sustaining relationships, with autonomy, justice and fairness, critical for achieving and sustaining self development and self-identity. The struggle to maintain harmony with others as well as fairness to oneself involves a delicate balance of sensing what and how much to surrender to preserve the relationship, and how to protect fairness to oneself. In identifying the human dilemmas at play in maintaining close relationships, Julia invites us to ponder the complexities and subtleties of personal choice.

By re-examining and reconstructing classical Confucian norms and moral imperatives for contemporary relevance, this final chapter challenges us to search out some of our cultural roots to discover for ourselves the extent to which they give meaning to present-day concerns.

The Search for Meaning

A common thread that runs through the chapters on clinical practice and research is a search for meaning. As the spouses recount their experiences that continue to cause pain, they and the social workers, whether in counselling, research, or through the group process, explore a range of possible interpretations of what has happened in their lives. This representation of experience is a process of "constructing history in the present" (Anderson and Goolishian 1985, 37), whether this is a family-of-origin experience, childhood trauma, or sense of loss and deprivation from infidelity or divorce. The recall and review facilitates the emergence of new meanings to reorient the individual, and to "open up new courses of action more fulfilling and more adequately suited to the individual's experiences, capacities, and proclivities" (Gergen and Kaye 1992, 175).

A Search for the Self within a Relational Context

This discovery-oriented process in the search for meaning leads to a reconfiguration of the sense of self. The Chinese self is embedded in a network of relationships, and meaning is derived from interaction and reflection from this network in interface with the acculturated self (Hall and Ames 1998). The self is perceived as carrying a personal history and a unique cultural legacy. It is dynamic, holistic, and open to multiple influences, which in the Chinese context have to harmonize with others in a close relational complex from which one derives status and a sense of belonging. However, in this emphasis on relatedness, the self can become submerged. In a society that maximizes responsibility and empathy for others, and minimizes self-needs and interests, the development of the individuated self is often underplayed.

A recurrent theme and the essential thrust of clinical intervention in many chapters is the recovery, rebuilding, and reconstruction of the self. Facilitating growth, through differentiation, and the establishment of a self-directed, autonomous, integrated person with unique strengths and vulnerabilities, promotes self-definition. Personal growth requires the development of self-definition integrated with the development of interpersonal relatedness, which facilitates the capacity for more mature loving and intimacy that can be sustained in circumstances of adversity and ambivalence (Blatt 1996). Rather than a static entity, the self, though stable and constant in some aspects, is continuously evolving, and there are many possibilities of who the self can be and can become. This is a perspective that echoes the Confucian idea that self-transformation and self-cultivation are ceaseless (Tu 1985).

However, while close relationships enhance self-esteem and can be sustaining, they can also give rise to pain and suffering and open us to risks of vulnerability and hurt (Noam 1996). In this context, it is worth noting the extent to which the spouses in these accounts struggle to repair and protect their relationships while preserving a sense of self-dignity.

Harmonizing the Self with Others

Endeavours to harmonize the self with others can be achieved through various pathways. One is through reflective self-transformation and self-cultivation, calling forth and developing personal resources and resiliency in dealing with everyday life concerns, as revealed by the remarried spouses in their adaptation to their "second spring". A relational pathway is possible from partners helping each other to overcome old vulnerabilities, as portrayed by the husband reassuring his wife disturbed by flashbacks of early sexual abuse. Another pathway could be facilitated in therapy or in research by the unfolding process of recall and review, paying attention and focusing exploration on a variety of possible viewpoints of the same incident. This moment-by-moment reliving of experiences is illustrated through the family-of-origin exploration and the painful process of letting go and reclaiming self-harmony in forgiveness work. Another approach is to encourage a bottom-up exploration by the spouses, the therapist stimulating the process rather than directing the creation of meaning (Young 1997, 197–200). This is somewhat different from the top-down authoritative diagnostic assessment so critically debated in a soul-searching trialogue by Hoffman (Gergen, Hoffman, Anderson 1996). Yet another pathway would be the sharing of experiences in similar peer groups, thus expanding appreciation of the range of possible meaning from other people's perceptions, allowing for revision or reaffirmation of one's own perspectives, as in the empowerment groups designed for divorced women.

Cultural Determination of Meaning

The thrust of this publication is to ask questions and to raise debate. It could well be asked how it is that social workers, trained in casework and problem-solving and familiar with systems and varied theories of the personality, carefully avoid imposing their own views on the client. Instead, they adopt a therapeutic approach focused on facilitating the client's search for meaning, an approach that promotes the emergence of alternative meanings more conducive towards adaptive responses in their particular circumstances.

My sense is that this has been in response to the clients who present their dilemmas and difficulties in terms of the meaning that these have for them. And the meanings that they make of their experiences are highly coloured by cultural considerations. It is difficult for a Chinese person to appreciate the extent to which our beliefs and behaviour are affected by the strength of our cultural conditioning. Whether we accept, oppose or reject certain cultural mores and norms, they contribute importantly to our construction of meaning. This is clearly brought out in the analysis on traditional values and norms, in the discussion on gender perspectives, in the discussion on divorced women's and divorced men's marital experience, and in the debate on men's and women's differences in participation in counselling and enrichment groups. In the context of this compelling acculturation process in Chinese society, the theoretical position of constructionism offers an approach for reconstructing beliefs and values to liberate from their constraints and to generate more creative sets of meaning appropriate to our experiences. This is not a rejection of our culture. Our culture constitutes our survival kit. It is the accumulation of generations of learning and wisdom, and highly prized. By activating and inhibiting us in various ways in our response to life demands, our cultural guidelines enable us to adapt to changing circumstances. However, certain aspects can become irrelevant, some can be limiting in the way they reflect the dominance of our patriarchal past, and require revision calling for a search to reconstruct meaning in a way more helpful to a person at a specific point of time.

In this regard, the articles presented here reflect a gradual shift towards a viewpoint that meaning is multifaceted, relational, contextual, and constantly evolving in social interaction. This theoretical stance that meaning is socially constructed and that the self is constructed and reconstructed in relationships throughout life is integrated with our cultural formulation that also views the self as embedded in relationships with others.

> "Wishing to establish oneself, one establishes the other,
> Wishing to enlarge oneself, one enlarges the other".
> 已欲立而立人
> 已欲達而達人
>
> *The Analects* 6: 28

Indeed, it is our relationships with others that offer diverse pathways through which we can search out a way of life to be lived within various relational connections.

The Search for Direction

The final two chapters on marriage ideology and traditional values constitute the background context for a rethinking of marriage and relationships. Lam Chiu Wan and his team discuss the mindset helpful for reviewing various possibilities. Julia Tao reminds us of the traditional norms and moral imperatives deeply embedded in the Chinese culture. Any debate on the future of marriage in Hong Kong will need to take these aspects into account.

This collection of articles on marriage examines three main themes in a search for direction. The first is to invite a redefinition of the values and ideology of marriage to reflect the many possibilities of different lifestyles and relationship arrangements more suited to the pluralism of modern life. The second is a call for the development of social policies and a societal ethos that reinforces the aspirations that promote continuing close relationships. The third is to encourage theoretical innovations and creative evolutions in marital work that facilitate growth, whether through marriage, divorce, or remarriage, and how these can assimilate different perspectives and new paradigms building on the family and kinship bonds which we still have in Hong Kong.

References

Anderson H. and Goolishian H. (1992). The client is the expert. In S. McName and J.Gergen (Eds.) *Therapy as social construction.* 25–39. London: Sage.

Blatt S.T. and Blatt R.B. (1996). Relatedness and self-definition: A dialectic model of personality. In G.G. Noam and K.W. Fischer (Eds.) *Development and vulnerability in close relationships.* Mahwah, NJ: Lawrence Erlbaum.

Chan E.K.L. (2001). Chinese culture and family violence: Face, help-seeking behavior and self-preservation of Chinese male batterers. Paper presented at the Symposium on Chinese Cultural and Social Work, University of Hong Kong.

Gergen K.J. and Kaye J. (1992). Beyond narrative in the negotiation of therapeutic meaning. In S. McNamee and K.J. Gergen (Eds.) *Therapy as social construction.* 166–85. London: Sage.

Gergen K.J., Hoffman L. and Anderson H. (1996). Is diagnosis a disaster? A constructionist trialogue. In F. Kaslow (Ed) _Handbook of relational diagnosis and dysfunctional family patterns._ New York: John Wiley.

Hall D.L. and Ames R.T. (1998). _Thinking from the Han: Self, truth, and transcendence in Chinese and Western culture._ Albany: State University of New York.

Jia Wen-Shan (2001). _The remaking of the Chinese character and identity in the 21st century: The Chinese face practices._ West Point. CT: Ablex Publishing.

Meijer M.J. (1971). _Marriage law and policy in the Chinese People's Republic._ Hong Kong: Hong Kong University Press.

Noam G.G. (1996). Conceptualizing maturity: The search for deeper meaning. In G.G. Noam and K.W.Fischer (Eds.) _Development and vulnerability in close relationships._ Mahwah, NJ: Lawrence Erlbaum.

Ocko J.K. (1971). Women, property, and law in the People's Republic of China. In R.S. Watson and P.B. Ebrey (Eds.) _Marriage and inequality in Chinese society._ 313–46. Berkley, CA: University of California Press.

Tu Wei Ming (1985). _Confucian thought: Selfhood as creative transformation._ Albany: State University of New York Press.

Wong F.M. (1972). Modern ideology, industrialization, and conjugalism: The case of Hong Kong. _International Journal of Sociology of the Family,_ 2: 139–50.

Yeung C. and Kwong W.M. (1998). A study of the attitudes of pre-marital couples towards marriage in Hong Kong. _Hong Kong Journal of Social Work,_ 32 (1): 71–84.

Young G. (1997). _Adult development, therapy and culture: A post-modern synthesis._ New York: Plenum Press.

2

Discovering the Spouse's Other-ness Through Family-of-origin Explorations and Re-inventing Partnerships in Marriage

Laurene L.P. Man and Natalie K.W. Law

In the intimate sharing of lives in marriage, some individuals have a strong tendency to personalize their spouse's behaviour and responses. When they take this perspective, the spouse's actions are seen as targeted and focused on their own persons. They quickly and reflexively react to each other in negative ways, feel extremely anxious and are unable to trust each other's intentions. Anger and animosity easily become the backdrop of their daily interactions. Such processes usually take place between couples who are emotionally fused or undifferentiated and who have a low degree of awareness that the other spouse is a separate and different person (an "other") apart from being a partner in marriage.

Doing families-of-origin explorations together with a couple helps them develop awareness that their spouses are separate and different persons who have unique histories of their own. Such awareness will give them new lenses through which they could read each other's behaviour differently: their spouses behave in ways they do, not because of them but because of the spouse's own life experiences. This new way of reading each other's behaviour will reduce the tendency to personalize it and will foster greater calmness and objectivity in the way the couple relates to each other. It will also help couples develop new mutual understanding and greater trust of and compassion for each other. This paper summarizes a case study of joint families-of-origin explorations with one couple, and the subsequent effects.

The Story of Us — Persons of Here and Now

Generally, couples first meet each other as adults. When a person comes for marital counselling with his spouse, he may complain that his spouse is a person with annoying characteristics that he perceives as static and fixed. He may feel "that is the way she is". He does not see that his spouse is a human-being-in-process, that she has been evolving from a past, and is still in the process of transforming into a person-to-be in the future.

The former is a frozen view, but the latter is much more tentative and fluid and provides more room for change. The person who sees his partner as "that's the way she is" does not have any expectation or hope for change in his partner. Whatever weaknesses he sees in his partner may be seen as unchangeable and frozen flaws, disabilities and defects. In addition, he may very likely adopt the same static view of himself. Though he may outwardly deny that he has such weaknesses, he often secretly believes he has them and feels ashamed of them. His natural outward tendency is to defend his sense of self as it is and to fight changing. In order to protect his sense of self, he may intensify his focus on the perceived permanent flaws of his partner, giving her little room to try new behaviours and to change. Both partners end up being stuck with their current patterns of relating, feeling little hope for change.

The Story of Us — Only One Identity: Role as Spouses

Very often also, illogical as it may sound, a spouse who comes to therapy assumes that his spouse (or partner) has only one identity: his spouse. He has known his partner only as "a-person-in-relation-to-me". He will tend to interpret his partner's behaviour as related to him, focused on him, because of him, or targeted to him. From such a subjective and personalized perspective, his partner's behaviour could not be about anything or anyone else except "me" (i.e., him).

This view of his partner often causes him to miss out on a much broader picture, that his partner is a person who has a life of her own apart from him. He may have difficulty realizing that, apart from being an agent who affects his life and who "does things to him", his partner may also be a passive recipient of many other influences, and is a product of her past. Failing to see this, he may see his partner as having complete control over her behaviour and so interpret her behaviour as always deliberate. He may feel that the reason his partner does not change is that she does not want to, so he may not be able to entertain the possibility that sometimes his partner may not be capable of changing and controlling her behaviour, though she may want to. He may believe that she chooses to neglect or ignore his needs, that "she does not care about me" or that "she does not love me".

(Note: Though the masculine pronoun has been used, the same could be said of women.)

Differentiation and Family-of-Origin Explorations

The realization that self and other are two separate and different persons, each with his or her unique developmental history and each a product of experiences in a unique family-of-origin, constitutes what Bowen refers to as "the differentiation of self" (Kerr and Bowen 1988). When a person's differentiation of self increases, his tendency to personalize the other person's behaviour is reduced. He will have a greater capacity to respect the other person as a person in her own right and to let the other person just be. Two persons with a high level of differentiation will be able to get along much more calmly, more respectfully, and much less reactively. There will be less need to be critical of the other or to defend self from perceived criticisms.

Bowen proposed that reviewing one's own family-of-origin experiences as an adult will enable a person to understand members of his family-of-origin afresh (Bowen 1978; Guerin and Pendagast 1976). He will have an adult's perspective and ability to comprehend interpersonal relationships in his family much better than when he was a child. This process will help to revise his family story into a more mature one with more complete information and enable him to see for the first time that his parents were not only his parents but were also human beings in their own right, struggling with their own lives. Thus, what his parents did or did not do was less about him and his inadequacies, or his inherent badness or unlovable qualities as a child, but more about the parents themselves and their struggles. They had their own needs and were struggling to look after those needs. They were dealing with their own insecurities and were trying to fulfill their own dreams at the time he was still a young child. This realization will help him reduce his tendency to personalize his parents' behaviour as having been provoked by him, and reduce his later tendency to feel the same about the parents' current behaviour and that of other people, including that of his spouse in marriage.

The process of reviewing one's family-of-origin experiences with the partner as a participant listener will bring many benefits to the marital relationship, if the couple is ready to listen to each other and if done in an atmosphere of calmness and mutual acceptance. It is expected that the partners will come to understand each other, not only as their spouses but also as separate persons who have unique histories.

Moreover, they will come to realize they have a lot more in common than they realized. They may come to appreciate that they share a *common* longing for the warmth within the family and appreciate that they both care about their family, that they both want to be good parents and that they both experience frustrations and disappointments but also hopes and dreams. With professional facilitation, this process may promote a greater resonance and compassion between a couple, and increase trust in each other's positive intentions behind the *differences* in their behaviour. There will also be greater readiness and curiosity to understand more about the thoughts behind the other person's responses. As their shared inner sentiments meet, superficial behavioural differences seem easier to accept. All these processes will provide a solid foundation for better and more open communication.

Structure and Process of the Approach

After a year of counselling in a family service agency over difficulties in parenting, Mr and Mrs Chan's counsellor, Natalie Law, believed they might be ready for couple therapy. Laurene Man joined in at this point as co-counsellor for marital therapy, and the couple was seen for seven one-and-a-half-hour interviews, each time jointly by the two counsellors. Over a period of six months, Mr and Mrs Chan participated in four couple sessions, followed by two individual sessions, one with each spouse, and a final couple session.

Our plan was to focus on family-of-origin explorations around three themes regarding:
1. Parent roles
2. Couple communication
3. Handling differences.

For each of these areas, we focused our attention on:
1. Their current experience in each of these areas
2. Their observations of their parents in these areas
3. What they would like to retain, and what revise, from their family-of-origin exploration
4. The connections between their family-of-origin experience and their present experience in their nuclear family relationships.

There was no intention to undertake direct or deliberate intervention to change the presenting difficulties in the marriage. The belief was that changes around these difficulties would come when the couple saw and experienced each other differently in the course of the joint family-of-origin explorations.

The verbatim excerpts of the counselling dialogues quoted in this paper are condensed from the original dialogues and therefore do not reflect the actual counselling flow. They are presented in a condensed form mainly to illustrate the themes under discussion.

Therapeutic Positions

A preliminary assessment of the couple's suitability for this work was undertaken before proposing this approach. In spite of their difficulties, there was enough love and trust between Mr and Mrs Chan that they were open and ready to listen to each other without feeling excessively insecure and reactive or always perceiving attack. If they had had these tendencies, joint family-of-origin explorations would not have been suggested.

Our conscious goal was to create an emotionally safe atmosphere in which the couple could feel secure and comfortable enough to share even their inner thoughts and feelings and to share their family-of-origin experiences without feeling afraid of being disrespected, ridiculed or shamed. We also encouraged the couple to focus on sharing about self and not on criticizing the other person, and to avoid put-downs and censure of the other person. If they did any of these things, we interrupted them. We took responsibility for the exploration process, asking questions to help the couple review their family-of-origin experiences, examined overlooked areas, and explored issues and themes as they emerged in the clients' sharing. We did not ask questions with expected answers in mind, nor did we propose interpretations to the clients.

We tried to adopt a research stance, somewhat like reporters doing fact-finding research of the couples' experiences in their current family and in their respective families-of-origin. We tried not to get emotionally involved or overly excited about particular aspects as they arose. It was not our goal to modify undesirable behaviour or change personality; instead, we left it open to the clients whether and how to change themselves. Both of the authors have been trained in and have been practising Bowen's Family Systems Theory, and we adopted the conceptual framework and practices proposed by this theory.

The Couples' Relationship before Family-of-Origin Exploration

To protect the confidentiality of the couple and family, names and other identifying information have been changed, but essential clinical features of the case are retained. Mr and Mrs Chan, both forty-three, had two sons, aged eight and five. The older son had problems with bedwetting and with learning disabilities one year ago, and doctors suggested it was related to stress. This problem improved after a few sessions, and after one year of counselling service on parenting issues, the original counsellor, Natalie Law, felt that some work on their marriage would be beneficial, and the couple were invited to participate in further work on their relationship.

Mrs Chan worked half-days in the morning. She described herself as a nervous person. She tended to be lenient and protective of the children, especially the older son, and tended to shelter him from his father, who was strict with him. She was quite unhappy with her husband's strict disciplinarian way of handling their older son. She hoped he could be warmer and more flexible, and that he would talk and reason with him more, be less critical and less of a disciplinarian. She acknowledged, however, that he was a devoted father who spent a lot of time with the children.

Mrs Chan was quick and direct in saying what she thought. At times, she could come across as blunt, and was perceived by her husband to be inconsiderate. She might not have been aware of her husband's resentment of her quickness and bluntness. Mrs Chan longed for a closer relationship with her husband, and appeared to be a pursuer in the relationship. She felt hurt and frustrated by her husband's reserve, quietness and distance, and she took these as his indifference, lack of care for her, or even rejection. She turned instead to her friends for support.

Mr Chan was a high achiever in his family of origin and was the only one of his siblings to study to a level higher than primary school. He was a very quiet person and found it hard to be open and expressive. Being a secondary school teacher himself, he had trouble accepting his son's learning problems. He liked to have things tidy and organized, and was strict with the children, particularly with the older son. He believed that children should learn to be independent and be accountable for their own behaviour and parents should not pamper them too much. Therefore, he took a firm and strict approach with his children. Mr Chan was angry that his wife disagreed with him in front of their sons and felt that she interfered with his relationship with his sons, especially the older son. He felt she had made it hard for him to father his sons. He was not happy that his efforts in parenting were not appreciated by his wife.

The family seemed to have divided itself into two camps, mother and older son in one, and father and the younger son in the other. The lack of communication between the couple created problems for parental cooperation, and the children often turned to their mother for approval and support. Mr Chan felt distant from his wife and his children and felt isolated and lonely in the family.

Summary of Complaints

Mrs Chan's Complaints	Mrs Chan's Feelings and Responses
a) Parent Role: Mr Chan's over-focus on the children	She felt ignored and abandoned.
b) Couple Communication: Mr Chan's reserve, seldom talking and distancing	She felt he did not care. She longed for closeness but felt she did not get it.
c) How they handled differences: Mr Chan's strictness with their older son	She felt she had to protect her son from his father.

Mr Chan's Complaints	Mr Chan's Feelings and Responses
a) Parent Role: Mr. Chan thought Mrs Chan was too lenient with the children	He felt children should learn to be independent and responsible.
Mrs Chan's interfering with his discipline of his older son	He felt he was sabotaged.
b) Couple Communication: Mrs Chan's bluntness, disrespect, and lack of appreciation	He withdrew and distanced himself from the family.
c) How They Handled Differences: Mr Chan felt pressured to talk and express himself.	He felt disrespected, resentful and angry.

Summary of the Couples' Interaction Patterns

Just before couple's work began, they were mutually critical and their complaints about each other loomed large in their consciousness; there was little exchange of positive appreciation. Both were immersed in their own hurt, and they could not sympathize with the other. The couple easily reacted to each other emotionally, and tended to generalize negatively about each other's intentions, over even very small day-to-day interactions. For example, Mrs Chan concluded that Mr Chan did not love her because he turned off the fan she had turned on, and Mr Chan concluded that Mrs Chan criticized him when she queried why he did not open the window.

Mrs Chan felt very hurt and emotionally abandoned by her husband's quietness, his reserve, and their lack of couple time. She felt frustrated and helpless and further burdened by having to take care of the two boys, one of whom was suspected of having learning difficulties. As a result, she was extremely anxious and had to take medication. Mr Chan found Mrs Chan's desire for open and expressive discussions between them very threatening and uncomfortable. He perceived criticisms in his wife's straightforwardness, and he withdrew in response. He also tended to avoid open conflict, by not talking. Disagreement over parenting was a constant area of struggle, as Mrs Chan tried to protect her son from her husband's strict discipline, and Mr Chan felt resentful over his wife's sabotage of his attempts to parent their sons.

Mr Chan's Story and His Major Themes

The relationship had become so unpleasant that they had both chosen to distance themselves from each other in order to avoid conflict. They were caught in a vicious cycle: the more they withdrew from communication, the more negative assumptions they accumulated about each other; the more they became alienated from each other, the harder it became for them to resume connection.

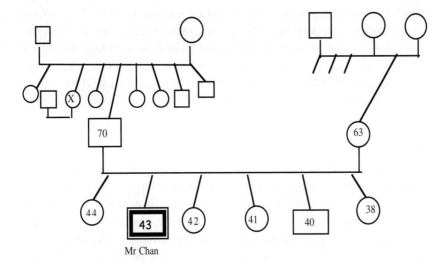

Mr Chan

Family Composition and Background

Mr Chan is the second child in his family. His father was a sailor when he was a small child, and the family lived with the paternal grandparents. His mother stayed at home until the birth of his youngest sister, when he was about five; then she started working. Around this time, his father started working in a shipyard in Hong Kong, far away from home. He stayed overnight at the shipyard most of the time but returned home sometimes. After his mother started working, young Mr Chan and his siblings were taken care of primarily by their grandparents. When his mother returned from work everyday, she was very busy with the chores and could not spend much time with the children. It was his mother's and the family's pride, however, that twice the family won the Clean Household Award in the housing estate where they lived. There were constant arguments and conflicts between his grandmother and his mother, and his father tried to stay away from these conflicts.

He was the only successful student of all his siblings and was considered the family scholar. His siblings turned to him for help with their children's schoolwork or to read English documents.

Longing for his father

Mr Chan did not get to be with his father very often. Throughout his sharing in the sessions, we heard an obvious and consistent admiration of and fondness for his father and a longing for a close relationship with him. Mr Chan remembered crying as a young child in the middle of the night and asked his mother where his father was. He described staying in the kitchen to watch his father cook, and he shared the view that this was his way of finding a chance to spend more time with him. He started to help his father cook, when he was in Primary 5. Mr Chan had warm memories of his father returning (not more than once a week) from work in the shipyard and bringing fresh fish and ice cream home for their dinner.

Wish for closer supervision and guidance

His father was not always home, and his mother started working when he was five. The six children were taken care of by their grandparents. He did not remember much about how he was taken care of but repeated many times that they used to play outside the house with the neighbours' children. Every day, when his mother got home from work, she was very busy, doing the laundry for the entire family of ten, getting the six children bathed one by one, and tidying the house (to a level of cleanliness that twice helped them win the Clean Household Award in the public housing area where they lived). There was not much time left to attend to the children. The children were taught to help with household chores, to look after themselves, to do their own homework, and to entertain themselves by playing with the neighbours' children outside the house. He was used to leading a very independent life, to keeping things to himself, and to solving his own problems. He defended his parents by saying, "In those days, all the parents were busy and most children grew up the way we did".

Consistently, however, he expressed a longing for more family time together, for more nurturing and closer supervision and guidance from his parents, especially from his father. He had positive memories about special times when his parents took turns taking the children out in groups to see movies in the theatre. In the following excerpt, such longing is obvious:

> **Interview Excerpt (condensed): <u>On Parent Role</u>**
> **Mr Chan:**   **"I would like to have more nurturing and care from my parents and I am trying to give my children what I did not have."**
>
> (LM is Laurene Man; NT is Natalie Law)
> Mr C: Our parents seldom took care of us directly. Most of the time our grandparents took care of us. If somebody could be there to care more, it would be better. Now, I do it myself, and I won't leave it to the Filipino maid.

(Later in the interview)

LM:	If you could spend more time with your parents, how would the picture be different?
Mr C:	Maybe I would have a closer relationship with my father.
LM:	What do you imagine you might do with him?
Mr C :	(Long pause) Father liked to pay chess; he liked fishing. He had a lot of interests. I always knew. But I never had the chance to do them with him. Never played chess with him, not even once.
LM:	I hear a longing.

Determination to provide active guidance to his children

Now that Mr Chan has become a father himself, he has tried to make himself available to his children as much as possible and was determined never to leave them with the Filipino maid. He made sure that either he or his wife would be in the house at any time. This had deprived the couple of time alone and made his wife rather unhappy. He believed that the parents' active involvement in the children's lives was very important. He wished to prepare his children adequately for their future and was anxious that they might fall behind in society (probably like his own siblings). Because of these concerns, he guided and disciplined them strictly.

> **Interview excerpt (condensed): <u>On Parent Role</u>**
> **Mr Chan shared his feelings that it was important to be an actively involved parent.**
>
> | | |
> |---|---|
> | Mr Chan: | (Referring to his older son) His biggest problem is that he does not concentrate. Whenever he has to memorize something, he will be disadvantaged. This is what I am worried about. My wife tends not to correct his mistakes and lets the teacher correct him, but I always insist that he correct them himself … My family did not do anything deliberate about my education. All my brothers and sisters, they all studied only up to primary school. I was the only one who managed to continue to a higher level. Now I tend to be strict with my boys. |
> | LM: | No one supervised you when you were young, and now you feel it is important to supervise your children? |

Mr Chan: When they (his children) are young, they don't
          know how to supervise themselves. I don't want
          them to waste time playing. I am stricter. Their
          mother is more lenient. We both value parenting,
          but we do it differently. She thinks that I am harsh.
LM: You feel you are harsh, too?
Mr Chan: A little.

Mr Chan realized that, although his father did not say much, he was an interesting person

Initially, Mrs Chan complained about Mr Chan's quiet reserve, and Mr Chan was himself somewhat apologetic about it. Mr Chan described himself as being like his father. In his descriptions of his father, he said that his father bought gifts to his mother, bought ice cream home, cooked good food, and made furniture for the family. These were ways through which his father involved himself in his family and expressed his care, and ways that were deeply appreciated by Mr Chan as a child. Like his own father, Mr Chan demonstrated his care less through words and more through action and behaviour. Though he was not an articulate person, his love for his family became more apparent to his wife in the process of sharing.

He also came to appreciate how a quiet man like his father could also be interesting, despite his quietness. He had from a young age always admired his father for his having a lot of interests and skills. He remembered his father's chess-playing, interest in fishing and in listening to music. He was also a good cook, and Mr Chan loved the food he cooked. As a child, Mr Chan was very interested in him. This helped to change Mrs Chan's view of equating her husband's quietness with dullness, distance, and inability to contribute to family life. Quietness in personality no longer needed to be a hindrance to their marriage and family relationships, as the couple had thought.

Interview Excerpt (condensed): <u>On How They Handled Differences</u>

Mr Chan: Family life could be fun and relationships could be close, even in a family that did not talk much

(LM is Laurene Man; NL is Natalie Law)
Mr C. talked about his parents' interests:
NL: How about your mother? What was she interested
          in?

Mr C:	She also liked to listen to songs. She collected small samples of wine bottles, put them on the shelf and cleaned them when she had time. And dad would go shopping with mom.
NL:	It seemed that, although they were so busy and so independent, they valued time with the family.
LM:	In your family, people might not talk much, but to understand your family we have to see it in action with our eyes and not so much by listening with our ears.
Mr C:	I think so. We don't talk much. We express feelings through action more. Yes, you are right.

Mr Chan's picture that women were strong and that men had to withdraw

Mr Chan got the idea sometime while he was growing up that his mother did not like children. He grew up in a household in which the only two adult women, his mother and his grandmother, argued constantly. He saw as a young child how his father got caught between them and how he withdrew. He might have found the two women too strong and intimidating, and similar feelings might be easily produced when his wife talked to him in a direct and straightforward tone. He and his wife became aware that, like his father, he had a tendency to withdraw and distance himself from arguments.

Mrs Chan's Story and Major Themes

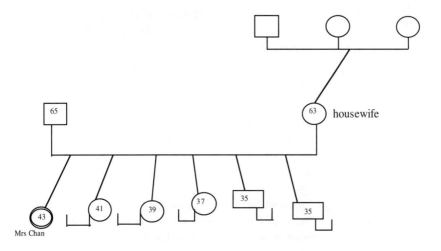

Family Composition and Background

Mrs Chan grew up in a nuclear family as the oldest of six children. In her description of her family, the first thing that came to mind was her close relationship with her father. She was his favourite child, "daddy's girl", and she felt specially loved by him of all her siblings. We came to understand how Mrs Chan longed for closeness and nurture from her husband, which was what her father used to give her, and the disappointment and the lack of fulfillment she felt when her husband did not meet this need.

She was weak and incompetent and needed to be protected

Her parents, particularly her father, were described by her to be very nervous people, always feeling unsafe and frightened in the world. They were always scared of the outside world. In addition, her parents, especially her father, saw her as weak and needing protection. One of the first things her father said to her husband when they first met was, "my daughter needs to be protected". She thus came to believe that she needed to be protected, looked after, and encouraged. This had contributed to her insecurity, and she was full of anxiety in her daily life. When she became a mother, she found the responsibility overwhelming and stressful. She was very anxious over the development of her children, and she tended to overprotect them, especially the older son, who was reported to have problems. She was so nervous that she had to receive psychiatric help. In the following interview excerpt, she describes the relationship with her parents.

> **Interview Excerpt (condensed): <u>Sharing Differences</u>**
> **Mrs Chan:** "I am weak and incompetent, and I need to be
>   protected."
>
> (LM is Laurene Man; NL is Natalie Law)
> Mrs C: (Recalling what her husband said about
>   appreciating her being sociable in the last session)
>   I have never heard before that he chose me
>   because he liked that about me. Involvement in
>   church, having good interpersonal relationships
>   etc ... I never knew that I have something that he
>   appreciated. I was happy to hear that.
> NL: Did your family praise you, too?
> Mrs C: Seldom. I was useless. Of all my family, I was
>   weak, never smart. My health was not good; I was

	often sick and very weak. That's why I was not confident.
NL:	How about other family members? Were all of them smart?
Mrs C:	Yes! The sister who is a nurse, she's really smart. She earned her own school fees, and finished university in Australia. Another sister is doing business, though she has not had much education. The youngest sister is now in seminary and was a secretary before. They are all very tough.
LM:	You said "tough"?
Mrs C:	And I am never tough. I am no good at anything. I always withdraw.
LM:	Since when did you begin to see yourself this way?
Mrs C:	(cries) Always.
LM:	You seem not very happy.
Mrs C	Yeah, I am so useless.

(A few minutes later)

LM:	They saw you as fragile and that you need to be protected? How do you feel about this?
Mrs C:	Not very happy, of course. They just feel that I am incompetent, for example, when I had my two children.

(In another session)

Mrs C:	As I have shared with you before, my father is a very nervous person, and so am I. I am now still taking medicine for psychiatric problems, and whenever there is a lot of time pressure in my life, like lately when I have to go to lessons, my mental condition becomes worse.
LM:	What does he worry about?
Mrs C:	About very little things, and then he could not sleep.
LM:	You said earlier he protected you very much?
Mrs C:	Yes, in the past. He still worries about me.
LM:	If he is not so worried about you, would that make any difference to you?
Mrs C:	Then I would not feel so stressed.

Strong tendency to focus on the negative and pitfalls

Perhaps because of her anxiety, she had a strong tendency to focus on the negative and the possible pitfalls and risks, and this had caused her to overlook the positive and interfered with her ability to appreciate her son as well as her husband.

Her tendency to protect her son from her husband

There was a parallel between how she saw herself and how she saw her older son. She saw her son as weak and incompetent. A lot of her protectiveness and ways of handling her children came from her anxiety. She tended to see herself and her children as fragile, hence needing to be protected. Her fears might have caused her to easily exaggerate her son's learning disability and to protect him from harm. This might be why she tended to be lenient with both sons.

She was also frightened of her husband when he was firm and strict with their older son, and she felt she had to protect him from his father. Strictness was something she had not experienced in her own family. On the contrary, protection was what she had always assumed to be something that a parent should do for a child. In her anxiety, she often felt the need to act and do something to help, and it was a challenge to her to give her husband and children space to relate to each other in their own ways, without her immediate intercession.

Interview Excerpt (condensed): <u>On Parent Roles</u>
Mrs Chan shares her feelings about Mr Chan's discipline of the children

LM: You are afraid of his harshness, but do you think your children could stand his strictness?

Mrs C: It's more difficult for the older son. He would be more afraid.

LM: You want to protect him from Mr C?

Mrs C: I am worried.

LM: Do you think this would make a difference, whether you are afraid or not? Would this affect whether your son is afraid of his father?

Mrs C: I think so. That's why recently I have been trying to stay away and let him handle the child.

(Later in the session)

Mr C: This would help our relationship. I appreciate her trying. Before, we could have no discussion at all. She just sabotaged what I was doing right there while I was handling my son. Now I hope slowly we could coordinate a better way of working together.

Mrs Chan describes herself and her family as blunt

Mrs Chan described herself as blunt. She also shared that, in her family, members were used to being loud, direct, and blunt with each other, and they had a rough and tough style of relating with each other. We do not know if this was their way, possibly not consciously used, of dealing with the sense of vulnerability, fear, insecurity, and anxiety they felt in dealing with the outside world. Mrs Chan used this style as well, and it caused her some difficulty when she needed to be gentle to invite gentleness and nurture from her husband.

As Mrs Chan shared this, Mr Chan came to understand that her bluntness did not necessarily reflect the negativity or animosity that he previously perceived she felt toward him.

Changes In and Between the Couple

Interview Excerpt (condensed): <u>Handling Differences</u>
Mrs Chan's describes her increased ability to self-focus and reflect on her own processes in her relationship with Mr Chan. She is also better able to see, respect and handle their differences.

LM: How has it been lately between you and Mr Chan?

Mrs Chan: Pretty good. I have been more patient. Once after an incident, I thought back on it and thought that I had been impatient; then I talked to him and apologized for being impatient. I think he liked that … . It has been quite obvious that he has been quite different this last month. He smiled more and talked more.

LM: You seem happy! You have to tell us more. How have you been different, to make it possible for him to become different?

Mrs Chan: I think he minds very much that I don't accept him and that I don't appreciate him. One point was quite obvious: how come I could not appreciate in him something most other people appreciated?

NL: What was that?

Mrs Chan: His tidiness. It's not that I don't appreciate it; only he overdid it sometimes.

LM: So how have you been adjusting to this?

Mrs Chan: I never criticized him about that, but I think he was not happy that I did not appreciate him.

NL: How have things been in the last month?

Mrs Chan: He was more relaxed. I became more relaxed. Our relationship has been less tense, and I became less uptight, for example, about our older son.

(About half an hour later)

Mrs Chan: Before, I really felt annoyed with the way he (husband) taught our son. Now I feel he has a point in having expectations, only if he could be gentler and explain to him more.

LM: Do you have to intercede a lot of the time?

Mrs Chan: Most of the time I don't, because I know there won't be good results. Also, I don't want my son to disrespect his father. So I kept silent. Before, I would get mad. Now I would just leave it, and just let him do it.

NL: Could you talk with him about it afterwards?

Mrs Chan: Yes, we did and we could talk. I used to think that I was right and he was wrong. Now I changed my view. Now I know that he is my son's father, and it's not like he does not love him. He wanted to teach him well, and he cannot be all wrong. Only his method of handling is not the best.

Interview Excerpt (condensed): <u>On Couple Communication</u>
Mrs Chan remarks on her experience of family-of-origin explorations and her new appreciation of her husband's quietness.

NL: We have done some exploration into your relationships with the older generation. Has this affected your relationship in the marriage?

Mrs Chan: Some of the things I seldom noticed. But now I understand more about him. His father was very much like him. I had never thought about thsis.

LM: What have you discovered?

Mrs Chan: I never thought about what kind of a person his father is.

NL   So, what do you think they have in common?

Mrs Chan: Their quietness and not being sociable, and their style of communicating. But his father loved his mother also.

LM: In spite of his quietness?

Mrs Chan: Their personalities, they have pure hearts, are not busybodies and won't gossip.

NL: How would these new understanding affect how you will relate with him?

Mrs Chan: I've come to appreciate him more.

LM: What is it about him that you appreciate?

Mrs Chan: I accept him more. Now I see the good side of his quietness; he wouldn't think about the bad side of people and is not suspicious of people.

NL: You did not notice these before? I remember you used to be very unhappy about his quiet personality. Now you feel different?

Mrs Chan: Perhaps it's because I have increased my understanding of him and of myself. There must be reasons behind what he does. Before, he did not talk much, and I did not try to understand. Now I am older, I would think, learn, ask, and listen to other people, and understand why he does things a certain way. Before, when I did not understand, I would use my own thinking to interpret. Now I understand more about him. Also he has been talking more, too, recently.

Interview Excerpt (condensed): <u>On Parent Role</u>
Mr. Chan demonstrates increased ability to look at his harshness from his son's point of view and talks about how he wanted it to be different.

LM: I was not there when you were harsh, but behind your harshness could there be nervousness and worry (you talked about earlier)? Do you think your wife and your sons get the chance to see the care and concern and gentleness in your heart which you have shared with us?

Mr Chan: Some, but not much.

LM: When you are soft, what do you think they would see? I heard you share it just now. But what a pity if they don't see the softness, they don't know you care, and they don't know you love them. It's a great pity.

(A few minutes later)

NL: Do you want your sons to be afraid of you as they are growing up?

Mr Chan: Of course not. Then they would be afraid to talk
              to me.

LM: And avoid you, but in their hearts, they wanted
              to be close to you like what they had drawn in
              their pictures earlier. It's such a pity. You love and
              care about them so much, and you want to help
              them, but all they could feel is that you are harsh
              and strict. It's such a pity!

LM (later):   Have you ever thought about how you would like
              your children to see you?

Mr Chan: Like a friend, so that when they have difficulties
              they will come to me.

LM: This is very important. Now he is nine, very soon
              he will be ten, eleven and twelve; if he could see
              his father as his friend, he could always come to
              you when he meets challenges, and you can be his
              guide. But if he resists you, rules you out, treats
              you as irrelevant, counts you out, he will lose you
              as a very important resource!

NL: It seems both you and he would want to become
              closer to each other, but if he is afraid of you, that
              won't happen. What do you think you can do to
              remove that barrier?

Mr Chan: Play chess, play ball; we can become more relaxed.
              When he is relaxed, he will talk to me and ask me
              a lot of questions.

Interview Excerpt (Condensed): Handling Differences
Mr Chan is more ready to listen and understand his parents.
He is also more open to seeing his wife's positive intentions
in spite of her bluntness.

Mr Chan: (In response to the counsellor's question to him
              about how he had felt about the counselling) The
              atmosphere was satisfactory. Sometimes I would
              think about what we had discussed and tell
              myself: "maybe I did not understand the full
              picture or maybe my views have been biased".

NL: About what?

Mr Chan: My own (nuclear) family. I've come to accept my
              family more, their personalities.

LM   How so?

Mr Chan: Sometimes her (wife's) intentions were good.

Only her tone of voice, use of words, and her habit of being direct, and she is a little blunt.

(Later)

Mr Chan: Now I observe my own parents more.

LM Have these observations increased your understanding of them?

Mr Chan: Yes, but sometimes I didn't know how to communicate with them.

NL: What do you find difficult?

Mr Chan: Maybe they are older now; sometimes they repeat and repeat themselves. They may not change.

NL: Your new discoveries, did they change how you communicate with them?

Mr Chan: I listen more; sometimes I find it tiring but I try to listen.

LM: Compared to the past, you feel you are listening more?

Mr Chan: Before, I did not understand them; now I want to be closer to them, but I don't know how. I'm learning.

Interview Excerpt (condensed): Respecting differences
Mrs Chan has increased her ability to respect herself and her husband as unique, separate persons.

LM: (In the last session) Before we close, we would like to ask you how you have experienced these sessions. This is part of our study, and we hope to include your views in the report.

Mrs Chan: In the past, I never thought about the older generation.

LM: What happened after you learnt all that?

Mrs Chan: I understand him more and can accept him more. He is a separate person.

NL Understanding him more helps you accept him more?

Mrs Chan A little, because he is actually a separate entity.

LM: You begin to see that he is a separate entity, that he has his own history?

Mrs Chan I try to understand him, this person.

LM: This person who is not only my husband but also a separate person. How about you?

Mrs Chan: My father and my mom. It got me to think about

NL: what influences they might have on me and what aspects of my present reflect these influences. I discovered that I do resemble them in many ways, even my gesturing (laughs)!

NL: So our discussions gave you an opportunity to reflect?

LM: Did it help you understand your own history more?

Mrs Chan: A little. It's more like it helped me understand my own personality more.

LM: Would that help you accept yourself more?

Mrs Chan: Yes. Especially when other people did not accept me. Like this morning. I told you before I was a nervous person. This morning somebody said to me, "You have gone to class for only one day, and then you become so tired?!" I did not feel very good listening to that. But … (laughs) well, that's me! And that (pressure) is as much as I can take.

LM: So you could just tell yourself that?

Therapeutic Effect on the Couple's Marital Relationship

The new understanding that Mr and Mrs Chan gained of themselves and their parents through exploration of their families-of-origin experiences affected the ways they saw themselves and their parents. It also affected the ways they related to each other.

Each of them could take the other person's behaviour and styles much more calmly and less personally. They came to *appreciate the other person's positive intentions* and to find the other person's *behaviour* much less annoying. Although the counsellors had not made any deliberate interventions in their behaviour, there were some dramatic changes. They came to understand each other's difficulties and were more able and ready to give emotional support. There was much more compassion. Trust gradually developed, trust in each other's positive intentions, care, and commitment. Sometimes, even though such trust was not expressed, there was enough of it inside each of them to sustain them for long enough to suspend premature suspicion and negative interpretations and avoid escalating negative cycles.

In spite of the differences in their personalities, which had been annoying to both, a feeling of warmth gradually emerged. Contrary to common belief, couples that have different personalities do not necessarily have to break up because of them, if they can find a way to respect those differences and use them to enrich their lives together. Shame and defensiveness were reduced. At the beginning of counselling they were accusing each other, agreeing with the accusations from each other, and felt quite defensive. But as the sharing progressed, they came to take the stance, "It's OK, you are like this and I am like that, and we are different", and they were able to *acknowledge and respect the differences* that existed between them. There was increased general acceptance of their own styles and the other person's styles. They came to appreciate that there were no good or bad styles. They were just accepted as different styles, developed from each of their unique histories. They were learning to allow the self and the other to just BE, without feeling a great pressure to change.

Interestingly, both of them came out of the process less bound by their own habitual styles. There was no longer any need to defend their usual responses by saying "I just can't help it." There was an increased interest and curiosity in self and in the other person, and in how each came to be the person he or she is. They became interested in observing their own family as well as the other person's family. The latter was an interesting surprise to the counsellors. Because of greater acceptance of their own past, they developed greater self-acceptance, and they now feel more open to exploring different options and to making choices about who they want to be. There was more openness in both of them toward exploring what other ways are available and could be considered. There was also greater readiness to try these other new ways of handling the same problems in relating to each other. There was lower reactivity and much better cooperation. They could also give each other more space to handle their inadequacies with new compassionate tolerance instead of responding with disapproving criticalness or sulky withdrawal, which in the past only added fuel to the fires of their struggles.

In spite of all the above changes, both Mr and Mrs Chan still felt some disappointments and a sense of loss when they realized that there would still be times when the other person could not be the person they wished and needed them to be. They will have to come to terms with this and find their own ways of looking after their own unfulfilled needs, when such fulfillment does not come from the other person. This in fact is the essence of "differentiation", that we accept our spouses are different and separate persons with their dreams and struggles, as well as limitations, and that they do not exist solely for the purpose of satisfying our needs.

There can be many ways of understanding marital difficulties. They can be seen as the result of skills deficits, clash of needs, and personality differences, and unresolved pain and hurt. In our work with the Chans, we have not attempted to teach the couple communication skills. We have not attempted to help them fulfill each other's emotional needs. We have not helped settle their personality differences or helped resolve the unresolved pain and hurt. Therapeutic interventions were far from complete in this focused family-of-origin exploration. Rather, the process described is only a beginning of further work by the couple, with or without professional help. In spite of this, because of the lowered reactivity, the increased calmness and openness to each other, the additional trust in each other's positive intentions, and the new ability to appreciate each other, the increased compassion and warmth, the reduced shame and defensiveness, and new mutual acceptance, new curiosity and interest to understand, they now have greater readiness to change, a better awareness of choice and options, better cooperation and more hope in improving their marriage. Family-of-origin exploration might not have removed all their marital difficulties, but it seemed to have helped them set a new *foundation for the discovery and experimentation* of different solutions to their problems, as confirmed by the couple in the concluding session.

Discussion: Therapeutic Effect of Family-of-Origin Exploration

The Powerful Influence of Families-of-Origin Experiences

The Bowen Theory or the Family Systems Theory postulates that our experiences in our families of origin play an important role in shaping our sense of who we are and shaping our first formulations about what it means to be in a family. Such influences affect us through a number of processes.

From early childhood, our families have been influencing us through day-to-day interactions and through the nature of the emotional atmosphere in the home. Sometimes, like Mr and Mrs Chan's parents, parents were not able to give their children everything that the children needed, be it material provision or emotional care and attention, or they might not have been able to demonstrate a sense of safety in their world. When these children grow up, they develop deep yearnings to make up for such deprivations. When the children grew up and become parents themselves, some of them might vow that they would not let their children repeat their own stories.

Sometimes, we pick up from our family experiences messages about who we are. As young children, we tend to personalize adults' responses to us. We believe that their behaviour and responses to us are related to us, because of us, or that such behaviour is targeted at us. We believe that we are the centre of the universe. We come to believe that we are not good enough, we are stupid, we are weak, we are not pretty, we are inferior, and we come to believe a whole range of positive or negative things about ourselves.

In addition, we form images of objects and people and relations external to us, but these images are actually only *our perception of* these objects, people and relations, which might be incomplete, inaccurate, and very different from what they objectively are. A person's experiences in the family of origin provide scripts about how he should conduct his own life; they also shape expectations about what kind of a husband and what kind of a father he wants himself to be. Further, they set up expectations in his mind about what kind of a wife he wants his wife to be and what kind of children he would like his children to be. Starting from the way we react to our families, we transfer similar reactive patterns of responding to other people, including our spouses. These scripts and expectations are assimilated into our experience in the course of our development and in the context of certain special times and under certain special circumstances in our history, such as conditions of war, Cultural Revolution or emigration. There are reasons behind how they were initially incorporated, but by the time we reach adulthood, the unique times and circumstances have gone, yet the acquired behaviour and expectations stay on. Some of these scripts might have outlived their original relevance and usefulness. Unfortunately, however, these scripts and expectations are the only ones we learnt and experienced. Without deliberate reflection or assessment, we continue to conduct our lives and involvement in relationships in the only ways we have ever known. Such scripts are so deeply ingrained that they feel really natural and taken for granted, and we may not be aware that we could have other possibilities.

Reconnecting with History and Discovering Self and Other as Separate Persons

The family-of-origin approach deals with the perceptions and experiences underlying communications and behaviours not only in the here-and-now exchanges between couples but also in the subjective scripts and beliefs that were programmed in the marriage partners a long time ago. These constitute the powerful driving forces behind their current behavioural habits, styles and patterns of relating with each other. Because of this, the approach puts less emphasis on hurrying clients into behavioural change and more on cognitive change in their understanding of themselves and the partner's behaviours as products of their history. The hypothesis is that, after they learn more about themselves and their partners, they would come to realize and to accept that such behaviour that was relevant and useful in the past might not necessarily continue to be relevant and useful now. They will realize that they have a choice. Often, such a realization provides people with the impetus to make some new choices about their individual behaviours and the way they relate to each other, without too much direct intervention on their behaviours by the counsellor.

Developing Resonance and Compassion over Shared Human Experiences

In the process of sharing their different families-of-origin experiences, couples will also have a chance to listen to each other's wishes, desires, dreams, disappointments and struggles. They will find a new sense of resonance around their common humanity: the fact that they are two human beings struggling to fulfil common human longings and desire for love, connection, and sense of worth, each in his or her own ways. These ways may be the only ways they know, the only ways they have learnt so far, although they may be clumsy ways that might not have worked perfectly. As they listen, they will come to feel a greater sense of compassion for each other, as one struggling human being feels towards another struggling human being. This resonance over their common humanity will often balance the previous heightened awareness of differences and polarity, which often breed feelings of anger, hostility, and mistrust in the other's intentions.

Increased Mutual Acceptance Reduces Resistance against Change

When both partners realize that their spouses are *separate and different* human beings sharing *similar* human sentiments, they will come to accept their spouses more, just as they are. As they come to feel more assured of their spouse's acceptance and respect, there is less need to defend who they are. When they feel less need to defend themselves or to insist on continuing their current behaviour, they are more ready to acknowledge that there are some things they want to change, and are more ready to entertain other possibilities. Change has now become something that they want and choose to go for, and not something that was forced on them by their spouses or by the counsellor.

As couples began to experience each other in this new way, they have, without realizing it, set foot on a new journey, an exciting, possibly lifelong one, of growing together as mutually supportive partners in marriage.

(*Note*:   The authors would like to point out that joint family-of-origin exploration work is not suitable for all couples. We would like to advise that it should not be conducted with couples who have decided to terminate the relationship, with highly reactive couples who easily engage each other in escalating patterns of attacks and counter-attacks, with couples who feel too much negativity and too little trust in their relationship, or couples with a great deal of unresolved individual issues and who are emotionally too fragile or sensitive. It is definitely not suitable for couples that are dealing with violence in their relationships. Also, the counsellor should have received proper training in the use of the approach.)

References

Bowen M. (1978). *Family therapy in clinical practice.* New York: Jason Aronson.

Bowen M. (1974). "Toward the differentiation of self in one's family of origin." In *Georgetown Family Symposium*, Vol. 1. F. Andres and J. Lorio (Eds.) Washington, DC: Dept. of Psychiatry, Georgetown University Medical Centre.

Carter B. and McGoldrick M. (1980). *The family life cycle.* New York: Gardner Press.

Freeman D.S. (1992). *Multigenerational family therapy.* New York: Haworth Press.

Guerin P.J. and Pendagast D.G. (1976). Evaluation of family system and genogram. In P.J. Guerin (Ed.) *Family therapy.* New York: Gardner Press.

Kerr M. and Bowen M. (1988). *Family evaluation.* New York, Norton Press.

Lerner H.G. (1985). *The dance of anger: A woman's guide to changing patterns of intimate relationships.* New York: Harper & Row.

Lerner H.G. (1989). *The dance of itimacy: A woman's guide to courageous act of change in key relationships.* New York: Harper & Row.

Lerner H.G. (2001). *The dance of connection.* New York: HarperCollins Publishers.

McGoldrick M. and Gerson R. (1985). *Genograms in family assessment.* New York: Norton.

Napier A. and Whitaker C. (1978). *The family crucible.* New York: Harper & Row.

Papero D. (1990). *Bowen family systems theory.* Boston, MA: Allyn and Bacon.

Richardson R. (1984). *Family ties that bind.* Vancouver, BC: Self-Counsel Press.

Richardson R. and Richardson L. (1990). *Birth order and you.* Vancouver, BC: International Self-Counsel Press Ltd.

Skynner R. and Cleese J. (1984). *Families and how to survive them.* Oxford: Oxford University Press.

Stone E. (1989). *Black sheep and kissing cousins: How our family stories shaped us.* New York: Penguin Books.

Tolman W. (1969). *Family constellation.* New York: Springer.

3

Long-term After-effects of Childhood Sexual Abuse on Married Life:
Implications for Practice

GRACE MI-HAR CHAN

This chapter attempts to discuss the significant after-effects of childhood sexual abuse in the married life of adult survivors. These are difficulties in trust, deficiencies in couple communication, problems over intimacy and sexual relations, and the possible risk of intimate partner violence. Implications for treatment are then explored. Some clinical issues are also addressed.

Introduction

Hong Kong, like many societies, has been slow to respond to the vulnerabilities of children who have been sexually abused. Though the plight of abused children led to the founding of a non-government society, Against Child Abuse, in 1979, and the establishment of a government Child Protective Services Unit in 1983, the Task Group on Handling Procedures on Child Sexual Abuse under the auspices of the Health and Welfare Branch was not formed until 1995. The vulnerabilities of adult survivors of child sexual abuse, however, have received even less recognition, and it has been very much left to the individual endeavours of professionals working with their particular client or patient groups.

In this paper, the author discusses a few significant areas of after-effects of childhood sexual abuse in the interpersonal relationships of adult survivors, in particular their relationship with intimate partners.

Case illustrations are cited. Those quoted are mainly of female adult survivors, though there is a brief reference to the impact on male survivors. To protect the survivors, names and identities have been changed. The intervention process is then highlighted and some clinical issues addressed.

Long-Term Effects of Childhood Sexual Abuse on the Survivor's Marriage

The long-term effects of childhood sexual abuse have also been of concern to professionals in other countries. The impairment of trust, deficiencies in communication, fear of intimacy and sexual dysfunction seem to be the most prevalent effects of abuse within relationships (Busby *et al.* 1993; DiLillo & Long 1999; Hunter 1991; Margolin 1999). Recent research indicates that childhood sexual abuse is very likely a contributing factor in a variety of impairments in social and interpersonal relationships (Davis 1991; DiLillo 2001; Engle 1991; Gil 1992; Stark 1993). Marital discord as a long-term effect of childhood sexual abuse has also been documented (Jehu 1988; Finkelhor 1990; Firth 1997). Similar findings are reflected in the author's work in one of Hong Kong's counselling agencies.

Distorted Belief and Difficulty in Trust

Researchers studying the cognitive processes of sexually abused adult survivors consider their distorted cognition to be a likely effect of the disturbances they experienced as children (McCann & Pearlman 1990; Fine 1990; Finkelhor 1990). In their childhood, during episodes of abuse, they experienced mixed emotions such as fear, pleasure, anger and confusion. At the same time, as children, they were often threatened or tricked by the abusers not to tell anyone about the "secret". Sometimes, when the abuse experience was disclosed, they were not believed. It is common for survivors to be blamed for the sexual abuse.

Not being validated, the abused children very often questioned their own judgement. Carrying these confusing messages in their upbringing, they may have developed a pattern of relating to the world based on confused cognition and distorted beliefs (Sgroi & Bunk 1988). The world may no longer be perceived as safe or in their control. They gradually develop mistrust in others. This sense of mistrust is often complicated by the fact that the survivors were frequently abused in childhood by someone they knew and trusted. Yet, their trust in the abusers was manipulated and betrayed. Even worse, incest survivors often felt not only betrayed by the abuser but also commonly by their family members, who were perceived to be aware of the abuse but had not taken action to intervene. The survivors, with such experiences of betrayal, may develop negative beliefs and attitudes about people, particularly males, seeing others as untrustworthy. Such mistrust directly affects the survivors relating to their partners in later married life. It is difficult for survivors to tell their partners of the history of abuse, because they would be extremely vulnerable if their partners used the information as a weapon against them in times of conflict. Yet, without trust, the couple relationship is hampered.

Working with the survivors in therapy groups and individual counselling since 1995, the author has observed that many of the survivors experience great difficulty in trusting others. It has taken much more time and effort for the author to establish a trusting working relationship with them. When therapist-client rapport is established, the latter often acknowledges difficulties in trusting others, including even the husband.

> Yan, a married survivor of numerous childhood sexual abuse experiences by different perpetrators, explained that her difficulty in trusting others made it hard for her to develop intimate relationships with the opposite sex. Once male friends appeared to show more affection to her, she could not help thinking that they wanted to take advantage of her. Though married, she acknowledged that she still felt distant from her husband and could hardly believe that he really cared for and loved her.

In the same way, another survivor — Marilyn Van Durber, an incest survivor and former Miss USA — also revealed that she had told her fiancé that she could not even trust him after she had undergone a period of therapy (Video "A Story of Hope").

Besides developing a sense of mistrust, the survivor may manifest distorted beliefs such as perceiving him or herself as being no longer worthy of love. On the one hand, the survivor yearns for love. On the other hand, he or she perceives him or herself as not deserving love from others.

> Sum, a survivor of intrafamilial sexual abuse, acknowledged she could hardly think of herself as being lovable. She yearned for love, but she believed that she was "damaged goods" and

not worthy of others' loving her. Her mother told her so when she revealed to her during puberty that she had been abused sexually. She often felt guilty for not being a virgin when she married. Therefore, when her husband blamed or even hit her in later married life, she believed that she deserved such treatment.

Couple Communication Deficit

Another adverse effect of childhood sexual abuse on a couple's functioning is problems in communication. As mentioned, the issues of esteem and distorted beliefs such as "I am damaged goods" or "nobody is trustworthy" are complex issues for the survivors. Such issues directly and/or indirectly affect the survivors' communicating with their partners in an effective way. At the same time, their difficulties in trusting others also directly and indirectly negatively affect the relationship and communication with their partners. As many survivors were forced to keep silent about the abuse experience, secrecy may have become a developed pattern. Such a pattern in life gradually results in less direct and less open communication as adults (Davis 1991). In one study, it was found that twenty-three percent of the survivors reported "no meaningful communication" with their partners, whereas only six percent of the non-abused control group reported this (Mullen *et al.* 1994).

Problem with Intimacy and Sexuality

Survivors commonly have problems with intimacy and sexuality. A prerequisite for forming a sexual relationship is the ability to develop an intimate emotional relationship. However, survivors cannot really trust others, so it is difficult for them to take risks to develop intimate relationships, not to mention sexual relationships. Even if they choose to become intimate with someone and choose a partner, as Kirschner *et al.* (1993) point out, two general types of dysfunctional marital pattern seem to emerge. The first pattern is for the survivor to find a withdrawn or non-relational spouse who will not challenge her to deal with her childhood sexual abuse trauma. The second pattern is for the survivor to select an abusive partner who outwardly resembles the abuser. No matter which choice of partner the survivor makes, neither pattern can foster intimate relationships but gradually leads to dissatisfaction in married life. However, from my observation, the choice of partner could be one from anywhere along a continuum from less withdrawn to more withdrawn, and from less abusive to more abusive, rather than at the extreme ends.

Various studies indicate that childhood sexual abuse has a great effect on varying aspects of a person's sexuality, such as sexual preference, body image, sexual lifestyle and sexual functioning (Kinzl *et al.* 1995; Maltz 1991; Tharinger 1990; Westerlund 1992). These sexual difficulties include decreased sexual satisfaction and increased sexual dysfunction. Victims may perceive sex to be dirty, are troubled by sexual anxiety, have difficulty with arousal or vaginismus, experience flashbacks during sex, guilt after sex, and difficulty in achieving orgasm. To them, small events can trigger fear reactions about the sexual abuse. They may still have sex with their partners. Yet, it is common for them to have sex out of a sense of duty or generosity to their partners rather than for pleasure.

> Lai, a bright and charming woman in her forties, came for counselling about her sexual difficulties. She felt greatly disturbed by her sexual relationship with her husband. She found she was reluctant to have sex with him, for she believed that sex was dirty. Yet, as someone's wife, she thought that she had the obligation to "give" her husband sex. During the counselling process, she acknowledged that she was sexually abused by her uncle, who forced her to have sex when she was eight or nine years old. Very frequently while having sex with her husband, not only could she not enjoy the process but she was disturbed by flashbacks when the couple became physically very intimate. The flashbacks were sometimes in the form of intruding images of her being abused sexually as a child, or sometimes simply the sensation of helplessness and powerlessness. This made her suffer greatly, as these flashbacks interfered with and interrupted moments of intimacy in her marriage. She was distressed as well by strong guilty feelings for being unable to satisfy her husband. At the same time, her husband felt frustrated and sometimes confused with anger and self-doubt while being "rejected" by Lai. The couple's relationship was negatively affected.

Lai's case is not an isolated one. In fact, a number of married survivors also reported not wanting to have sex because they feel it to be disgusting. They were also disturbed as flashbacks of scenes, thoughts and feelings of being sexually abused in their childhood would emerge out of their control, and they would feel frightened. Some women survivors even took drugs to numb themselves before having sex with their husbands.

Whereas female survivors often find sex disgusting, sexual problems for male survivors often include having strong sexual drives and very commonly an image of reduced manhood, which threatens their perception of their masculinity (Dimock 1988). In a qualitative study of ten male survivors, six claimed that they used sex to avoid being drawn into intimate relationships. They perceived themselves as performing rather than engaging in sexuality (Gill & Tutty 1999). The author has encountered only three male survivors so far in her professional life, yet they all expressed strong sexual drive. One male survivor, who was abused by a male perpetrator, once confided that he used sex to show his masculinity, because he was afraid that he had lost his manhood.

Risk of Intimate Partner Violence

As mentioned, some survivors tend to choose partners who resemble the abusers. Research findings indicate that survivors of childhood sexual abuse have an increased risk of suffering later intimate partner violence (Banyard et al. 2000; DiLillo et al. 2001; Russell 1986). In the study by DiLillo (2001), it was found that childhood sexual abuse survivor respondents were twice as likely as non-abused women to report at least one incident of physical violence in their current couple relationship, that is, thirty-four percent verses seventeen percent. This corresponds to the study report of Russell (1986), indicating twenty-seven percent of the incest survivors had husbands who had been physically violent to them, whereas only twelve percent from the non-incest control group so reported. It is also interesting to find from DiLillo's study (2001) that a significantly greater number of relationships of childhood sexual survivors were involved in physical violence committed not only by their spouses but by them as well. There have been cases of acts of violence by female survivors against their male partners, even when their partners did not reciprocate. In the author's clinical experience, it is also interesting to observe similar patterns in couple violence among the married survivors. A possible explanation may be that the survivors are generally hyper-vigilant. The violence may be the result of the survivor thinking that the relationship with the partners poses for them an imminent threat, so that they initiate violence or fight back as a defensive act. At the same time, survivors' families-of-origin are often characterized by marital dysfunction (Mullen et al. 1994). This may suggest that many childhood sexual abuse survivors may not have many opportunities to observe and learn effective conflict resolution from others. When they get married, they may relive the same pattern of conflict resolution as their parents had.

Research indicates that intimate partner violence in the survivor's married life may be predictive of later separation and divorce (Rogge & Bradbury 1999).

The Intervention Process

From the author's clinical experience, intervention with the survivors is observed to evolve in stages. In the first stage, it is essential to establish a trustful therapeutic alliance, so that the survivors can then take risks in working through their emotions and the after-effects of the childhood sexual abuse experiences. In the second stage, intervention endeavours to help the survivors deal with the after-effects of the childhood abuse, such as the issues of responsibility, self-blame with cognitive restructuring of distorted beliefs, recognizing and expressing feelings, working through the grief and distress. The third stage focuses on acknowledging and building on the survivor's strengths. The fourth stage draws together the working-through processes towards integration.

Revelations of childhood sexual abuse usually surface in the course of therapy, seldom as a presenting problem at the beginning of therapy. Whatever presenting problem the survivor brings to counselling, building a trustful therapeutic attitude is of paramount importance.

Building of Trust

As mentioned, childhood sexual abuse survivors experience great difficulty in trusting others, because of the repeated betrayals they experienced in their upbringing. In emphasizing the importance of establishing a trustful therapeutic relationship with the survivor, Sgroi and Bunk (1988, 159) suggest a useful approach for preparing and building trust. The therapist can say to the survivor: "It will probably be a long time, if ever, before you feel that you can trust me ... That's okay ... it is only necessary that we all behave in a trustworthy fashion". The author, from her clinical experience, finds that such a statement helps to give permission to the survivors to take time to build up trust in the counsellor. Very often when such a statement is made, the survivors will feel understood and respected. This will encourage and help them to move forward. As time passes and the counselling proceeds, the survivors may gradually risk opening themselves up by further disclosing their childhood sexual abuse trauma.

Anxiety over being out of control is another important issue of the survivors, as many things were not in their control during childhood, not even their body. Again, the approach suggested by Sgroi and Bunk (1988) offers reassurance to the survivors, giving them a sense of being in control and being helpful in building trust within the therapeutic relationship.

Helping the Survivors to Articulate: Their Personal Belief about the Meaning of the Experience

Once the sense of safety and security is established so that the survivor is enabled to acknowledge and constructively deal with early experiences and the after-effects, the therapeutic process can address the effect of childhood victimization on current functioning (Sgroi & Bunk 1988). At this point, it may still be appropriate to offer separate interviews to the couple before going into couple therapy.

All through the counselling process with the survivors, it is helpful to understand the belief system they have evolved, how it was affected by their childhood sexual experiences and how the meaning they make of these abusive experiences may be contributing to their current marital functioning.

Very often, the survivors believe that they are responsible for the abuse. The nature of this belief, and other distorted beliefs, is influenced by the age at which the abuse occurred, the level of cognitive maturity of the child at that time, the turmoil experienced, the relationship with the abuser, whether force was used during the abuse or any tricks or threats imposed, whether the abuse was disclosed, as well as the responses of others. All these factors contribute to children's interpretations, or rather misinterpretations, of what happened, which continue to affect them in adult life. This tendency in distortion of belief has also been observed by other therapists (McCann & Pearlman 1990; Sgroi & Bunk 1988). Examples of common distorted beliefs include:

> "I did not refuse his sexual advance. I should be responsible for it."
> "As I wasn't forced into the sexual abuse, I must have allowed it to happen."
> "Why did I not tell others right away? As I have kept it a secret for so many years, I should bear responsibility for the abuse."
> "The world is dangerous. People who get close to you are going to take advantage of you."
> "Sex is dirty and disgusting!"

Those who received material returns from the abuser before or after the abuse, or whose body responded to the abuse with physical pleasure, showed even stronger guilt and shame. They strongly believe that they are responsible for the abuse.

To aid the survivors in challenging these distorted beliefs, cognitive restructuring techniques could be adopted. For those who feel guilty for not having refused the perpetrator's sexual advance in childhood, the author has found that inviting the survivors to bring photos of themselves that date to around the same age as the onset of the abuse can be particularly empowering. The survivors, visualizing the little girl in the pictures, are normally more able to realize cognitively how fragile and helpless they were at that time in refusing the advances of the abuser. For those unable to find a photo of themselves at the age of abuse onset, an alternative with comparable empowering effects is to invite them to observe children of a similar age as they were at the time of the onset of abuse.

> Ming was sexually abused when she was seven years old by a neighbour of over fifty years of age who was thought to be a nice man who loved children. Ming had a strong belief that she was responsible for the abuse, because she had accepted that neighbour's candies before letting him fondle her the first time she was abused. Afterwards, she was given $1 or $2 or candies after the abuse.

When the author invited her to bring a photo of herself at around the time she was abused, Ming suddenly realized while looking at the little girl in the photo how young she was at that age to resist that man's deception. That experience was a great breakthrough to her. In later sessions, she was better able to comprehend the childhood experiences and to blame herself less.

After challenging their own distorted beliefs, the counselling process can assist the survivors in replacing their distorted beliefs with other definitions. For instance, the alternative perspective for those who feel responsible for the sexual abuse because they kept it secret for so many years may be: *"I kept it a secret for so many years because I was told not to tell when I was a child. Just because I feel responsible doesn't mean I am responsible."* Similarly, for those who believe that their body had betrayed them because they had physical excitement while being abused, the alternative can be: *"My body has not betrayed me. It has responded in a normal physiological way to sexual stimulation only. It's the abuser who has betrayed me."* Similarly, for those who see sex as dirty and disgusting, the alternative belief can be *"Sex is natural. It is not dirty".* *"It is not sex itself that caused pain or panic, but the sexual abuse. Sex can be enjoyable."*

In the process of facilitating the survivors' exploration of the meaning of their childhood experiences for themselves, the author finds that encouraging them to write their own story of childhood abuse enables them to examine their own feelings and thoughts in between counselling sessions. It helps them to express their feelings and thoughts and to organize and clarify their perception of the meaning of the experience. Reviewing these very personal journals together helps the survivors and the counsellors to appreciate the implications of the abuse in a developmental context.

Childhood sexual abuse is always an experience of loss — loss of security, of childhood innocence, of self-esteem, identity and confidence, loss of other attachments and healthy relationships (Cruz and Essen 1994). The survivors need to be helped in understanding and grieving these losses properly. The writing exercises in the form of letters or self-dialogues with their inner child are also helpful to the survivors in giving expression to the meaning of the childhood abuse to them.

When survivors have a better understanding of their own belief system and the effects of the childhood sexual abuse on their current functioning, they can then better integrate the experience, reclaim their body both physically and psychologically and move forward towards self-nurturing, self-appreciation and self-determination.

Working on Survivors' Strengths and Resources to Survive Childhood Sexual Abuse

While working with survivors, whether in individual or in couple work, highlighting and building on their strengths is found to be effective and essential. Survivors often bear guilt and shame, believing that they are responsible for the abuse and are damaged goods. Enabling them to see that whatever means they may have taken to survive the abuse (even means that may appear to be negative) highlights the fact that they have the courage to survive and is of paramount importance. Survivors are generally very persevering in making a life for themselves. Validation and positive reflection of this perseverance is often empowering to the survivors. The author enjoys using a "courageous warrior" metaphor to describe the survivors as they have been persevering enough to survive all the pain, fear and hardships for so many years and have not given up. Sometimes, using the cactus plant as a metaphor also seems meaningful, as a cactus can survive in a very harsh environment.

All survivors have their own internal strengths and resources. While working with them, it is important to encourage them to mobilize these internal strengths to help themselves. Using the "building a powerful part of self" technique introduced by Macdonald *et al.* (1995, 203–5) to identify a powerful person who is capable of providing support and a solution to his or her problems can be very effective. The counsellor can ask the survivor to imagine that she is now a caring elder with wisdom and power. If her "older, wiser self" were to write a letter to her, what comforting words, what advice would she give her? When the letter is written, the counsellor can invite the survivor to read it silently or aloud, whichever she prefers, and then remind her that this powerful person is part of her. It is particularly empowering if the survivor can be given time to absorb a sense of this powerful self. Then, going home, the survivor can continue practising this as homework, consulting her "older, wiser self" through such dialogue and building a powerful part of herself between sessions.

The following is a letter written by a survivor from her "older, wiser self":

> Dear Shan,
> I can understand your feelings and your fears. At this moment, I want to say to you: "You are very safe now. What you need is to feel with your heart and not your head. Get in touch with the need for "breaking free" deep down in your heart. Try to do this. I'm sure you can make it! Don't let your head rule over your heart. Just listen carefully to the voices from your heart. Slow down and don't rush. You don't have to always be a perfect person. ... I wish you every success.
>
> Older, wiser self

Throughout the counselling process, and particularly at this stage, the survivors are encouraged to nurture themselves better. They will be encouraged to give compliments to themselves daily, engage in positive self-talk/self-affirmations. In group settings, the survivors' self-affirmations will be shared publicly, with other members reiterating the affirming sentiments to the survivor. Affirmation cards with positive messages specifically tailored for adult survivors would also be shared with the survivors. Key messages include *"Being abused sexually was not my fault"*, *"I am a valuable and courageous person"*, *"I can allow myself to have anger"*, *"I will better nurture myself"*, and so on. One survivor, during the course of counselling, bought herself a very lovely little notebook. She proclaimed it her "Success Bank". Daily, she would put in the "bank" the little successes she achieved and what she had done for self-nurturing.

Such practices build on the strengths and positive potentials of the survivors and contribute to boosting self-belief.

Apart from mobilizing the internal resources of the survivors, activating the supportive network such as a supportive partner, discussed later, can surely be an integral part of working with the strengths and resources of the survivors.

Towards Integration

The endeavours to re-establish trust in relationships, the articulation and redefinition of the meaning of the abuse experience, the building of strengths and resources, all contribute to helping the survivor deal with what has happened, and in moving forward in self-nurturing and self-appreciation. At this stage, as the survivors review their growth through counselling and reflect on what they consider to be the next step forward, the issue of forgiveness or claiming justice may arise. Yet, every survivor is unique, and not everyone wishes to forgive the perpetrator or claim justice. Rather, as long as the survivors can properly deal with their fear, hurt, anger and grief, forgiving themselves, setting themselves free from the guilt and shame that has engulfed them for years, they have more choices for their life. The author's work with survivors has shown that a few may choose to claim justice by confronting the perpetrators, but more survivors resolve the childhood trauma by just letting go.

For those who choose to confront the perpetrators, a thorough assessment with the survivors on the purpose of their confrontation, the perpetrator's possible reaction, the possible consequences, and what they hope to achieve for themselves are of paramount importance. With this assessment, and if confrontation is the choice, preparation and rehearsal are still necessary. Then the follow-up after the confrontation must also be taken care of.

The survivors who decide to forgive can choose to write a letter to themselves, to the perpetrators, or to tell the latter in person. If they do write a letter to the perpetrator, they can still choose to have the letter sent or not. Whichever way they choose, to stay at peace with themselves and befriend their own selves is the ultimate concern. Premature suggestions of forgiveness are by no means helpful and indeed can cause perturbation to some survivors.

At the stage of integration, it is common that many would like to contribute in some way to encourage other survivors still struggling with the impact of childhood sexual abuse, to realize that being abused is not their fault and to seek help. They also commonly wish to educate the public and to promote public awareness of the impact of childhood sexual abuse, suggesting helpful responses should survivors wish to disclose childhood experiences in confidence. Some survivors volunteered to share their experience with others in person as peer counsellors. Others were willing to be interviewed on TV and in the press. A few years ago, some survivors the author worked with in group therapy also chose to compile their personal stories and have them published as a book. They formed an editorial board with the author and her colleague, and a book entitled *No More Secrets* (不再是秘密) was published in 1999. The book was the first local one containing the personal stories of local childhood sexual abuse survivors, their struggles, their growth and their voices. Those who contributed articles to the book said that they found that, by doing so, they moved another step forward in the healing process towards integration. The book also encouraged many other survivors and educated the helping professionals working with the survivors.

Inclusion of the Partners

Whether to work individually with the survivor or to involve the partner is a question that every therapist has to resolve. Douglas *et al.* (1989) suggest individual therapy before paving the way to couple therapy. Maltz (1988) suggests couple therapy, as this "gives validation and a voice to the suffering of the partner" (169). Johnson (1989) highlights a preference for Emotionally Focused Marital Therapy (EFT), as it offers a flexible balance of individual sessions with each partner as well as couple therapy. Clinical experiences indicate that the intervention approach selected depends on whether the survivor comes to counselling service for marital relationship difficulties as the presenting problem or for her own childhood sexual abuse concerns, whether the partner knows of these early experiences, and whether the partner knows that the other is in counselling.

In fact, the effects of childhood sexual abuse on the partner, the effects of the survivor's therapy on the partner, and the role of the partner in the survivor's healing process have been receiving increasing concern. Whereas survivors seem to have more outlets to solicit support, the partners may feel neglected or left out (Firth 1997; Reid *et al.* 1996). Strictly speaking, partners are victims, too, and they are affected by what the survivors are going through. They also need to be reassured that the issues raised by their survivor partners are not about them personally. Firth (1997) listed the issues faced by the partner. They include:

- Feeling bewildered and quickly falling into a "carer" role for the suddenly "sick" partner;
- Feeling hurt at being misidentified with the abuser;
- Feeling angry at the powerlessness to have intervened in the abuse;
- Insecure, anxious and fearful of abandonment;
- Having conflict between feeling robbed of a good sexual relationship and feeling selfish for wanting this;
- Sadness at the loss of physical and emotional closeness with partner;
- When the partner in therapy becomes more independent and assertive, it may be difficult for both parties to adjust to the different dynamics within their relationship.

Many partners find it hard to put aside their sexual relationship. A partner once said: "I understand she (the survivor) needs to withdraw from sex when dealing with a painful memory or dream. It can feel abusive to have sex immediately following a dream from the past, but to cut off the partner sexually for indeterminate lengths of time is not in anyone's best interest. Men need to know they are loved and desired too." If sex is refused, the partner's frustration or anger may contribute to the survivor's experiencing her partner as the powerful abuser. This association with the original perpetrator may bring additional resentment to the partner. Helping the couple to discuss and negotiate their needs and expectations has to be undertaken.

From the author's clinical experience, it seems that the partners who know of the spouse's childhood sexual abuse welcome being involved. They want to support the survivor. They are eager to understand more about the after-effects of childhood sexual abuse, the therapeutic direction, and the part they can play in the recovery process. If not involved, some partners may feel the counsellor to be a competitor. Even worse, positive change in the survivor may lead to unnecessary fragmentation of the marriage, if the partner and the relationship do not develop at the same pace (Bacon & Lein 1996; Kirschner et al. 1993). As Bacon and Lein (1996) wrote: "Changes in the survivor during psychotherapy, such as enhanced self-esteem, increased assertiveness, or a desire for reallocation of roles within their primary relationship, are considered to be progress, but may require that partners accept and adapt to these changes" (3–4).

What, then, is the most effective approach in working with a couple when one partner is an adult survivor of childhood sexual abuse? A number of studies highlight group therapy for partners as an effective means in the healing process (Firth 1997; Jehu 1988). Firth (1997) identifies sexual dysfunction, emotional difficulties and interpersonal problems as the main targets for treatment of the survivors and the partners. While involving the partner, the meaning of the childhood sexual abuse to both partners can also be explored. Psycho-education about the effects of childhood sexual abuse and the process of the treatment can be covered. It is a pity that there is no such group therapy for partners of survivors in Hong Kong. Yet, the author tried to run two sharing sessions last year for the partners of the survivors who were participating in the therapeutic group for survivors. Feedback from the few partners who joined the sharing sessions was positive, and the survivor/wives were observed to have greater improvement than did the other group members whose partners did not participate in the group process. When appropriate, social workers can carefully endeavour to include some partners in couple counselling.

> With reference to the case of Lai who came for counselling about her sexual difficulties in her marriage, the husband was later included in counselling, with Lai's consent, after some therapy sessions with Lai individually. The husband expressed his conflict. On the one hand, he knew that it was normal for his wife as a survivor to avoid having sex with him. On the other hand, he had sexual needs and felt extremely frustrated when turned away while having sex. Psycho-education was rendered to facilitate the husband's increased understanding of the common effects of childhood sexual abuse on the survivor. The couple was encouraged to identify the triggers of the flashbacks. They were prepared so that, when Lai had flashbacks during sex, the husband would try to bring her back to the here and now by asking her to look slowly around the room, telling her that the one she is now with is her husband and not the abuser, telling Lai her present age, and reassuring her that she is safe at this time. With this understanding, the husband was more accepting of Lai's emotional responses, and his action to support her when she had flashbacks gradually helped her to have fewer flashbacks. Their sexual relationship gradually improved, as did their communication.

It should be emphasized that the involvement of the partner in the therapeutic process is rather delicate and has to be handled with care. When the partner is involved, the survivor may be worried. She may worry that her husband will not love her when he knows some of her defenses. She may also worry that the counsellor may like her partner more than the counsellor likes her.

> Sze, another survivor, was concerned that, though her husband
> knew her history of being sexually abused as a child, the
> information he had concerning her past history of abuse was
> rather limited. She was worried that, if her husband was
> involved and she disclosed more, she could not face him.

In such situations, working sensitively with her on the implications of
her worry and the options available is important. When is the appropriate
time to involve the partner? The author agrees with Kirschner *et al.*'s
(1993) stance that it is strategic to engage the partner when the survivor's
symptoms subside, when she is able to become more assertive and to
develop new behaviours and skills.

Clinical Issues

In working with couples or with the partner who is a survivor of
childhood sexual abuse, some clinical issues have to be taken into
consideration.

Transference and Counter-transference

In the counselling process, pacing and timing are very important. The
survivors are often very sensitive to rejection. Their progress in the
counselling process also fluctuates greatly. This requires patience from
the counsellor. Also, it should be noted that, during the therapeutic
process, the complicated dynamics of "eroticization of hate" may emerge
(Loris 1998). The survivor in the childhood abusive relationship has been
involved in a pattern of love accompanied by hate. In the therapeutic
relationship, then, these dynamics can be re-experienced in counter-
transference. The counsellor may feel the survivor's unconscious pressure
of turning the worker-client relationship into a "loving hate". Herman
(1992) also states that the eroticized transference- counter-transference
is one of the most complex dynamics that may occur within the
therapeutic relationship with adult survivors. In such a situation,
appropriate empathetic responses such as inviting the survivor to tell her
feelings, validating the possible overwhelmingness of these feelings for
her and inviting her to tell more can be of great help. To frankly clarify
and acknowledge the feelings and needs of the survivor is helpful in
changing the "loving hate" dynamics. This can sometimes initiate a
forward move in the therapeutic process.

Physical Contact

It is common for social workers to have, at times, physical contact with their clients as a form of support to the latter. However, it should be noted that any physical contact with the adult survivors, either in individual or couple therapy sessions, should be done with extreme care and caution. As the survivors have been physically and sexually abused and betrayed as children, any physical contact may trigger flashbacks or be interpreted as potential abuse. From past experiences of working with the survivors, the author has learnt that the counsellor should ask permission before making any physical contact. This practice is in a way empowering for the survivors, allowing them to have stronger sense of control, which they lost in childhood when they were unable even to control their own body and feelings.

Vicarious Traumatization

Dealing with childhood sexual abuse trauma is an intense emotional experience for the survivor, the partner and the counsellor. One can hardly be unmoved or unaffected by listening to the survivors' stories. A counsellor working with childhood sexual abuse survivors may have, as a natural result of the investment in caring, the experience of vicarious traumatization (Geib & Simon 1994; Herman 1992; McCann & Pearlman 1990). This is recognized as a form of post-traumatic stress or a sense of secondary victimization experienced by the counsellor. Courtois (1988) refers to this as contact victimization. Although Post Traumatic Stress Disorder symptoms are normal for those who have experienced trauma, they can be just as normal for those working intensively with survivors on their childhood trauma. Counsellors can find themselves emotionally and mentally overloaded, or as defensive and avoidant as the survivors are. Experiences such as these are normal. To prevent being overwhelmed by vicarious traumatization, the counsellor must have clearly defined boundaries, both internal and external, and must differentiate between personal feelings and client feelings. As well, the author finds that keeping a journal to track one's own feelings and thoughts, doing exercise and other means of self-nurturing are just as important for the counsellor as for the survivor. Surely, keeping a healthy supportive network should not be neglected.

Gender of the Therapist

Practical issues, such as the gender of the therapist, need to be carefully considered in working with couples that have one partner having experienced childhood sexual abuse (Wilson & James 1992). Generally, studies recommend female therapists for female survivors, whether for individual or group treatment. In the meantime, it should be noted that we should not assume the survivors must prefer a same-sex therapist. Instead, the wishes of the survivors are important and should be respected as far as possible. When the partner is involved and in couple therapy, it is beneficial to both the clients and the counsellors if a male and a female counsellor can pair up, thus making more resources available.

Conclusion

This paper is an attempt to discuss the complicated after-effects of childhood sexual abuse on the adult survivors' later married life, and examines the various stages of the treatment process. Involving the partners in treatment increases support and resources for healing, and needs to be implemented in planning treatment. Similarly, training to increase the sensitivity of marriage and family counsellors in recognizing indicators of childhood sexual abuse would enable adult survivors to be heard and responded to with respect, when they are ready to share painful experiences.

To end the paper, the author would like to cite a poem written by a survivor to her loved one (in Simon 1998, 132), which reflects the approach-avoidance conflict in a survivor and her difficulties in communicating with her partner.

For my love

It happened such a long time ago,
I kept it inside, not letting anyone know,
The fear and fright would never let it out,
You made me tell you when I heard your doubt.

I never told anyone; they'd think I might be lying,
So a wall I built around me,
Sometimes showing through anger, hate and crying,
"What's the matter?" people would say,
"Nothing" I'd reply, "leave me alone — go away".

But that's not the answer; you've got to tell,
Or you'll end up living a lie, living in hell,
It's really hard to tell, even the people you trust,
But you taught me how,
And now I'm trying — I must.

Don't run away; don't try to hide,
Reveal your feelings from deep inside,
If I'm the one that matters the most,
Why do I feel you're a living "ghost"?
Please come and talk to me today,
Before we drift too far away.

~ G.E. ~

This expression of yearning, from someone longing to be heard, and needing to be withholding at the same time, needs to be recognized by each of us, whether as spouses, partners, family members or professionals. We need to listen with an open mind, tuning ourselves in to be receptive and respectful of the underlying pathos striving towards healing. As a local survivor in Hong Kong wrote:

Finally, I'm longing for a pair of warm and gentle hands,
To give me hugs ...
Telling me, "You are lovable. You are precious.
It is not your fault. May peace be with you."

~Anonymous~

最後，我渴望有一雙慈愛溫暖的手，
給我擁抱。
……它可以告訴我：
「你是可愛的，你是有價值的，
這不是你的錯，願你平安。」

Caritas Family Service 1999, 31

May peace be with all the survivors in their relationships with their partners and others, and with themselves in particular!

References

Bacon B. and Lein L. (1996). Living with a sexual abuse survivor: Male partners' perspectives. *Journal of Child Sexual Abuse, 5* (2), 1–15.

Banyard V.L., Arnold S. and Smith J. (2000). Children sexual abuse and dating experiences of undergraduate women. *Child Maltreatment, 5,* 39–48.

Busby D.M., Glenn E., Steggell G.L. and Adamson D.W. (1993). Treatment issues for survivors of physical and sexual abuse. *Journal of Marital and Family Therapy, 19,* 377–92.

Chan M.H., Tam S.W., Chan S.K., Ko G. and Petty (Eds.) (1999). *No more secrets: Voices of survivors of childhood sexual abuse.* Hong Kong: Caritas Family Service. (In Chinese).

陳美霞, 譚素姁, 陳淑琴, Grace K. 及 Petty 編 (1999). 不再是秘密：童年曾經歷性侵犯之重生者的心聲。香港明愛家庭服務出版。

Courtois C.A. (1988). *Healing the incest wound: Adult survivors in therapy.* New York: WW Norton.

Cruz F. G. and Essen L. (1994). *Adult survivors of childhood emotional, physical, and sexual abuse: Dynamics and treatment.* Northvale, NJ: Jason Aronson Inc.

Davis L. (1991). *Allies in healing.* New York: HarperCollins.

DiLillo D., Giuffre D., Tremblay G.C. and Peterson L. (2001). A closer look at the nature of intimate partner violence reported by women with a history of child sexual abuse. *Journal of Interpersonal Violence, 16* (2), 116–32.

DiLillo D. and Long P.J. (1999). Perceptions of couple functioning among female survivors of child sexual abuse. *Journal of Child Sexual Abuse, 7* (4), 59–76.

DiLillo D. (2001). Interpersonal functioning among women reporting a history of child sexual abuse: Empirical findings and methodological issues. *Clinical Psychology Review, 21* (4), 553–76.

Dimock P.T. (1988). Adult males sexually abused as children. *Journal of Interpersonal Violence, 3* (2), 203–21.

Douglas A.R., Matson I.C. and Hunter S. (1989). Sex therapy for women incestuously abused as children. *Sexual and Marital Therapy, 4,* 143–59.

Engle B. (1991). *Partners in recovery: How mates, lovers, and other pro-survivors can learn to support and cope with adult survivors of childhood sexual abuse.* Los Angeles, CA: Lowell House.

Fine C. (1990). The cognitive sequel of incest. In Kluft, R.P. (Ed.) *Incest-related syndromes of adult psychopathology.* Washington DC: American Psychiatric Press.

Finkelhor D. (1990). Early and long-term effects of childhood sexual abuse: An update. *Professional Psychology: Research and Practice, 21* (5), 325–30.

Firth M.T. (1997). Male partners of female victims of child sexual abuse: Treatment issues and approaches. *Sexual and Marital Therapy, 12* (2), 159–72.

Geib P. and Simon S. (1994). Trauma survivors and their partners: A gestalt view. In G. Wheeler and S. Backman (Eds.). *On intimate ground.* San Francisco, CA: Jossey-Bass Publishers.

Gil E. (1992). *Outgrowing the pain together: A book for spouses and partners of adults abused as children.* New York: Bantam Books.

Gill M. and Tutty L.M. (1999). Male survivors of childhood sexual abuse: A qualitative study and issues for clinical consideration. *Journal of Child Sexual Abuse, 7* (3), 19–33.

Herman J. (1992). *Trauma and recovery.* New York: Basic Books.

Hunter J.A. (1991). A comparison of the psychosocial maladjustment of adult males and females sexually abused as children. *Journal of Interpersonal Violence, 6,* 205–17.

Jehu D. (1988). *Beyond sexual abuse: Therapy with women who were victims in childhood.* Chichester, UK: Wiley.

Johnson S.M. (1989). Integrating marital and individual therapy for incest survivors: A case study. *Psychotherapy, 26,* 96–103.

Kinzl J.F., Traweger C. and Biebl W. (1995). Sexual dysfunctions: Relationship to childhood sexual abuse and early family experiences in a nonclinical sample. *Child Abuse and Neglect, 19,* 785–92.

Kirschner S., Kirschner D.A. and Rappaport R.L. (1993). *Working with adult incest survivors: The healing journey.* New York: Brunner-Mazel.

Loris M.C. (1998). A case of "loving hate". *Journal of Child Sexual Abuse, 7* (1), 65–80.

Maconald K., Lamble I. and Simmonds L. (1995). *Counseling for sexual abuse: A therapist's guide to working with adults, children, and families.* New Zealand: Oxford University Press.

Maltz W. (1988). Identifying and treating the sexual repercussions of incest: a couple therapy approach. *Journal of Sex and Marital Therapy, 14,* 142–70.

Maltz W. (1991). *The sexual healing journey: A guide for survivors of sexual abuse.* New York: HarperCollins Publishers.

Margolin J.A. (1999). *Breaking the silence: Group therapy for childhood sexual abuse — A practitioner's manual.* New York: The Haworth Press.

McCann L. and Pearlman L. (1990). *Through a glass darkly: Understanding and treating the adult trauma survivors through constructivist self-development theory.* New York: Brunner-Mazel.

Mullen P.E., Martin J.L., Anderson J.C., Romans S.E. and Herbison G.P. (1994). The effect of child sexual abuse on social, interpersonal, and sexual function in adult life. *British Journal of Psychiatry, 165,* 35–47.

Reid K.S., Wampler R.S. and Taylor D.K. (1996). The "alienated" partner: Responses to traditional therapies for adult sex abuse survivors. *Journal of Marital and Family Therapy, 22 (4),* 443–54.

Rogge R.D. and Bradbury T.N. (1999). Till violence does us part: The differing roles of communication and aggression in predicting adverse marital outcome. *Journal of Consulting and Clinical Psychology, 67,* 340–51.

Russell D.E.H. (1986). *The secret trauma: Incest in the lives of girls and women.* New York: Basic Books.

Sgroi S. and Bunk B. (1988). A clinical approach to adult survivors of child sexual abuse. In S. Sgroi (Ed.) *Vulnerable populations,* Vol. 1, pp. 137–86.

Simon D. (1998). *Guiding recovery from child sexual abuse: Horizons of hope.* Philadelphia, PA: Jessica Kingsley Publishers.

Stark K. (1993). *Helping the adult survivor of child sexual abuse: For friends, family and lovers.* Racine, WI: Mother Courage Press.

Tharinger D. (1990). Impact of child sexual abuse on developing sexuality. *Professional Psychology: Research and Practice, 21* (5), 331–37.

VanDurber M. (1999). Video on "A Story of Hope" *(Chinese Translation Version).* Hong Kong: Caritas Family Service.

Westerlund E. (1992). *Women's sexuality after childhood incest.* New York: WW Norton and Company.

Wilson K. and James A. (1992). Child sexual abuse and couple therapy. *Sexual and Marital Therapy, 7,* 197–212.

4

Tackling the Intrinsic Dilemma in Marital Infidelity

Anita Yuk-Lin Fok

When a couple seeks counselling over an affair, they address a series of choices. The task of the therapist is to enable them to reflect on and to struggle through the personal and relational dynamics underlying this dilemma of choices, in order to search out what the marriage means to them and whether there is a basis for maintaining the relationship.

This chapter proposes a model of marital work that engages the couple through a process of personal reflection and focused decision-making, and no presumption of reconciliation. This is followed by a marital review in which they undergo an exploration of their experiences within the marriage and address the issues requiring attention, to discover for themselves where they stand as regards the future of their relationship.

Introduction — Challenges to the Marital Therapist

Several characteristics of couples struggling with infidelity challenge the therapist's clinical stance, ethical position, and epistemology of human needs, intimacy, and meaning of the marriage and of existence (Tuch 2000; Weeks & Hof 1987; Humphrey 1983; Young & Long 1998; Pittman 1989; Brown 1991; Glass & Wright 1988). Many couples caught up in the throes of tackling infidelity experience multiple layers of ambivalence, at the moral, behavioural, psychological and emotional levels, about themselves and others. At the same time, their turbulence sometimes produces drastic responses from the extended family, friends, church members, and work associates, so that what goes on outside the couple system shapes and alters their relational dynamics. At the stage of intense involvement with the third party, the couple is often pushed to the point of marital breakdown. The partners are so torn apart by these disruptions and disturbances in their daily life that they become ambivalent about what they would like to happen, so that they change their minds constantly, wanting alternately to be "in" or "out" of the marriage.

In such a situation, the marriage therapist may be led to assume that the couple should follow implicit expectations of commitment to marriage, that the husband should end the extramarital relationship, return to the marriage, and the wife should forgive the husband. Or, the therapist may also be ambivalent, remain neutral to "watch" what is going on and whatever might arise. Many therapists stand in between, frustrated about being pulled and pushed by circumstances. In the end, the stronger forces shape the outcome of the relationship.

This article proposes an approach to couple counselling based on the concept that to maintain self-respect, a person has to be accountable for his or her actions, despite the extenuating circumstances. Just as we trust that a violent person has the ability to be non-violent and not to hurt others, the person in an affair has the choice of engaging or not engaging in an extramarital relationship. To hold the person responsible for his or her choices with an emphatic non-blaming attitude is the clinical stance of marital therapy in such situations. Participants in affairs have various "choice-points" for deciding one way or another. The struggle over these choices and the marital work this calls for can be examined through the experience of Susan and Jim.

The Proposed Model for Marital Work

The case of Susan and Jim illustrates the process of the proposed approach, which works through: the initial stage of engagement of both partners, focused decision counselling and personal reflection, invitation to a marriage review and pre-review sessions, a marital review, and, if that leads to a recommitment to the marriage, trust rebuilding. Should there be no recommitment to marriage, the parties would have participated in a careful review of their circumstances, to be somewhat prepared for a less hurtful separation and divorce. The couples could then be referred to a mediation service to work towards a calm separation and cooperative co-parenting.

Susan and Jim are a young couple that have been married for six years. Jim was having an affair with a female colleague. Susan sought assistance. At the beginning, she manifested the emotional turmoil, intense insecurity, fear and disorientation of someone who has suffered greatly from betrayal and trauma. Her pain was validated, she was supported with empathy, some general knowledge of the psychology and behaviour in affairs was shared, and the participation of both partners to engage in counselling was suggested. Careful and calm responses to Susan's distress and the sharing of clinical insights were essential to stabilize the chaotic situation at its initial stage.

Note: In this article, the terms affaired party, the spouse, and the third party are used. The affaired party can be either the husband or the wife, although in Hong Kong the larger percentage of affaired parties is male. For convenience in this discussion, the affaired party is referred to as "he" and the spouse as "she".

The Initial Stage of Engagement

The affaired party, due to guilt, shame, as well as a sense of pride and a wish to present the perspective that he could manage the situation, was very reluctant to enter counselling. Appropriate invitation and genuine respect for him is essential to ensure his engagement. By treating Jim as the person who was crucial to an understanding of the situation, the counsellor successfully engaged him in the session. He was, in the beginning, aloof and defensive. When he was given respect to fully present his "version" and his "perspective", he gradually felt secure and acknowledged his internal struggles. In the second session, he was able to release his mixed feelings of guilt, anger and despair about the marriage and about the situation.

The technique of experiential exercise of being "torn apart" was used to uncover his inner tension. Jim was assisted in holding tightly to a door handle or a window frame with one hand (any object that could bear the weight of his body). Then, the counsellor would hold his other hand tightly. Jim was instructed to try to stay in such a situation for a minute and get in touch with his experiences. Such an experiential exercise helped the client to focus on his existential experiences of being "torn apart" by the demands of the family and of the third party. From these experiences, he became aware of his disorientation and that he was in need of personal space to centre himself. Also, he was aware that any movement on his part, such as clinging to or letting go of either party, would create tension and reaction from others. Jim, like other clients, appreciated from this exercise his many dilemmas and his need to be self-focused to handle the situation with great care.

There are two decisions the affaired party has to struggle with. The first is the secrecy of the affair. The second is the decision of staying or leaving the marriage. This second hurdle of the decision to divorce or not is very often hidden. In the face of this possible "hidden decision" (Brown 1991, 174), it would be a pretence to continue marital therapy. However, the surfacing of the hidden decision would upset marital equilibrium, and intense consequences might result. The party left behind would experience intense shock and fury. She needs time to sort out what has happened and what it means. Any sudden revelation of one party's unilateral decision can, in extreme cases, prompt mental breakdown or suicidal thoughts.

At this point, it is quite unlikely that the couple is able to consider in a calm and rational manner the "pros and cons" of separating or staying. Should the couple have such rational ability and cohesiveness, the relationship would not be so volatile. The decision counselling and personal reflection processes proposed in this model puts a hold on making this decision until some of the difficulties and dilemmas have been addressed. The couple's struggles raise several points of concerns and reality, at the psychological, relational, and moral levels. The counsellor's therapeutic neutrality means careful consideration and exploration of the reality of all these levels. The focused decision counselling and personal reflection enables both spouses to face their reality safely, squarely and realistically.

Counsellor's Reflection:

At this point, the counsellor is usually trapped into becoming either "persuasive", to prompt the affaired party to face up to the marital problem to ease his guilt, or "neutral" and detached, to allow the party time and space to make decisions on his own. In the past, the writer has used both these approaches and found both to be unproductive. In the former stance, the affaired partner may be "persuaded and encouraged" to go through marital counselling to ease his guilt of hurting his wife. However, he then tends to become "emotionally absent" in the counselling room, worried that any show of the slightest good intentions would be misunderstood as love and reconciliation. Because of such anxieties, he would behave in a "cautious" and "uninvolved" way, or his behaviour would go "back and forth". Should a counsellor take the latter stance to become "neutral" to allow the decisions to emerge, the counsellor fails to take advantage of the "time" element. Discovery of infidelity constitutes a crisis for the couple. Timely interventions at critical moments are crucial in crisis. Otherwise, the relationship may deteriorate fast, and the party who comes to seek help feels desperate and in despair. Thus, non-intervention is an ineffective intervention.

From clinical reflection, the writer, inspired by Professor Guldner, has improvised an effective, non-blaming and efficient intervention, inviting the affaired party to be centred and "focused" on his own decisions. The above technique is a powerful tool that moves the affaired party forward and stops him from reprocessing his hesitation.

Focused Decision Counselling and Personal Reflection

These sessions have to be regular, intensive, focused and purposeful, to provide the affaired party time and space for personal reflection. Should the issue of trial separation be raised, the writer would discourage physical separation from the spouse, as this heightens anxieties, opens opportunity for the affaired party to turn to the third party for comfort, and in the long run increases the risk of divorce. However, separation of beds and comfortable distancing and silence are encouraged. The spouse has to be fully informed of the purpose and duration of the counselling. The main task is to reduce anxieties and to stabilize the emotional system.

Focused decision counselling runs from three to four sessions. The sessions are designed as a free-floating experience for the affaired party to "pour out" the dreams and secret longings he has cherished for so long and kept to himself. The counsellor creates a secure space for the affaired party to be in touch with his inner yearnings and emotional vacuum. The pressure of hidden fantasies and anxieties evaporates a bit when it is shared in an open and calm atmosphere, and allows the client to examine his situation with more energy and rationality. There is a Chinese saying: "to push the boat along the current" ("順水推舟"). In this personal reflection, the process is carried along by the psychological current, the counsellor easing the momentum of the boat/client. Several supportive individual sessions for the spouse can be done at the same time. She should be informed that the counselling sessions would be focused on enabling the affaired party to explore his many dilemmas. The affaired party would share the end result with her afterwards, but the content and process are protected by confidentiality as a general rule of therapy.

In this focused decision therapy process, the client experiences and appreciates the paradoxical "both-and" of his own human nature. In our culture, the affaired person is sometimes viewed as irresponsible and neglectful of his commitment and his family. However, when viewed from a "both-and" perspective, he is both a liar and a protector, who lies to protect his wife. He is both unfaithful and dedicated, unfaithful to his previous commitment and dedicated to the search of a dream. He is both greedy and single-minded, greedy to fulfil his insatiable desire and single-minded in not being hindered. He is both indecisive and stubborn, indecisive in which loving relationship to choose, and stubborn in circling around. It is in the safety of the relationship with a supportive counsellor that he is able to reflect on the nature of his many contradictions.

The counsellor listens to the *recurrent themes and patterns*. In a brief overview of previous intimate relationships, the writer was working with a man who kept pursuing "cool and aloof" girls. Through reflection, he found resonance of inner emptiness in his perception of coolness and distance. In Jim's case, he was a good rule-abiding boy. He failed several times in courtship, for he was too timid to take the initiative. He regretted his "cowardice". Unfulfilled aspiration, hurt feelings and fear of failure had to be explored. Otherwise, these "hidden unfulfilled emotions" would build up resistance in the subsequent counselling sessions.

Very often, recurrent themes emerge in the empty-chair dialogue. This technique is very helpful in *elucidating inner struggles*. For instance, Jim repeatedly queried why he was deprived of the tender feelings that he so longed for. He also questioned what kind of person he was that he did what he did not intend to do. He was self-blaming but also resented being misunderstood by others. The empty-chair technique revealed these struggles. From the struggles, the counsellor is able to elicit his perception of the affair, his concept of love, and an appreciation of the significant influences of other factors — the family, children, community, and friends.

The affaired party was then asked to think of five things that he would most like to obtain before the end of *his life journey*. This technique proved to be highly effective. It helped him to temporarily escape from his current difficulties and to link up his dilemma with his future stance. Roger Scruton (1986, 335), in his discussion on sexual morality, refers to this as an act of deliberation which "enables the present self to incorporate its own future into its practical reasoning, so as to pursue, not merely that which is presently desired, but also that which is conducive to satisfaction". From the writer's experiences, all affaired parties welcome this intervention, as it offers them an opportunity to really project in an overall manner what they are looking for in life.

The sessions have to be kept short, focused, purposeful and free of pressure. After several sessions, the party is usually still ambivalent and no decision is likely to be made. This is to be expected. However, following this personal reflection, the counsellor would collaborate with the party *to formulate a way to make his decision* with certain explicit principles. Perhaps, if this could be meaningful to the client, it would be helpful to share with him the concept of a "solid self" as proposed by Bowen. "The solid self is made up of clearly defined beliefs, opinions, convictions, and life principles. These are incorporated into self from one's own life experiences, by a process of intellectual reasoning and the careful consideration of the alternatives involved in the choice. In making the choice, one becomes responsible for self and the consequences" (Bowen 1978, 365).

The following principles, jointly derived in discussion with Jim, are then made explicit. The decision is to be totally *voluntary*, for he has to bear the consequences of his decision. The decision is *not to be regretted* when reviewed in the future. The result of the decision *creates the least hurt to all parties*. The decision endeavours to *render fair treatment to every person involved*. In Western culture, the marriage decision is treated very much as a personal decision, perhaps a reflection of an individualistic ethos. From the literature, there is a lack of clinical guidance for the decision to divorce. Therefore, the writer has tried to design a clinical guide for a divorce decision, to assist affaired parties in their cognitive and emotional turmoil (see Appendix 1).

At this critical point, the affaired party is always "blank" about what to do next.

Counsellor's Reflection:

When a person has another lover, he is inclined to desire the new lover more than, or at least as much as, he desires his wife. In this dilemma, he is at a dead end. In the conventional approach, the client is assisted in weighing the pros and cons of staying with or leaving his spouse. This balancing of the merits and benefits of two women, to make a decision about breaking a former commitment, is a mishandling of a decision of human destiny.

The existence of a marriage is based on a decision, honestly made, whether it turns out to be good or bad, wise or foolish. If one does not learn from the first decision, how can one be so bold as to trust a second decision of whether to leave or stay with the marriage? To safeguard a "better" decision confronting a second watershed, one has to respect and honour the first decision. To follow the logic of the past, one has to review the history that one is already a part of. No one can jump out of history. Every page of history has an influence on the next page. Should the new lover render hope and promise of a bright future, one should handle the present and past with care, respect and honesty.

For the well-being of the parties involved, including the third party, the proper way of handling the decision of relationship commitment is to review and settle the history. Therefore, the party is invited to suspend development with the third party and to give himself some time to undergo a marital review. The marital review has to be a fair, neutral, transparent and non-coercive process.

Invitation to a Marital Review, and Pre-review Sessions

Based on the above philosophy, the writer would invite the affaired party to consider entering a marital review. Before undertaking this intervention process, there are a few crucial skills that require mental and practical rehearsal to prepare "how to tell the third party about going through the marital review". The sharing has to be non-threatening, calm, considerate and completely honest. If this step is treated carelessly, the subsequent intervention will stumble. Sometimes, the affaired party, governed by the fear of losing the third party, creates an implicit sense of false hope of settling the "divorce" with his wife and then returning to the third party. Any such elusive message has to be gently challenged. If the situation is mishandled, the reactivity of the third party will largely obstruct the ongoing process.

What exactly is the meaning of the "marital review"? The married couple might not be at the same point of the uncoupling process. Rather, it could be that "one wants in and the other wants out". In this scenario, the spouse who wants to reconcile is very tense and tends to try to draw the counsellor to her side to save the marriage. The other spouse, who is inclined to leave the marriage, will try to persuade the counsellor to assess the negative side of marriage, tends to reject reframing techniques, resists being open, and is highly sensitive to any hidden agenda. He is fearful that the slightest acknowledgment of the strengths of the marriage may drive him back to the marriage. In such a case, this triangulation to involve the counsellor restricts space and energy for all concerned to face complex relationship dynamics freely.

"Marital review" is a counselling process with a clear objective of reviewing the past marital relationship with no hidden agenda of reconciliation. Therefore, both parties have to learn to face the situation and each other honestly. When Susan chose to enter the "marital review" session, she was fully aware of the likelihood of separation after the process. If she is not ready for such uncertainties, she has the right to decide to get a divorce because of non-acceptance of her husband's disloyalty. Should each party be fully informed of the other party's tendency and situation, the personal agency is heightened. Psychological defence and manipulation will be minimized to a large extent. The couple is then required to make the decision together after the review has been done. No coercion towards either direction is implied. Only then can the couple be released to be free and open to the reality of their history. This stance of honesty and consistency itself helps the affaired party to demonstrate trustworthy behaviour, which itself also heals the hurt of all parties, regardless of whether the result is divorce or reconciliation.

Conducting the "Marital Review"

In the first session, the parties are still tense with emotional turmoil and uncertainty. The calm, open and transparent nature of the session is most important. First of all, voluntary entry to the review is made explicit between the spouses. In this case, Susan was fully informed of the ambivalence of her spouse. Sometimes, a quantified description is helpful in making the picture fair and clear. For instance, Jim clearly stated that he had a sixty percent inclination to leave the marriage. However, out of responsibility to his marriage commitment, he agreed to suspend his decision until an open-minded "marital review" had been done. Susan was given time and space to consider whether she was willing to participate in the marital review, being fully informed of a lack of 100% guarantee of reconciliation. With this understanding, she was prepared to tune her expectations and emotions to correspond with reality. Because she had suffered from disruption of trust within the marriage, every move in the counselling process had to be honest and free from collusion, to rebuild trust. Also, this openness prevented any subtle triangulation to involve the counsellor, and the counselling sessions could be more effective.

The parties were encouraged to make decisions together, so that the determination of the future of the marriage was experienced as a mutual decision. This is a difficult, controversial part. In general, people who do not initiate divorce feel "abandoned". The implicit understanding of the marriage commitment is that the couples support each other for life unless a disaster happens. As Brown points out from her rich clinical observation, the hidden decision to leave the marriage "will be the choice of one spouse and rarely both" (Brown 1991, 175). The feeling of abandonment hurts as much as the decision itself. So, both parties are assisted in considering in a matter-of- fact way that, should the marriage break apart, this would be a mutual and transparent decision to reduce hurt and guilt.

For Jim and Susan, seven weekly sessions of the marital review were conducted. In the first session, the writer suggested *rule setting* to respect and protect the counselling process. The first rule was that the affaired party agreed not to contact the third party, in order to help him to concentrate in the process. Very often, the writer would use the "gesture" of moving her head towards and away from the spouse frequently to show the effect of losing focus in the session. Therefore, his mind had to be focused in one direction, or the counselling would not be effective. However, separation anxieties with the third party sometimes also drew his attention away from counselling. Then, the couple was encouraged to negotiate an informed mutually agreed minimal contact method to reduce anxieties. The second rule was that the content discussed in the counselling process was not to be shared with the third party. The writer derived this rule from the observation of Glass and Wright (1988), who used the metaphor of building a wall around the couple with a window open to the third party.

The marital review was also guided by another piece of research done by the writer (Fok 1999). This research indicated the divorce decision process to be a dynamic one, running along a downhill satisfaction slope. However, the process can be reversed, though going through a period of turmoil, as long as the spouse has not reached the "point of no return".

In the marital review session, marital problems were unveiled and explored in the relational context. The current *conflicts were translated as differences*. The differences were further translated into underlying emotional needs. In the above case, Jim was annoyed that Susan queried him about his daily activities. Susan was upset that Jim sometimes showed his temper and shouted at her. Susan was fearful; she was in need of physical contact, comfort, connecting and reassurance. However, Jim was worn out and disoriented. He was in need of space, solitude and autonomy to handle his internal turmoil.

With a better understanding of the needs of each of them, the writer opened the exploration to trace *how they had handled their differences in the past*. Furthermore, the writer traced how different coping methods had affected their relationship. In this way, the past recurrent pattern of unresolved conflicts was unveiled. Jim had always accommodated Susan's needs, for he wanted to perform the duties of a good husband. However he restrained his own grievances, which he felt were unrecognized. Susan was ignorant of Jim's grudges and reached out even more. For her, her show of concern and his response was a sign of a good relationship, which earned a lot of compliments from friends. The writer thus acknowledged their good intention to protect the relationship. She used intervention of reversal techniques to shift and stabilize the system. Jim was allowed full space and self-control to take care of Susan in his way and in his time. Susan was instructed to observe instead of querying, to listen instead of questioning. The relational pattern was thus altered.

In the following sessions, the *context in which the problems arose was explored*. The pursuing and accommodating relational pattern was working fine until more family stress was experienced. The couple had different opinions about having a baby. Jim wanted a baby and Susan was worried about the responsibilities of motherhood. She recalled her observation of her tired and overloaded mother. The couple wavered over the issue and suffered from the pressure the in-laws put on them. Susan relied on the traditional gender role expectation that the husband should stand up to his family to shelter the wife. Thus, Jim found himself receiving a great deal of unfair blame and criticism. He used denial and rationalization to cope. As a result, Susan was free from worries and totally ignorant of Jim's pent-up anger. The pattern repeated itself, and grievances accumulated.

In the last three to four years, the situation was aggravated by changes at work. Jim suffered a lot of humiliation because of his career. He experienced unemployment and adjustment to a new job. Jim was not used to asking for comfort and help. His philosophical outlook, learnt from his mother, that "everyone has to stand on his own", further reinforced his helplessness and loneliness. Susan misunderstood, thinking that Jim was in need of solitude and space. As she turned more of her attention to her friends and social circle, Jim was more alone. He was unable to articulate his conflicting needs of having personal space as well as companionship and comfort from his wife. He became more depressed and lonely. In the last few years, Susan was successful in her career. She pursued evening studies. As a result, the couple rarely had a chance to eat dinner together at home. Jim once again suffered from his pattern of being unable to justify and voice his needs. He treasured dinnertime as a symbol of warmth and cosy family life. However, he internally argued with himself that a strong man should be able to be flexible, to adjust and to protect his wife. It was unreasonable to request dinner at home if his wife was too tired because of her studies. Once again, all these internal struggles and dialogue were totally unknown to Susan. Susan sometimes felt their relationship was distant, but no concrete problems were identified. Therefore, she turned her attention more to career and friends. In this vicious cycle that developed, Susan aired complaints once in a while, but Jim was uptight and had a hot temper. In the end, the hidden conflicts were unresolved.

When Susan and Jim found their vague sense of unhappiness *translated into contextual and interactive difficulties,* both of them felt relieved. At the same time, they also felt regretful of what had happened. Validation, generalization and explorations of fluctuations in the intimacy cycle were useful to support the couple in the hope of change and relief of self-blame. The couple was encouraged to revise their philosophy of life inherited from parents and shaped by social norms, to fit their life circumstances. As the sessions went on, Jim obviously changed to become more outspoken, more aware of his needs. Susan struggled to learn to adjust to a more assertive husband. But she was happier to be able to understand her husband more deeply.

As trust gradually built up, the *hidden problem* of sexual discontentment surfaced. The couple suffered from "poor" sex since the first week of marriage. Susan was fearful about pain during intercourse, Jim was highly accommodating during sexual intimacy. They had not had successful intercourse for one whole year. Also, often suffering from vaginal infection, Susan tried to avoid sex. Jim was extremely upset; his anger and sense of incompetence accumulated. Again, all these hidden grievances were suppressed and denied. Years on, Jim even developed a disinterest in having a sex life. This actually was a big issue that arose on and off. Once again, it remained unresolved, though Jim felt intense anger.

An individual session was held to heal Jim's wound. In the individual session, Jim admitted that he had a totally different sex experience with the third party. This was the first time in his life that he discovered sex could be so easy and so amazing. Jim was depressed at the discovery. The counsellor took great care to uphold and to contain Jim's anger. On the one hand, the counsellor had to show genuine human empathy for all his sufferings. On the other hand, the counsellor had to contain Jim's feelings in order that Jim is not too overwhelmed, which would make the situation worse. To come to Jim's rescue, the counsellor emphasized Jim's philosophy of not hurting others and of being a good husband. This called for a delicate balance on the counsellor's part and required quick-witted discretion to handle such intense past grievances with a couple who had yet to decide to reconcile or not.

In the subsequent sessions, more *toxic events were shared.* Many were based on misunderstandings and misperceptions aggravated by the interactive pattern. One issue was traced to early courtship. When Jim tried to express his love to Susan, Susan wavered and postponed her response several times. Jim felt hurt and rejected. He always wondered whether Susan really loved him wholeheartedly, or if he was the second best. Susan was surprised to hear this buried secret. She immediately affirmed her deep love for him. Her perceptions and the underlying dynamics of her behaviour in courtship were explored in detail. Susan was an obedient girl. She acted according to family and school teaching. She was worried about courtship at a young age. Her mother also instilled in her a philosophy of being reserved and to present a façade. She was inexperienced and sometimes avoided responding, to cope with the tension. The event was thus detoxified with this new meaning. Jim and Susan were a compatible couple who were rule abiding, obedient and responsible (Guerin et al. 1987; White 1989, 1990).

At times, Jim's emotions would fluctuate, disturbed by grief and guilt. Susan's resolve also fluctuated, beset with insecurities, a tendency to pursue, to doubt, and to become emotional. When the counsellor steered the boat in the right direction, the ocean waves seemed to be more under control. The couple was given a chance to revisit their history with new light and new perspectives. New energy was generated.

After the marital review had been done with care, concern and the right professional balance, the harder work was ahead. After reviewing the marital history clearly and honestly, how should the couple take the next step forward?

Counsellor's Reflection:

As I have mentioned, the marital review has to be fair, respectful and neutral. The process of the review, done with minutely tender skills, could itself reveal the inherent strength of the marriage. Very often, couples that have been married for more than three years owned certain relational strengths. Through the marital review, the relationship could be revisited and regenerated. However by this time, Jim was even more ambivalent than he was before counselling for he has less justified excuse to leave the marriage! At the beginning, he stated he was sixty percent inclined to leave the marriage. After the review, the issues addressed and detoxified, the emotional system of the marriage was back on track. Susan learnt to change a lot because of insights gained. Jim was now forty percent inclined to leave the marriage. The third party was waiting for his answer after the review. He was now under great strain.

Decision-making Transition

At the transition, one individual session was given to Susan. This was to support her, to calm her anxieties, reassure her of positive changes in the relationship, and to encourage her to regulate her pace and be patient for the decision. Three individual sessions were given to Jim. His internal struggles surfaced again. He struggled between "right" and "wrong", "good" and "bad". He also struggled with the possibility that his feeling towards his wife had diminished; he had little faith that the feelings could be rekindled. He also struggled with the social script and his own musings on liberalism: "when you have come across precious feelings of true love, why should you be tied by past miseries? Why don't you follow your heart to pursue your dream? If you have lost the love feelings towards your wife, why should you cheat yourself and follow obligations mechanically? You should take charge and lead your own life as you wish".

At this point, the counsellor should not argue with the client. She also should refrain from making any moral judgement. The counsellor faces the challenge of having sufficient understanding of various life philosophies to understand how they contend with each other. Human life is complex; human psychology addresses just some aspects of human behaviour. Human destiny and life choices involve an understanding of the individual's philosophy and ideology that transcends the level of psychology. As well as support and empathy for his difficult dilemma, one session was specially focused on Jim so he could iron out his internal contradictions. The process resembled the experiences of enlightenment. No teaching or education was given. Reflective questioning was asked to stimulate an honest self-examination. After the session, the main themes and discussion were summarized in a letter sent to Jim for his reference (see Appendix 2).

Marriage Rebuilding Phase

Eventually, Jim made a *voluntary* decision to leave the third party. The above counselling process took about six months of work. The counselling had entered a different phase: the marriage-rebuilding phase. This is briefly summarized to accomplish several tasks, such as:
1. Handling the aftermath of infidelity.
2. Grief work for the affaired party over discontinuation of the relationship with the third party, and anger work for the other spouse.
3. Trust-rebuilding work.
4. Understanding the meaning of "infidelity" for the couple and work for marriage enhancement.
5. Forgiveness counselling and a farewell ritual and recommitment pledge, when both parties felt ready to let go of their mixed emotions about the affair.
6. A review after three months confirmed that the couple had recovered and regained the momentum in their intimate relationship.

It takes another six to nine months to work through the above processes. Further innovative interventions have to be improvised and put into effect. For instance, the couple would write a letter to the third party and sign it jointly, to show the termination of the affair. The couple was requested to write a new marriage oath/pledge to express and signify the new birth of their marriage. This second phase of work is not much easier than the first phase of work. Emotional ups and downs do emerge. But the work has already shifted from decision ambivalence about the marriage towards rebuilding of the marital relationship.

Counsellor's Reflection:
    My work with couples affected by extramarital affairs is challenging and turbulent. I learn as I work; my learning informs my work. This model, which evolved naturally, has helped many couples to reconcile when they were at the brink of marital breakdown. I hope the approach will be beneficial to other practitioners and assist more couples in surviving life's hurdles and in avoiding unnecessary marital disappointment.

Other Outcomes

The clinical model articulated above is specific and precise; the process itself is difficult and turbulent. What about other cases in which the outcome is different from Susan and Jim's?

Different Pathways after the "Marital Review" and "Divorce Decision"

What if the affaired party refuses to leave the third party or is unable to recommit to the marriage? From my clinical experiences, there are two types of situation in which the couple is unable to work towards rebuilding the marriage. First, the marital bond is so weak that "marital review" cannot be carried through without prior intensive individual counselling. Both parties are highly reactive due to an unfulfilling past, so that more space and time is required for individual counselling. Second, the third party is unable to leave the scene. For instance, she is pregnant, or she is a very competent and indispensable assistant of the affaired party at work. I have tried to tentatively identify the positive and negative factors that affect the reconciliation or separation of the couple (see Appendix 3).

    In the event that the affaired partner is unwilling to recommit to the marriage, the spouse, though angry and in despair, may be more able to recover her self-esteem after having worked through the joint marital review and the shared decision counselling process. She would need further support, no less from her own self-stigmatization and from being affected by stereotyped labels. These could include suggestions that the extramarital involvement occurred because she had not been a good enough wife, had ignored his sexual needs, or that she is hot tempered, so it is understandable that the husband seeks to fulfil his needs elsewhere. Thus, the non-affaired party suffers from the loss of the husband's loyalty and from blame as the cause of his disloyalty, a double punishment. Again, using the analogy of domestic violence in a marital relationship, no matter how unsatisfactory the marriage, it is the violent man's full responsibility if he raises his hand to inflict violence. Similarly, regardless of how unfulfilling the marital relationship, the affaired partner is responsible for being disloyal in the marriage. Such a clinical stance would buffer the remaining spouse from unjust "double punishment" during the separation process. It may also provide the perspective to help the affaired party face up to his responsibility and handle his guilty conscience accordingly.

When both parties fail to recommit to working towards rebuilding the marriage, the marital counsellor could introduce mediation service to assist the party to separate in a supported and less hurtful manner. If they have children, the above counselling process and the divorce mediation service would help to prepare the couple for future co-parenting (Chow 2001; Irving 2002). The therapist may remain a counsellor to help the parties cope with post-divorce adjustment.

The Needs of the Third Party

Whether the same therapist should work with the third party is a controversial clinical question. Those who subscribe to the viewpoint that the third party is a significant element that cannot be ignored may offer contact and interview sessions. However, many therapists consider interviews with the third party undesirable. The reason is that the therapist will be triangulated by the third party and the couple subsystem that is basically in conflict. Some therapists remain neutral and flexible in their practice.

After much clinical reflection, the writer holds the stance of not working directly with the third party. However, the third party is encouraged to receive help from another counsellor. In this model, the needs and reactions of the third party are attended to indirectly, through the therapist's recognition of the presence and the importance of the third party, by talking about her and explicitly acknowledging her effect on the couple dynamics. For instance, the affaired party would be given time and space to air his affection and attachment to the third party, even including the history of their "falling in love".

The interest of the third party is also taken care of by raising the question of what would create less hurt to her. For instance, in Jim's case, when he was indecisive after the "marital review", he was asked to consider what would hurt the third party more: holding out false hopes and ultimately finding out that Jim did not wholeheartedly love her, or suffering an honest understanding that he could not develop an exclusively faithful relationship with her, because of his many dilemmas. The process of including a rehearsal on "how to inform the third party about the marital review" and the discussion of having an agreement of minimal contact with the third party during the marital review reflects concern for her and acknowledge her importance in the counselling process.

However, direct work with the third party is not favoured. Firstly, the affaired party in general would cherish a hope that the therapist, on meeting the third party, could directly observe and make a comparison for him to see which woman suits him. It could also be the means to prove that the third party is not a "bad" person. This is a trap for the therapist. At the philosophical level, different people are not to be compared, for they are not commodities to be exchanged if found unsatisfactory. All parties should be respected. The conflict of interest between the married partner and the third party obviously puts the therapist in an ethical quandary. Therefore, the clinical perspective is not to work with the third party directly but rather refer her or him to another therapist, as circumstances require.

Challenges for All Parties

This paper proposes a model of working with couples coping with infidelity in their marriages, and discusses some of the many challenges confronting all parties involved, including the therapist. The personal values and the philosophical stances likely to determine decisions and behaviour in these situations, as well as the many contradictions and conflictual needs and yearnings inherent in tackling infidelity, have to be addressed. These may surface at various stages of the counselling process.

When the affaired party takes the initiative to approach the therapist about his extramarital affair, the therapist has to be absolutely clear about the affaired party's motivation. It could be that he has decided to leave his spouse but worries that she may be depressed or suicidal. In this scenario, the therapist will be trapped into taking care of his emotional wife so that he can leave with a better conscience. Another possible scenario is that the affaired party has a hidden motivation in leaving the marriage, so he merely "performs" the necessary procedure to "try" marital counselling to ease his guilt. After the trial, the affaired party's conscience is soothed, as he can convince himself that the marriage has been observed by the marital counsellor as basically not workable.

The non-affaired party also poses certain common traps for the marital counsellor. The spouse with a strong belief in "professionalism" tries her best to drag her husband to the counselling room in order that the therapist would save the marriage for her. In this scenario, the therapist is psychologically flattered by the high expectation of the spouse and becomes triangulated within the emotional forces at play. Another common scenario is that she may be so hurt and angry that she expects the professional to help to "punish" the "villain". The therapist would be triangulated to another difficult position. The working model proposed above addresses these hidden and covert needs associated with these scenarios and avoids being triangulated into conflictual systems.

The Therapist's Own Emotions

The writer, as a practitioner, trainer and supervisor, has found that the therapist's own emotions and value system deeply hinder the effectiveness of the martial intervention. Supervisors may be trapped into going to two extremes. Many therapists feel angry with the affaired party. This hinders a genuine connection with the client, increasing difficulties in entering into his internal dilemmas. Failure to work with the affaired party leads to failure of work in tackling marital infidelity. Very often, this means the worker is confined to individual work with the non-affaired party, helplessly watching and waiting for the case to deteriorate. Some therapists go to the other extreme and support the affaired party in order not to lose contact with him. The support offered without philosophical reflection can evolve into a placating stance to the affaired party, so that he can avoid confronting his dilemmas. Instead, it is possible that the non-affaired party is then coached to be "patient", to "change", to become "feminine" to win the husband back. As a result, the work with both spouses is ineffective.

The therapist needs to be constantly alert to relational dynamics. Intensity and a sense of crisis are essential in moving the affaired party forward to face his situation; otherwise, he tends to avoid struggles over critical dilemmas and difficult choices. Thus the therapist has to exercise careful discretion to balance her work and not over-function to ease the tension and foster a means of escape for either spouse to avoid the predicaments they have to contend with.

Working with couples over infidelity can trigger strong emotions in therapists. Some may choose to take a detached stance. However, non-intervention is itself an intervention, and in such instances, the case usually degenerates without proper professional assistance. This work requires the therapists to work through their own experiences in marriage, get in touch with their attachment experiences and feelings about issues of trust and betrayal. Otherwise, intense reactions could directly affect the case.

Counsellor's Reflections:

As I review my work with couples suffering from marital infidelity, the faces and stories of different people appear in my mind. My struggles and difficulties in becoming an effective marital therapist will be reflected in the experience of other conscientious practitioners striving to respect clients' perspectives and demands, as well as their own values and beliefs. I believe that intimacy is precious. It is so precious that it can be earned not only by love feelings but through utmost integrity.

References

Bowen M. (1978). *Family therapy in clinical practice.* New York: Jason Aronson.

Brown E.M. (1991). *Patterns of infidelity and their treatment.* New York: Bruner/ Mazel.

Brown E.M. (1989). Getting the message. In *Family Therapy Networker,* May/June.

Carlson J. and Sperry L. (1999). *The intimate couple.* Philadelphia, PA: Bruner/ Mazel.

Chow S.L. (2001). 調解有關撫養權與子女生活安排. In *Family Mediation Handbook of Hong Kong,* HKCMAC.

Dattilio F.M. and Bevilacqua L.J. (Eds.) (2000). *Comparative treatments for relationship dysfunction.* New York: Springer Pub. Co.

Dym B. and Glenn M.L. (1993). *Couples.* New York: HarperCollins Publishers.

Fok Y.L. (1999). *Unraveling the riddle of the decision to divorce through the narrative accounts of divorced women — an attempt on an integrated model of divorce decision process to inform practice.* M.Soc.Sc Dissertation. University of Hong Kong.

Glass S. and Wright T.L. (1988). Clinical implications of research on extra-marital involvement. In R.A. Brown and J.R. Field (Eds.) *Treatment of sexual problems in individual and couples therapy* (pp. 301–46). New York: PMA Pub.

Glass S.P. and Wright T.L. (1997). Reconstructing marriages after the trauma of infidelity. In W.K. Halford and H.J. Markman (Eds.) *Clinical handbook of marriage and couples intervention.* New York: John Wiley & Sons.

Guerin P., Fay L., Burden S.L. and Kautto J.G. (1987). *The evaluation and treatment of marital conflict: A four-stage approach.* New York: Basic Books.

Humphrey F.G. (1983). *Marital therapy.* Englewood Cliffs, NJ: Prentice-Hall.

Irving H. (2002). *Family mediation — theory and practice with Chinese families. Hong Kong.* Hong Kong University Press.

Kell C. (1992). The internal dynamics of the extra-marital relationship: A counselling perspective. *Sexual & Marital Therapy,* Vol. 7, No. 2.

Lawson A. (1988). *Adultery: An analysis of love and betrayal.* New York: Basic Books.

Lusterman D. (1989). Marriage at the turning point. *Family Therapy Networker,* May/June.

Moultrup D. (1989). *Husband, wives and lovers — the emotional system of the extramarital affair.* New York: Guilford Press.

Pittman F. (1989). *Private lies: Infidelity and the betrayal of intimacy.* New York: W. W. Norton & Co.

Pittman F.S. and Wagers T.P. (1995). Crises of infidelity. In N.S. Jacobson and A.S. Gurman (Eds.) *Clinical handbook of couple therapy.* New York: Guilford Press.

Scruton R. (1986). *Sexual desire — A moral philosophy of the erotic.* New York: Free Press.

Spring J.A. and Spring M. (1996). *After the affair: Healing the pain and rebuilding trust when a partner has been unfaithful.* New York: HarperCollins.

Tuch R. (2000). *The single woman-married man syndrome.* New York: Jason Aronson.

Weeks G. and Hof L. (1987). *Integrating sex and marital therapy: A clinical guide.* New York: Brunner/Mazel.

White M. (1988/89). The externalizing of the problem and the re-authoring of lives and relationships. In *Dulwich Center Newsletter,* summer, pp. 5–28.

White M. (1990). *Narrative means to therapeutic ends.* New York: W.W. Norton.

Young M.E. and Long L.L. (1998). *Counselling and therapy for couples.* Pacific Grove, CA: Brooks/Cole Publishers.

Appendix 1

Guidelines for Divorce Decision

1. Do not make important decisions when in high emotional turmoil.
2. Ask yourself five important things you want to achieve by the end of your life over which you will not feel regret afterwards. These could be, for example, integrity, peace of mind, a warm and happy family, happiness, not to have a wasted life.
3. Try to prioritize your values.
4. List resources that may help you, such as your friends and family.
5. Try to imagine the advice that they might give you.
   Fill in the boxes:

	Person	Advice	Rationale	Accept/Not Accept	Reasons
1.					
2.					
3.					

6. Make a decision that you can live with and not hurt another person.
   Set out principles for decision-making: a decision to live your life towards harmony and integration instead of disintegration, a decision that conforms to the three highest virtues "真善美".
7. Draw out your dilemma.
8. Try to discuss your dilemma with a mature person whom you trust.

Appendix 2

Letter to Jim, following Marital Review & Divorce Decision Counselling

Dear Jim,

Thank you for sincerely sharing your thoughts with me. I appreciate how difficult your struggles have been. As I promised in the session, I am sending you a summary of your queries and of our discussion, which may be useful for your reference and further consideration.

A.   You asked, "How should one make a decision? How can we make a decision that acts against some of my feelings?"

Our discussion on what one "ought not" to consider:

Do not make decisions solely based on feelings.

Rationale: Feelings are real and valuable. However, they cannot be counted on as a major basis for decision-making. Human feelings can waver and change with the changes of the environment, people's reactions and life circumstances.

Do not make decisions based on a comparison of your wife and the third party.

Rationale: Both your wife and your girlfriend are respectable and honourable persons. A comparison of their qualities implies a process of depersonalization and diminishes their value to that of comparable commodities.

B.   You asked, What considerations affect one's decision?
Considerations:
1.   How does a decision affect self and others — self, wife, family members of self and partners, friends, relatives, the third party?
     Considerations based on principles:
     a.   to minimize the hurt to all parties,
     b.   to build up and support others,
     c.   to consider the modelling effect and the social effect on others.
2.   How does one link one's history of the previous life pathway and the future life pathway?
3.   What is the meaning of marriage?
4.   What is commitment? What constitutes a breakdown of commitment? How can one be congruent to self, wife, third party and people who trusted us?
5.   Is there any over-arching principle that governs all these considerations? "Decision defines a person."

C. You asked, "Are these principles only designed for the "Great" person to follow, and not for ordinary common people?

Our discussion: These principles sound "great", but they are not extraordinary. They are just simple human principles that even a child can follow, for instance, not to hurt others, not to be unfair, not to take advantage of others, not to be dishonest, etc.

D. You asked, "If one identifies with these principles, but one is not willing to follow them, what can one do?"

Our discussion: According to Kohlberg, in the mature stage of moral development, a person departs from a desire for external approval. The mature person can internalize what he believes and act with joy and pride.

E. You asked, "Why is it so difficult to follow and act according to what one believes?

Our discussion: Perhaps the discussion has already entered into the depth of human nature and human existence. Should one believe a human being to be more than an animal, he is subject to a severe test of good and evil forces, regardless of his religious inclination. Human integrity survives the test. The person with such integrity warrants honour and respect. That is why "decision defines a person" as we postulated.

You have thoughtfully reflected on the five most important things you want to obtain by the end of this life are: (1) be a loving and honest person, (2) be trustworthy, (3) enjoy a good family relationship, (4) do not to feel regretful, (5) be happy in life. How you honestly pursue your life wishes will affect what you are going to obtain in life.

I hope that this review of our discussion supports you and gives you hope and strength.

Best regards,

Anita

Appendix 3

Factors that positively affect marital reconciliation

1. The couple has some positive recollection of good feelings in the past, even though these may have been forgotten or denied.
2. The affaired party has strong and healthy moral development.

Factors that negatively affect marital reconciliation

1. The affaired party is searching for manhood by breaking away from the marriage.
2. The couple's relationship has developed from emotional fatigue to absence of affection.
3. The couple basically has little hope and faith in life, and intimacy and is very often affected by the experiences of their family of origin.
4. The affaired party is "too guilty" to face the situation.
5. One party has experienced drastic changes of values or value disintegration.

Factors that remain neutral if the above positive factors exist

1. The couple is highly conflictual.
2. The couple has experienced an accumulation of toxic events.
3. The couple has had no sex life for a number of years.
4. One party is regretful of getting married.

5

Forgiveness in Marriage

WONG LAI CHEUNG

In the myriad activities of everyday living, people in close relationships may hurt or upset each other. This is generally overlooked or forgiven in the context of the emotional bond. However, it is common for a marriage counsellor to come across couples whose relationship is in distress because of unfulfilled expectations, emotional blackmail, betrayal, or loss of trust, over which forgiving is much more difficult. It is worthwhile exploring forgiveness as a way to heal these hurts and rebuild the relationship.

This chapter examines the cultural, moral, and psychotherapeutic bases of clinical work in promoting forgiveness between married partners. Forgiveness work could constitute a minor or a major aspect of a couple's counselling experience. In clinical practice, the working-through process of forgiving goes beyond simply righting a wrong or seeking recompense for injury. In a marriage, being forgiving and being forgiven deepens trust and commitment in a relationship.

The Cultural, Moral and Psychotherapeutic Roots of Forgiveness

The Cultural Roots of Forgiveness

Forgiving, a process of giving up or ceasing to harbour resentment for an offence is an inherent aspect of social living. This is reflected in many cultures from ancient Greek to Judeo-Christian times, and in the Taoist, Confucius, and Buddhist traditions (Kwan 1994). From early times, the *Tao-Te-Ching* has highlighted the value of "recompensing injury with kindness". Confucian teaching emphasizes benevolence, *ren* (仁) as the cornerstone of a harmonious society (Lee 1993, 275). *Ren* has been defined as 1) being self-controlled and compliant to social norms, 2) being considerate to other people, 3) being humble and embracing in interpersonal relationships, and 4) having the courage to take action (Wen 1971, 64).

Chinese people place a great deal of emphasis on "harmony". The practice of *fung shui* is the actualization of harmony between humanity and nature. Harmony is important in human relationships as well. In maintaining harmony, the interpersonal boundary is blurred, and fairness is forsaken (Suen 1992). This is confirmed by Lee (1993), who suggests that Chinese people's sensitivity regarding fairness decreases within the increased proximity of a relationship. Sampson (1985, 1988) described Chinese individualism to be a form of the self with an assembly of other people close to him, which he termed "ensembled individualism". This ensembled individualism facilitates the letting go of a need to be treated fairly more easily than in those cultures with self-focused individualism, such as in the American culture (Lee 1993). Feeling that one has been treated unfairly is a major block to forgiveness; forsaking such a need will seemingly facilitate the process of forgiveness among Chinese people, especially when they are in close relationships.

However, paradoxically, the practice of forgiveness is more difficult among Chinese people. Because of unclear interpersonal boundaries and an emphasis on self-sacrifice, people's expectations of one another will be very high, and these expectations will make the harmful act disproportionately more hurtful within close relationships. In fact, it is not the act *per se* that harms but, more importantly, who does the act. According to attachment theories, a profound psychological and physiological interdependence (Hazan & Zeifman 1999, 351) is formed in intimate adult relationships, so incidents in which one partner responds or fails to respond at times of urgent need seem to have a disproportionate influence on the quality of an attachment relationship (Simpson & Rholes 1994). The closer the relationship, the more vulnerable the involved parties are, and so the more hurtful the act will be (Kwan 1994, 1000). A paradoxical phenomenon occurs here. Chinese people appear to be very forgiving, but once the interpersonal harms exceed the threshold, forgiveness seems to be more difficult than in those cultures in which expectations are clearly spelled out in close relationships.

This difficulty is also complicated by the subtle tendency to hold onto a sense of moral superiority in social interactions among Chinese people. According to Suen (1992), this is a tendency to compete with others on a more superior moral position, to gain social legitimacy and power (135). Forgiveness includes a process of introspection; the need for moral superiority may hinder the forgiving process because introspection is blocked. As a result, forgiveness may appear as a form of "pseudo-forgiveness", in the sense that it is practised solely to maintain a superficially harmonious relationship rather than to achieve reconciliation through a genuine understanding of the people involved.

The Moral Roots of Forgiveness

Forgiveness is needed when moral standards in an interpersonal relationship are violated and the parties involved experience a sense of moral injury. This deep sense of moral injury leads to a sense of unfairness and injustice, and an urge for redress (Hunter 1978; Kohlberg and Power 1981; Brandsma, 1982). From this perspective, a wounded relationship can be rebuilt only when the moral dimensions of the relationship are restored.

The development of moral values is inevitable in every society, because these values inform people's lives, both directly in deciding what to do and indirectly in their comments and judgements on people and actions. Moral standards may vary across cultures, but there are some universal ones, such as empathy, fairness, duty and discipline, which are valued in human relationships all over the world (Wilson 1993). In Chinese societies, the practice of moral standards is demonstrated in concrete behaviours. Without action, *ren* is impossible (Wen 1971, 64). Within tightly structured human relationships, concrete actions are embedded as responsibilities in relation to one's role. Though the types of responsibility may have changed drastically as a result of the rise of feminism and individualism in contemporary Chinese societies, the ability to fulfil one's responsibilities is always considered as a criterion for judging a person. For instance, a husband is responsible for the family financially and a wife for being the caretaker. An inability to fulfil these role responsibilities may be considered a breach of relational morality. Apart from fulfilling these functional responsibilities as above are other moral standards such as fidelity, honesty, and duty that are valued in marital relationships.

Psychotherapeutic Theories of Forgiveness

The attention given to forgiveness as a psychological intervention was very limited until the 1980s. The construct had been considered value-laden; many thought it should be studied only in a religious context, such as Christianity. However, forgiveness has actually been proven to produce psychological health by freeing a person from bitterness, anger, resentment, and the erosion of one's personhood (Hope 1987; Flanigan 1987; Worthington & DiBlasio 1990; Hebl & Enright 1993; Al-Mabuk *et al.* 1995; Freedman & Enright 1996; Coyle & Enright 1997; Konstam, *et al.* 2000). Thus, forgiveness as a therapeutic intervention for clients who have experienced an emotional wound is now the subject of more attention and study. Some scholars, such as Flanagan (1991), also argue that moral philosophy needs to be more psychologically realistic. In other words, although forgiveness is a moral value, it should be realistic and practical in a psychological sense.

According to McCullough and Worthington (1994), theories of forgiveness can be classified into four categories. First are the psychological elements conducive to forgiveness, such as religious belief, thinking patterns, the ability to empathize, and the willingness to sacrifice for the relationship (McCullough 2000; Worthington & Wade 1999). Second is the process from non-forgiving to forgiving, as specified by Enright and the Human Development Study Group (1991), Flanigan (1992) and Coleman (1989, 1998). Third is consideration of the types of forgiveness, such as premature or instantaneous forgiveness, arrested forgiveness, conditional forgiveness, and pseudo- or pseudo-mutual forgiveness (Walrond-Skinner 1998). Finally, the developmental stages of forgiveness in line with the one's moral development have been delineated (Enright *et al.* 1992; Enright & Fitzgibbons 2000; Nelson, 1992; Spidell & Liberman 1981). Enright proposes a six-stage developmental view of forgiveness, from revengeful forgiveness, restitutional forgiveness, expectational forgiveness, lawful expectational forgiveness, forgiveness as social harmony, to forgiveness as love.

Forgiveness Defined

Genuine interpersonal forgiveness may be defined as a process by which one who has been deeply and unfairly injured by another chooses to give up the right to resentment and retaliation and instead chooses to view the wrongdoer with compassion, benevolence, and love (North 1987,

502). It may or may not lead to reconciliation, because it depends on whether the justice of the relationship and mutual trust is restored. Forgiveness is not excusing, condoning, forgetting or denying the wrongful act. Genuine forgiveness is a path to psychological healing by transforming and freeing the forgiver from hate, anger, and the erosion of personhood.

The Nature and Levels of the Hurt

How can the above theories be applied in marriage counselling? Many hurts occur during the interaction between the partners in a marriage. Yet it is very difficult to identify who the offending party is and who the victim is, when the hurt is mutually escalating and interactional. The issue is especially complicated when we know that an emotional wound can be better healed when an apology is given and received, to balance the emotional ledger. Given the interactional nature of the marital relationship, each party may feel that he or she is the one who has been hurt and the other is to be blamed. A marriage counsellor may be drawn into this struggle. I will try to delineate the steps in handling this kind of situation and the intervention that may be helpful. I will also try to identify, from my clinical observations, the elements conducive to facilitating forgiveness in a couple's relationship.

Delineating Levels of Hurt

The nature of the hurt needs to be assessed in order to guide the kind of forgiveness process needed. Borrowdale (1996) identified the following four levels of offences within family relationships:
1. *Misdemeanours* that are superficial and temporary. These could occur through misunderstanding, oversight, or failure to fulfil certain minor responsibilities. They are not likely to have lasting significance. Irritation may result, but this is actually part of normal family living.
2. *Negative behaviours* through negligence, weakness and undermining the other, which disrupt relationships, such as interpersonal insult, devaluation of the partner or lack of respect (Worthington & Drinkard 2000). The offending party may or may not mean to hurt. Such behaviour can be interpreted more as an inappropriate expression of inner needs and feelings than as a deliberate intention to hurt.
3. *Extreme hurt* caused by physical, sexual or emotional abuse. This damage has long-lasting effects. The offending party is believed to

have hurt intentionally, for instance, to revenge, to humiliate, or to manipulate. There is always damage to self-esteem at this level of hurt.

4. A *"state of sin"* stemming from a societal structure and culture that leads the individual to harm the spouse inadvertently, out of ignorance. For example, a controlling wife may think that what she does is to help a submissive husband, with the best of intentions. She may not realize that her actions in fact rob him of confidence and hurt his self-esteem. Another example is, in a society with gender inequality, a woman may make sacrifices for the husband and the family, depriving herself of opportunities for self-development. The result could be a devaluation of self, while the husband remains ignorant of his part in contributing to the gender inequality. This is classified as the most serious form of hurt, because the hurt is sanctioned by the larger societal and cultural context, and the individual's forgiving process is the most limited. The offending party is usually unaware of the hurt that is caused, but the victim will suffer for a long, long time without knowing the cause.

Perceived Seriousness of the Hurt

In actual practice, in the process of forgiveness, the perceived seriousness of the hurt often plays a more important part than the nature of the hurt. The perceived seriousness depends on:

1. the perceived intention of the offending party; the more the offending party means to hurt, the more difficult it is to forgive;
2. the lasting effect of the hurt; temporary irritation can be easily dealt with, but the destruction of self-esteem will take much longer to rebuild;
3. the possibility of involving the offending party in the forgiveness process; if the offending party (which could be both partners in the marriage) is able to admit responsibility for causing the harm, the possibility of forgiveness will be higher;
4. the perceived harm in the value of "self"; the more the injured party identifies personally with the hurt, the more difficult it is to let go.

Clinical Practice

Many hurts in a marriage are forgiven in a subtle way without being raised for explicit discussion. This is especially true for minor misdemeanours and acts of negligence or omission. The counsellor needs only to do some reframing, consolidating the strengths of the relationship, and inducing positive feelings between the couple. The couples themselves may recognize that conflict, anger, and revenge are counterproductive, and they may decide to adopt peaceful coexistence strategies (de Waal 1989). Others "bury the hatchet" and enter into amicable conversations, eventually finding that the hurt and anger have subsided (Worthington & Drinkard 2000). Some couples engage in sharing common tasks (Sherif *et al.* 1961); in mutually pleasurable activity, such as enjoyable sexual relations (de Waal 1989); or in adopting reconciliation strategies such as complimenting, stroking or making the partner feel good psychologically (de Waal 1989).

Certain hurts that couples have not been able to work through on their own or with assistance from their support network could be uncovered during the counselling process. Seldom do couples enter counselling with an identified issue or toxic event requiring forgiveness work. Rather, in the course of marital work, for instance regarding the continuation of the marriage or coping with the crisis of an affair, counselling may reach the stage at which working on forgiveness becomes necessary in order to deal with issues blocking intimacy or reconciliation.

Beginning Forgiveness Work

For a couple to articulate what really matters to them beyond the presenting complaints, they need to feel secure and safe in a relationship in which the counsellor appreciates that their complaints, however trivial, have important meaning and serious implications for them. Unresolved emotional wounds can be manifested in several ways; for instance, through blaming the spouse, withdrawing and not daring to take the risk to connect with the spouse emotionally, or manifesting denial and repressing resentment, entering into self-blaming, and losing the trust to confide.

A sense of security will help clients to identify the overwhelming emotions caused by the hurts, such as disappointment, anger, grudges, and blows to self-esteem, and will increase their awareness of the blocks to forgiveness. Initial work has to focus on the blocks that are stopping them from letting go, such as their need for fairness, their inability to see their own part in causing the hurt and accepting their own and their spouse's dilemmas and difficulties, or their possible misconception that forgiveness means denial or forgetting what has happened.

Sometimes, spouses may not be aware that forgiveness is needed, if they deny the hurt too easily. This also blocks forgiveness. Direct feedback about this tendency of denial may be helpful, or the counsellor may facilitate exploration to enable the spouses to get in touch with their feelings. Within this very supportive atmosphere, they may be more open to express their hurt.

Sometimes, partners are out of step in relation to the need for forgiveness. For instance, one may think that the matter is trivial, whereas the other thinks that it is very important. A process of co-construction is necessary. In other words, the issue is not a personal but a relational matter, because it blocks their intimacy. It is not the issue that matters, but the person who means a lot to the spouse is important.

Finally, if both partners feel hurt, there may be competition for the opportunity to grant or receive forgiveness first. It must be agreed that they will take turns to resolve the problems. From my clinical experience, I find that couples usually do not mind who goes first, so long as both partners are assured of the chance to resolve the issues they are concerned about.

Intervention: Couple Forgiveness Work When Both Parties Are Involved in the Process

There are times when the couple's trust is violated by infidelity and abuse, but there are also negative events that, even though they may be perceived as minor by outsiders, do cause a violation of trust in the attachment bond. These hurts also call for forgiveness. From observation, these events may have ended, but they still have significant adverse effects on the secure bond.

There may also be negative behaviours when the parties may not mean to hurt, or when they attribute their negative behaviours to circumstances beyond their control, but such behaviours still result in a perceived violation of trust. For instance, there are times when expressions of inner needs and feelings are intense, when one partner has an urgent need but the spouse fails to respond. These events often re-emerge in an acutely emotional manner, leading to negative interactional cycles, which could be repetitive. In therapy, the counsellor observes such impasses that call for going through the process of working towards forgiveness.

Towards Relational Reconnecting — Betty and Jimmy

Betty and Jimmy came for counselling because they wanted to communicate well. The presenting problems seemed quite trivial.

For instance, Betty complained that Jimmy never told her his whereabouts, whereas Jimmy said he wanted more personal space. The interaction cycle was very obvious. The more Betty pursued, the more Jimmy demanded his personal space. To the counsellor, two unresolved questions came to mind: 1) What made Betty so anxious to know Jimmy's whereabouts, even though he was always able to offer a convincing explanation for what he was doing? 2) Why was it so difficult for Jimmy to tell Betty where he was going? This cycle was played out again and again in their everyday lives. The counsellor decided to go beyond the presenting complaints. The counsellor validated Betty's anxiety and directly commented, "I guess if nothing had happened in the past, your anxiety about Jimmy's whereabouts would not be so high. Perhaps there are some reasons behind this?"

Phase 1: Uncovering the Hurt

The couple may need help to articulate the events that they experienced as hurtful. In this phase, the counsellor has to validate the painful experience. This is particularly so if one spouse is unable to do so as a result of being trapped in his or her own pain. The counsellor also helps the parties to decode the meaning of the hurt and how this hurt affects each partner, such as the feeling of being belittled, rejected or controlled. It is important at this stage not to push for an apology because both will stand by their positions and are likely to be defensive.

Betty burst into tears when she heard this question and told the counsellor with a trembling voice how she felt betrayed by Jimmy's suspected affair. However, Jimmy did not have an affair with the woman, who was his ex-girlfriend, but offered her some assistance when she was in trouble. Betty knew about the incident but started to feel uncomfortable when they saw each other frequently. Jimmy had promised to stop seeing the woman, but on one occasion Betty discovered that Jimmy broke his promise. After that, Betty became suspicious. She always told herself to trust Jimmy, but failed. Jimmy was more and more annoyed by Betty's "controlling" behaviours and became withdrawn. His withdrawal further aggravated the problem. Betty entered into a self-blaming and anxious pursuing dance. She also wanted to trust Jimmy, but she couldn't forget the past incident. Betty said: "He promised not to see that woman. Why can't he care about my feelings? Why does he lie to me?" Jimmy defended his position: "I didn't want to hurt you so I didn't tell you the whole story. My friend was really in a desperate situation and I felt obliged to help her. I swear that I am still faithful to the marriage". Jimmy had his own reasons to defend himself. Instead of rehashing Betty's need to be told and Jimmy's need for personal space, the counsellor solicited their commitment to working through this unresolved incident.

Phase 2: Committing to the Process

The benefits of forgiving could be discussed, to secure both parties' commitment to the process. Sometimes, the couple may present an indecisive or ambivalent attitude here. The commitment to involve oneself in the review and reflection process must be solicited before the forgiveness journey commences, because it is important for the parties not to take advantage of the spouse's opening up of vulnerabilities during the self-revelation. The counsellor will, from time to time, remind the parties of this commitment once the forgiveness process starts, as emotions may become heated and anger inhibits rationality. The counsellor acts as a captain to steer the ship towards constructive exchanges in the couple's exploration.

At the same time, the parties will be prepared to be forgiven as well. In considering how they have been hurt, and in preparing to grant forgiveness, they may be unaware that they also need to be forgiven.

Betty offered a prompt response, but Jimmy showed some hesitation. He wondered about the value of revisiting all the old pain. He was assured that it was not a process of finding fault but of removing any blockages to intimacy. The counsellor had a hunch that Jimmy also had his own story to tell. Perhaps with this understanding, Jimmy would feel more confident about entering into the process.

At this point, Betty's pain has been validated by the counsellor, but Jimmy was still unable to listen, held back by fears he could not articulate. It was obvious that he was hesitant to tell Betty his real thinking, but he had rushed to reassure her with a promise that had yet to be actualized. (Phase 1 work with Jimmy to uncover his hurt was called for.) The counsellor said to Jimmy:

"I observed that you are so concerned about Betty's feelings that you want to do anything to make her happy. Yet by so doing, you are fearful of telling her what you really want". Jimmy nodded and started to share his fear of conflicts. The fear arose from his family of origin. He explained how he was troubled by his parents' conflicts. In addition, as his parents were preoccupied by their own problems, Jimmy was a lonely child. He was not used to talking about what he thought, how he felt, and what he needed. "Who is there to listen?" Jimmy asked in a helpless voice.

Phase 3:   Appreciating Each Other's Perspectives

A speaker-listener technique (Markman 1994) can be introduced, both parties taking turns to be the speaker and the listener. The counsellor guides the speaker to voice the hurt in a non-blaming way and encourages the listener to paraphrase what is said without being defensive. It is an exchange of thoughts and feelings to facilitate better understanding of what has happened and why, so that a deeper appreciation of the matter may emerge to enable the parties to value each other's perspectives (Coleman 1998).

The process of opening up each party's pain was designed to let each appreciate the other's perspective. It was not time for an apology, because both wanted to be heard. The counsellor helped them to reframe their stories in a self-focused manner.

Betty desperately wanted to trust her husband but was held back by the past incident, which to her was a violation of trust. She had tried her own methods, such as self-blame, to suppress her pain, but what she needed was Jimmy's assurance and commitment to be transparent. Jimmy had never wanted to hurt or lie. Instead, he was so concerned about Betty's feelings that he used his own method to avoid conflicts. Moreover, the suffering in his childhood had made him lose trust in sharing with someone, and this experience had an effect on his marriage. Both partners listened, and felt that they were understood. Betty could not stop sobbing, because she finally had the chance to validate her worry without being accused of hyper-vigilance, and Jimmy's defensiveness was disarmed because Betty understood that he had not meant to hurt her.

Phase 4:   Acknowledging Responsibility

The spouses may now undertake "self-examination" (Clinebell 1993, 133) to identify their part in causing pain to the other. In this process, the phenomenon of "intimacy blindness" may become evident. When two people are close to one another, the ability to see how one's part contributes to the interaction cycle is blinded by the intense emotional atmosphere, inadequate personal distance, and vulnerabilities of exposing oneself. With adequate validation of each person's hurt and provision of a secure relationship, the partners can be helped to examine themselves from an emotional distance. During this phase, they may consider their family of origin and the possible carry-over effect of their upbringing on their current relationship (Coleman 1989).

When ready, each party could acknowledge the hurt caused to the spouse and then apologize for causing it. This is not assigning blame but acknowledging the importance of one's effect on the injured spouse. Admitting responsibility can also be a process of sharing one's limitations and vulnerabilities. Though a partner may not mean to hurt, acknowledging the spouse's pain and admitting responsibility for being unable to respond or for being insensitive to the spouse's needs will be very helpful. In the case of traumas such as infidelity or abuse, the offending parties need to undertake to stop hurtful behaviour. This commitment is essential, because it serves to demonstrate the perpetrator's sincerity in shouldering responsibility for his or her actions and acknowledging the pain of the other party. A mere verbal apology is not enough to rebuild the relationship. Each party has to be prepared to go through further ups and downs in their transactions. Change may not happen instantly and will take time. Setting too-high expectations and pushing too hard, or not allowing space and time for the change to take place, will result in another cycle of mutual hurt.

> It was after each had validated the other's pain that Jimmy was the initiator to apologize to Betty. He told her he had not meant to be hurtful, and he expressed empathy for Betty's hurt feelings. The counsellor highlighted what Jimmy said and asked Betty to express how she felt when Jimmy apologized. Betty said that she felt relieved, as it was the first time that he had shared his childhood story in that way. She had not realized how fearful he was of conflict, so that he tried so hard to avoid confrontation.

Phase 5:   Empathizing with Each Other

Both parties may now be able to empathize with each other, give and receive apologies, let go of the hurt feelings, and recommit to an intimate relationship. Sometimes trust-rebuilding is needed as well. An attitude of appreciation is encouraged to affirm each partner's progress (Worthington & Drinkard 2000).

> Betty was also encouraged to share what she could do to help Jimmy overcome his childhood fears. Betty said that she was there to listen. Jimmy then made a commitment to say what he really wanted and to keep Betty informed about what was happening to him. Meanwhile, Betty reaffirmed her intention to contain her concern and her queries over his whereabouts.

Phase 6:   Rebuilding Intimacy

This phase involves rebuilding intimacy and actively doing things to cultivate feelings of love, such as words of love, physical touch, and small surprises.

> Once Betty and Jimmy begin to empathize with and affirm one another, they were ready to respond to each other in revitalizing their marriage.

Intervention: Couple Forgiveness Work

Towards Constructive Uncoupling — *Ken and Susan*

> A divorcing couple, Ken and Susan, came to therapy because Susan wanted to save the marriage but Ken had decided to leave. Individual sessions were conducted with the couple, but unfortunately there was no room for reconciliation. The counsellor realized that, if forgiving work were not done at this stage, Susan would be very angry and full of hate towards Ken.
> Initially, Ken did not admit his part in contributing to their marital difficulties. Instead, he blamed Susan for not attending to his emotional needs when he was in trouble. Susan had apologized and wanted a chance to save the marriage. Yet, it was

too late for Ken, and he foresaw that it would take a long time for Susan to be emotionally sensitive. He could not stand the frustration in the marriage again. However, Ken could not face the reality that Susan would be very hurt by the divorce, and rationalized his decision as helping Susan to understand herself better. He wanted to help Susan to increase her self-awareness by passing this "assignment" to the counsellor.

However, it was pointed out to him that Susan's pain was unavoidable once he decided to divorce (Uncovering the Hurt — Phase 1). What Susan needed was not his rationalization but his acknowledgment of her pain and his responsibility in causing that pain. After serious consideration, Ken was committed to being involved in a direct conversation with Susan, which, it was hoped, might help Susan to forgive, though he could not demand that forgiveness (Committing to the Process — Phase 2). In the joint session, Ken made a genuine self-disclosure. He told Susan how he suffered when he knew that he could no longer return to the marriage and when he visualized the pain that this would cause Susan (Appreciating Each Other's Perspectives — Phase 3). This self-disclosure was very helpful for Susan, allowing her to empathize with Ken's limitations (Empathizing with Each Other — Phase 5). The counsellor helped Ken to apologize for breaking the marriage vows. When he did so, he cried bitterly, telling Susan that he was really sorry (Acknowledging Responsibility — Phase 4). Though the couple did not reconcile, Susan was more able to forgive Ken after his genuine apology.

From the clinical observations, it is very important for the couple to know that they are not there to find fault with each other. In reality, most couples need a validation of pain from the spouse, instead of faultfinding. Also, a genuine self-disclosure of one's vulnerabilities, whether they are fears, limitations or sadness, will help the partners to appreciate each other's perspective. This can only be done when both feel secure enough to do so. Thus, forgiving occurs when both partners are ready to disarm. It usually emerges from goodwill between the couple, and the counsellor has to be sensitive to this surfacing and take the opportunity to make it explicit.

Sometimes, individual sessions for both parties may be necessary when there is too much hostility and reactivity. They may need some personal space to work things out on their own. When both sides are in an easily agitated state, attempts at further communication may intensify conflicts. Rather, a contract could be made with both to confine any discussion on conflictual issues with the counsellor. In the meantime, if appropriate, tension-free and more enjoyable activities in their daily life could be encouraged to increase positive affects in the relationship.

Intervention: When only the Injured Party is Involved in the Process

In some situations, it is hard to involve the offending party in the forgiving process, or to expect him or her to acknowledge the hurtful act or to express regret, remorse or repentance. In order to heal the emotional wounds, the injured party can still go through a forgiving process, even without the presence of the offending party, in order to let go of the pain. Such a process has been proposed by Enright and the Human Development Study Group (1991). Genuine forgiveness may occur without an apology or even recognition of wrongdoing on the part of the offender (Coyle, http//www.holycross.edu/department/crec/forgiveness/coyle.pdf).

It should be pointed out that genuine forgiveness does not involve trading something for something in return, such as fear of loss of the relationship. Many injured spouses come for therapy because they have been betrayed or abused by their partners. They might want to feel instant forgiveness because they hope that, as a result of their forgiveness, their spouse will change. The counsellor might hear such statements as "I have forgiven him already, so he should come back to me", or "What can I do to let him know I have forgiven him so that he will know how good I am?" When the injured parties want to trade forgiveness for something in the relationship, they cannot truly be involved in a forgiveness process, as described below, leading to the healing of the emotional wound and the transformation of self.

Intervention: Individual Forgiveness Work

Towards Self-Relief and Empathy with Partner — *Mary*

When the work of forgiving has to be undertaken without the presence of the offending party, the working-through process requires some minor modification. This is delineated and illustrated by case examples in the following discussion.

Phase 1:   Uncovering the Hurt

When extreme hurts with serious implications are brought up in counselling, clients may need help to articulate, in their own terms, their definition of the injury and their feelings about how the hurts have compromised everyday life. For instance, the experience of betrayal could lead to a loss of trust in people and an inability to open up in new relationships; the experience of rejection may awaken self-denigration, self-blame, and depression.

> Mary came to therapy because of depression. After exploration, it was learnt that Mary was extremely guilty about her possible role in her husband's rejection of her. The husband had been very nice to Mary years ago, but his behaviour had recently changed drastically. He blamed Mary for pushing him away and vehemently refused to see a counsellor.
>
> At the initial stage of the counselling, it was gradually uncovered that Mary was extremely hurt by her husband's rejection. Instead of knowing how to be angry with him, she directed the anger towards herself. Whenever the counsellor asked about the marital relationship, Mary could not stop herself from crying, and she blamed herself for pushing her husband away.
>
> This pattern of serious self-blame was feedback to Mary, and she gradually realized it. Some family-of-origin work was done at this point. The themes of "rejection" and "self-blame" were very obvious. Coming from a working-class family in which both parents were busily engaged in their own work, Mary rarely felt emotionally acknowledged. She was rejected but was told that she was emotionally demanding. The aspect of being emotionally demanding was highly unacceptable to her, so she blamed herself. Once again, in the marriage, she was blamed.

Phase 2:   Acknowledging the Hurt

When the hurt is uncovered, there will be a painful effect. The injured party may either be very angry with the offending spouse or, going to the opposite extreme, may start blaming him or herself for getting into such a situation. When the injured party acknowledges the personal suffering, realization surfaces that some sort of resolution must be sought.

Mary realized that she was hurt emotionally by her parents and by her husband. She did not want to blame them, but she blamed herself. The counsellor helped her to acknowledge how painful it could be when she was rejected. Mary cried continuously whenever this pain was raised. There was an important turning point when Mary acknowledged that she was hurt by the rejection instead of feeling guilty about being "emotionally demanding" and thinking that she was not justified in feeling hurt.

Phase 3:   Decision to Forgive

The decision to forgive requires the injured party's commitment not to let the hurt compromise her life, and a commitment to set herself free. The injured party can then enter into a process to examine what forgiveness means to her.

There was a clear indication that Mary wanted to change. She did not want to be so emotionally demanding or to hate anyone. She was strongly determined to change herself. When Mary looked back, she thought that this determination was the most important factor for her to heal the hurt and, behaviourally, to cure her depression.

Phase 4:   Expanding the Narrative of the Hurt

To overcome the feeling of injustice and unfairness, the injured party needs to have a more thorough and comprehensive account of what has happened. Very often, the injured party will focus only on his or her own experience of being hurt, and will remain stuck in self-pity or a self-righteous position. By expanding the narrative account of the incident, the parties will have more perspectives and dimensions from which to view the incident. As a result, there is a new understanding of fairness and justice.

The process is indeed challenging work. Because other people are not involved in the process, the information provided by the injured party may be biased as a result of projection, denial or a confused memory. An absolute, true picture is unlikely to be formulated, but a story based on the injured party's honesty to him or herself can be expected. Given that it is not an investigation but a healing process, the subjective nature of the account of the event is acceptable.

Mary reviewed her marriage from a systemic perspective. She gradually developed a more thorough and comprehensive understanding of the interactional nature of the relationship. First, she considered whether her husband was having a mid-life crisis and was projecting some of his tensions and anger onto her. Second, she wondered if he was subtly trying to push her into a depressive and dependent state, as he had a strong desire to be needed. Third, she thought that he was using rejection to protect his own sense of vulnerability. Mary sensed that, deep down, he had an extremely low self-esteem and was jealous of her self-development. Mary acknowledged her part in not helping her husband to feel secure enough to confide in her. The more Mary developed an expanded narrative about the rejection, the more she was able to forgive herself and her husband.

Phase 5: Letting Go

When the angry feelings gradually subside, the counsellor guides the injured party in undergoing two processes. First, the client will be guided in entering the offender's world, to understand the vulnerabilities and weaknesses, unfulfilled wishes, and unexpressed needs and wants, which may have influenced the commitment of the hurtful offences. This could lead to a change of perception and affect, and the development of greater empathy and compassion towards the offender.

Then, in order to avoid a self-righteous forgiveness, the offended party also needs to undergo a painful self-examination. After entering the internal world of the offending party and understanding what vulnerabilities may be present, the injured party experiences the human side of the offender and begins to realize that he may have similar human weaknesses. It is a threatening process and often comes with denial and rejection. The counsellor's full acceptance is crucial to facilitate the injured party, who may not be prepared to be forgiven, or to forgive or accept him or herself. Forgiveness of oneself is sometimes more difficult and sometimes needs to come before the granting of forgiveness to others.

After the completion of the above two processes — entering the offender's world and undergoing a healthy self-examination — the injured parties will be more able to let go of their sense of grievance.

Mary had once said, "The awareness of my own imperfection helped me accept and forgive my husband's imperfection", and she gratefully thanked the counsellor for helping her achieve this level of genuine acceptance of herself and of others.

Mary experienced a sense of freedom and relief from letting go of her pain. As she developed more confidence in herself, her depression lifted. When she had rebuilt her self-esteem, she wrote a letter to her husband, sharing with him her experiences of self-exploration.

She sincerely invited him to have a genuine dialogue with her. She believed that only when her husband could appreciate himself and his part in the relationship could they rekindle their feelings of intimacy.

The above healing process took two years.

Phase 6:   Deepening/Transformation of Self

At this stage, the meaning of suffering may have to be addressed, to develop a new set of personal beliefs and a stronger faith in the meaning of life. The injured party experiences a sense of freedom by letting go of the pain. Whether reconciliation is possible depends on the offending party's acknowledgement of the harmful acts, feelings of remorse and commitment to stop the acts. Reconciliation requires the restoration of trust in an interpersonal relationship through mutual trustworthy behaviours (Worthington & Drinkard 2000). Reconciliation may come about over time. However, the process of letting go of resentment itself, with or without reconciliation to follow, frees the self for growth and further transformation.

In some situations in which continuous abuse is still present, divorce/separation may result. Forgiveness does not mean a distortion of self or a denial of personal safety. It cannot be manipulated by the offending party to justify harmful acts or to maintain the abusive relationship.

Intervention: Individual Forgiveness Work

Towards Letting Go and Becoming Free — Janet

Janet had a very different temperament from Mary's. Instead of self-blaming, she always felt a self-righteous anger towards her ex-husband, who had left her for another woman. Janet did not realize how the hurt of being abandoned was compromising her life. She only knew that she was full of anger and was easily provoked, resulting in poor social relationships. Janet's anger was explored and she gradually realized the hurt of abandonment (Uncovering the Hurt — Phase 1). The realization of such pain made her want to get revenge; she thought this was only fair. It was very difficult to calm her down at this stage, so the main thing the counsellor did was to acknowledge her anger and hurt (Acknowledging the Hurt — Phase 2). It was important for Janet to feel that her feelings of abandonment and unfairness were understood. As time went by, her feelings of anger became less intense. The counsellor was then able to suggest the letting go of pain (Decision to Forgive — Phase 3). Janet wanted this, but she thought that the only way was to forget the incident. The counsellor was able to help Janet expand her understanding of the marital breakdown (Expanding the Narrative of the Hurt — Phase 4). At one point, the counsellor asked Janet to consider what her husband might have been feeling when he wanted to share something but Janet refused because she was too busy. Janet's inability to attend to her husband's emotional needs appeared to be the thing that hurt him in the marriage. At first, Janet was angry because she did not think this was sufficient justification for him to leave the marriage. The counsellor agreed that it was not sufficient justification, but it was also a fact that he felt hurt. The counsellor understood that Janet seemed to have difficulty acknowledging the emotional wound experienced by her husband when Janet herself lacked the experience of being emotionally cared for.

Nevertheless, the confrontation appeared to be a turning point because Janet started to empathize with her husband's feelings. Her empathy reduced Janet's wish to take revenge, because she started to realize she had also done unfair things to her husband. As a result of the realization of the husband's emotional wounds and her own shortcomings, Janet was able to let go (Letting Go — Phase 5). After a time, the counsellor received a touching letter from Janet, saying that, although the divorce was painful, she experienced the "grace of life" even more (Transformation of the Self — Phase 6). She had finally set herself free from hating her ex-husband.

Intervention: When Hurts Arise from Societal Structure and Culture, Outside of the Couple's Awareness

Hurts in level four are the most difficult to deal with, because both parties may be unaware of the hurt caused by the subtle aspects in their society's structure and culture. This being the case, should the individuals be held responsible for acts of which they are unaware? There is no easy answer, and this question may require a long debate. Nevertheless, if the behaviour continues to be harmful, some moves towards abatement are called for. Forgiveness in this case will start with the victim's depersonalization of the suffering. Victims often blame themselves or are blamed for instigating their own suffering. In other words, they receive a double punishment from the harm: the direct pain induced by the offender's harmful acts and the psychological responsibility of bearing the blame. For instance, a submissive husband hurt by a controlling wife may feel guilty about his inability to meet his wife's expectations and demands, instead of seeing his wife's part in setting up unrealistic expectations and belittling him. Intervention would help him understand that his suffering is due to his wife's unrealistic expectations. In another example, a wife who misses out on opportunities because she makes sacrifices for her family is helped to see that her low self-esteem is not her fault but arises from the fact that she has been deprived of the chance of self-development. Validation of her suffering and an externalization of the problems will help free her from self-blaming and will help relieve some of her suffering (White & Epston 1990).

Working with the offending parties can be extremely difficult. It may not be easy for them to see their part in causing the spouse's pain or their contribution to the consequences. Even worse, they may be self-righteous in upholding their perspectives. Exploring with them the basis of these perspectives, reflecting on the detrimental effects on the spouse, and considering some of the beneficial effects on the relationship if some changes are attempted may lead to a review and an increasing awareness of societal pressures on their behaviour.

When the relationship has some value, or when there is attachment to the partner, awareness of their part in causing pain could lead to moderation of the hurtful behaviour. When there is self-interest in subtly upholding power over the other, the possibility of change will be low. If so, the injured party may have to go through an individual forgiveness process to let go of the pain and suffering. In this case, forgiveness may not lead to a rekindling of intimacy.

Readiness to Forgive

People who are more ready to forgive have been described as those with higher self-esteem, who find it easier to get out of the blaming game, who see their own part in the relationship, and who accept the limits of others and themselves. Also, those who are able to appreciate that they have caused harm to others find it easier to grant forgiveness. Someone who is able to enter the world of the offending party, and see the context in which the offence occurred, may experience a change of affect to appreciate the other's perspective. In summary, therefore, it would seem that those who are able to conduct an honest self-examination, are willing to assume responsibility for having caused harm, and are willing to be involved in genuine dialogue and empathize with others are more ready to engage in the process of forgiving. Also, couples with higher emotional involvement and satisfaction in the relationship will be more motivated to forgive in order to rekindle feelings of intimacy. Those from a religious background that extols the virtue of forgiveness will have greater conviction about the benefits of forgiveness (Witte 1997; Enright & Fitzgibbons 2000).

Couples who are still very angry, reactive, and emotional may not be ready to engage in the review and reflection required in working through forgiveness. Validating and working through their pain, feelings of injury, and subjective experiences and perceptions could help them to relieve the anger and resentment.

When there are blocks to forgiveness, such as feelings of unfairness, a need for revenge, or a need for self-protection, some pre-forgiveness work will be needed to clear these blocks (Wong 2001). For example, couples may misunderstand what forgiveness is, so a clarification will be helpful. Sometimes, the spouses may not see their part in causing the harm, like Ken, so the counsellor will help them to be honest with themselves. In other situations, fears about opening up old wounds, as in the case of Jimmy, are understandable. In this case, the counsellor reassured him and offered him a safe forum in which to be heard, and this seemed to be helpful. In other words, pre-forgiveness is the work of preparing the couples to enter into forgiveness work, by helping them to clarify expectations, to see the value of doing so, and to acknowledge their own part in the process. This preparatory work creates a sense of security.

However, when relational ethics and the levels of maturity between the couple are very different, undergoing a mutual process of forgiveness will be very difficult. It is difficult to carry on a relational conversation if both sides have radically different definitions of pertinent issues (Enright and Fitzgibbons 2000). Instead, working on forgiveness individually with a counsellor may be necessary to let go of and find relief from emotional pain.

The Benefits of Forgiving

People who undertake a painful review of their difficult circumstances in order to forgive can experience changes in their perceptions and emotional experience of the hurts. According to Simon and Simon (1990), forgiveness is a by-product of an ongoing healing process and a sign of positive self-esteem. Internally, a person experiences a feeling of wellness, freedom, and acceptance. Letting go of the intense emotions attached to incidents from the past and surrendering to grudges and resentments, hatred, and self-pity, lessens the wish to redress the wrong. Letting go frees the energy once consumed by holding grudges, harbouring resentments and nursing unhealed wounds, and allows the person to move to a new life.

McCullough *et al.* (1997) also reiterate the point that forgiveness facilitates the release of just anger and the wish for revenge, and moderates the desire to withdraw from or avoid the offender, opening the path to reconciliation. Though reconciliation can be achieved through forgiveness, forgiveness does not necessarily result in reconciliation.

However, the question is not one of forgiving and forgetting. Rather, it is a question of forgiving and remembering. Relationships are rebuilt, not as if no injury has occurred, but with that experience as part of the past, and with a commitment to relating differently in the future.

Challenges for the Counsellor

In the course of working through pain and injury towards forgiveness in a couple's relationship, the counsellor needs an appreciation of his or her own value basis and the couple's value and belief systems, as well as sensitive skills to search out the couple's experience and perspectives of the meaning of what has happened between them. Subjective responses to breaches in interpersonal expectations and trust can be coloured by ongoing circumstances in the couple's current life context, as well as unresolved problems from the past. Some problems even reach back to influences from the clients' families of origin. The counsellor needs to discern what these may be, and tune into each partner's beliefs about what is just and fair in their relational transactions and what may be beneficial to them and their relationship. The client may subscribe to the cultural value that forgiveness through letting go of negative emotions frees their energies to move on in life. They may value Christian and other religious beliefs in the grace and virtue of forgiving. Or, they may agree with the psychotherapeutic perspective that forgiveness fosters personal growth and relational healing. Any of these, or a combination of them, could guide the counselling process through the ups and downs in the journey towards forgiving. The important point is that it is the emphasis on the clients' values and belief systems that determines what is meaningful to them.

The challenge for the counsellor is to avoid the temptation to push for instant forgiveness or to condone the clients' desire to trade forgiveness for something in the relationship. It is also possible to overlook the power distribution in the relationship, one partner granting forgiveness out of fear because he or she holds a less powerful position.

Conclusion

It is inevitable that marriage counsellors will face many situations of relational hurt and damage resulting from a breach of relational ethics. Leaving them unattended would be to leave many unresolved issues buried, which carries the risk of explosion at any time. One of the major challenges for marriage counsellors is to tune in to the nature of the hurt and to discern each party's strengths and vulnerabilities in dealing with these painful interactions. This requires the counsellor to be aware of his or her own philosophical and ethical orientation. Unfortunately, these issues have been neglected in our training. The major focus in the training of marriage counsellors in Hong Kong is on the skill level, without due consideration for the counsellor's own values in examining relationships. The marital relationship is very complicated. Marriage counselling requires a respect for the clients' presentation, an appreciation of human frailties, and a belief in people's natural striving towards health and growth.

References

Al-Mabuk R.H., Enright R.D. and Cardis P.A. (1995). Forgiveness education with parentally love-deprived late adolescents. *Journal of Moral Education*, 24, 427–44.

Borrowdale A. (1996). Right relations: Forgiveness and family life. In S.C. Barton (Ed.) *The family in theological perspective*. Edinburgh: T&T Clark.

Brandsma J.M. (1982). Forgiveness: A dynamic theological and therapeutic analysis. *Pastoral Psychology*, 31, 40–50.

Clinebell H. (1993). *Basic types of pastoral care and counseling*. 2nd edition. Translated by Pauline Wu-Harris, Hong Kong: Chinese Christian Literature Council, Ltd.

Coleman P.W. (1989). *The forgiving marriage*. Chicago, IL: Contemporary Books.

Coleman P.W. (1998). The process of forgiveness in marriage and the family. In R.D. Enright and J. North (Eds.) *Exploring forgiveness*. Madison, WI: University of Wisconsin Press, 75–94.

Coyle C.T. (n.d.). *Psychological and interpersonal aspects of forgiveness*. (Online). Available at http://www.holycross.edu/department/crec/ forgiveness/coyle.pdf

Coyle C.T. and Enright R.D. (1997). Forgiveness intervention with post-abortion men. *Journal of Consulting and Clinical Psychology*, 65, 1042–5.

De Waal F.B.M. (1989). *Peacemaking among primates*. Cambridge, MA: Harvard University Press.

Enright R.D. and Fitzgibbons R.P. (2000). *Helping clients forgive — An empirical guide for resolving anger and restoring hope*. Washington, DC: American Psychological Association.

Enright R.D., Gassin E.A. and Wu C. (1992). Forgiveness: A developmental view. *Journal of Moral Education*, 2, 99–114.

Enright R.D. and the Human Development Study Group (1991). The moral development of forgiveness. In W. Kurtines and J. Gewirtz (Eds.) *Handbook of moral behavior and development*, Vol. 1, Hillsdale, NJ: Lawrence Erlbaum, 123–52.

Flanagan O. (1991). *Varieties of moral personality: Ethics and psychological realism*. Cambridge, MA: Harvard University Press.

Flanigan B. (1987). Shame and forgiving in alcoholism. *Alcoholism Treatment Quarterly*, 4, 181–95.

Flanigan B. (1992). *Forgiving the unforgivable*. New York: Collier Books.

Freeman S.R. and Enright R.D. (1996). Forgiveness as an intervention goal with incest survivors. *Journal of Consulting and Clinical Psychology*, 64, 983–92.

Hazen C. and Zeifman D. (1999). Pair bonds as attachments: Evaluating the evidence. In J. Cassidy and P.R. Shaver (Eds.) *Handbook of attachment: Theory, research, and clinical applications*, New York: Guilford, 336–54.

Hebl J.H. and Enright R.D. (1993). Forgiveness as a psychotherapeutic goal with elderly females. *Psychotherapy*, 30, 658–67.

Hope D. (1987). The healing paradox of forgiveness. *Psychotherapy*, 24, 240–4.

Hunter R.C.A. (1978). Forgiveness, retaliation, and paranoid reactions. *Canadian Psychiatric Association Journal*, 23, 167–73.

Jones L.G. (1995). *Embodying forgiveness — A theological analysis*. Grand Rapids, WI: Eerdmans.

Kohlberg L. and Power C. (1981). Moral development, religious thinking, and the question of a seventh stage. In L.Kohlberg (Ed.) *The philosophy of moral development*, San Francisco, CA: Harper & Row, 311–72.

Konstam V., Marx F., Schurer J., Harrington A., Lombard N. and Deveney S. (2000). Forgiving: What mental health counselors are telling us. *Journal of Mental Health Counseling*, 22 (3), 253–68.

Kwan W.C. (1994). Meta-physical basis of forgiveness — part I. *Philosophy and Culture*, 21 (11), 994–1003. (關永中 (1994) 寬恕的形上基礎 (上) 哲學與文化，21 卷 11 期，頁 994–1003).

Lee M.C. (1993). Understanding the interpersonal boundary of Chinese people from the concept of fairness. In K.S. Yeung (Eds) *Indigenous Psychological Development*, 1, 267–300. (李美枝 (1993) 從有關公平判斷的研究結果看中國人之人己關係的界限載於楊國樞主編本地心理學的發展，創刊號，頁 267–300)

Markman H., Stanley S. and Blumberg S.L. (1994). *Fighting for your marriage*. San Francisco, CA: Jossey-Bass.

Martin J.A. (1953). A realistic theory of forgiveness. In J. D. Wild (Ed.) *The return to reason: Essays in realistic philosophy*. Chicago, IL: Regnery.

McCullough M.E. (2000). Forgiveness as human strength: Theory, measurement, and links to well-being. *Journal of Social & Clinical Psychology*, 19 (1), 43–55.

McCullough M.E. and Worthington E.L. (1994). Models of interpersonal forgiveness and their applications to counseling: Review and critique. *Counseling and Values*, 39, 2–15.

McCullough M.E., Worthington E.L. Jr. and Rachal K.C. (1997). Interpersonal forgiving in close relationships. *Journal of Personality and Social Psychology*, 73, 321–36.

Nelson M.K. (1992). A new theory of forgiveness. Unpublished doctoral dissertation. West LaFayette, IN: Purdue University.

North J. (1987). Wrongdoing and forgiveness. *Philosophy*, 62, 499–508.

Sampson E.E. (1985). The decentralization of identity: Toward a revised concept of personal and social order. *American Psychologist*, 36, 730–4.

Sampson E.E. (1988). The debate on individualism: Indigenous psychologies of the individual and their role in personal and societal functioning. *American Psychologist*, 43, 15–22.

Sherif M., Harvey O.J., White B.J., Hood W.E. and Sherif C.W. (1961). *Intergroup conflict and cooperation: The robber's cave experiment*. Norman, OK: University of Oklahoma Book Exchange.

Simon S.B. and Simon S. (1990). *Forgiveness — How to make peace with your past and get on with your life.* New York: Warner Books.

Simpson J. and Rholes W. (1994). Stress and secure base relationships in adulthood. In K. Bartholomew and D. Perlman (Eds.) *Attachment processes in adulthood.* London: Jessica Kingsley Publishers, 181–204.

Spidell S. and Liberman D. (1981). Moral development and the forgiveness of sin. *Journal of Psychology & Theology*, 9, 159–63.

Suen L.K. (1992). The deep structure of Chinese culture, revised edition. Hong Kong: Writers' Publications (孫隆基著 (1992) 中國文化的紳層結構 (修訂版) 香港：集賢社).

Walrond-Skinner S. (1998). The function and role of forgiveness in working with couples and families: Clearing the ground. *Journal of Family Therapy*, 20, 3–19.

Wen S.Y. (1971). Discussion on Chinese national characters from the perspective of value orientation. In Lee, Y.Y. and Yeung, K.S. (Eds.) *Chinese Personality.* Taiwan: Central Research Institute, 47–78. (文崇一 (1971) 從價值取向談中國國民性載於李亦園、楊國樞編著中國人的性格台灣：中央研究院，頁 47–78).

White M. and Epston D. (1990). *Narrative means to therapeutic ends.* Adelaide, South Australia: Dulwich Centre.

Wilson J.Q. (1993). *The moral sense.* New York: Free Press.

Witte J. Jr. (1997). *From sacrament to contract: Marriage, religion, and law in Western tradition.* Louisville, KY: Westminster John Knox.

Wong L.C. (2001). Forgiveness in marriage. Hong Kong: Breakthrough (黃麗彰著 (2001) 婚姻中的創傷與饒恕香港：突破)

Worthington E.L. and DiBlasio F.A. (1990). Promoting mutual forgiveness within the fractured relationship. *Psychotherapy*, 27, 219–33.

Worthington E.L. Jr. and Drinkard D.T. (2000). Promoting reconciliation through psycho-educational and therapeutic interventions. *Journal of Marital and Family Therapy*, 26 (1), 93–101.

Worthington E.L. and Wade N.G. (1999). The psychology of unforgiveness and forgiveness and implications for clinical practice. *Journal of Social & Clinical Psychology*, 18 (4), 385–418.

6

Reaching the "Point of No Return": Tracking the Pathway to Making the Decision to Divorce

ANITA YUK-LIN FOK

This chapter reports on a study to search out the processes by which spouses come to the point of considering their marriage to have reached the point of no return, leading them to a decision to divorce. The experiences of the Chinese wives in this study indicate divorce to be a psychological process of disenchantment. When the wives experience the marriage as permeated with a prevailing sense of expectations unfulfilled and a subjective sense of entitlement of love unachievable, they engaged in a re-evaluation of the relationship. This evaluation focuses on a series of significant events that punctuate the downward decline in satisfaction. Each of these events has particular meaning and implications, leading to increasingly negative interaction, to globally negative characterization of the partners, and to the reversal of the attachment process.

When the reappraisal of the marriage resulted in a subjective sense of violation of core beliefs, values, life themes and self-identity, requiring a new reconstruction of the self and of their world view, these wives believed they had reached the verge of the decision to divorce.

As divorce is basically a "no-win" choice with a severe effect on the future life path, this discussion suggests that spouses seeking counselling at this point need to engage in a thorough divorce decision review at the historical, interactive and internal process levels to decide if they are at the point of no return.

Introduction

The rapid rise in the divorce rate is a worldwide trend, which is also reflected in Hong Kong. Marital dissolution poses a serious threat to family cohesiveness and stability for a society which values marriage as the basic foundation of family relationships. Whereas a good divorce can reduce unnecessary hurt and pain, and free energy towards the reconstruction of a new lifestyle in a different family form, the actual period when the decision whether to divorce is being made is clearly a critical period in the relationship. It is critical because another choice, reconciliation, may help the couple rebuild trust and heal wounds, and re-establish the relationship. The question arises of whether we can track the pathway to making the decision to divorce, so that the spouses facing the decision, and the marital counsellors whom they approach, can examine the extent to which the relationship is irretrievable.

No one intends to divorce when he or she marries. Nevertheless, more and more well-intended marriages do end in divorce. How does this decision to divorce come about? What pushes couples towards a destiny that they never intended or desired? How is it that some people in an acutely distressed relationship choose to stay in the marriage, whereas some push for divorce when their distress seems less acute to outsiders? Also, couples do change their mind about divorce decisions even after the papers have been filed. What exactly are the determinants of the divorce decision? Are there indicators to enable marriage therapists to help couples at the verge of marital breakdown, to avoid unnecessary marital dissolution?

Divorce as a Psychological Process of Disenchantment

The course of marital dissolution has been examined by many researchers and theorists (Duck 1982). Social Exchange Theory is a frequently cited theory in the investigation of divorce decisions (Donovan 1990; Kalb 1983; Edwards et al. 1981; Albrecht et al. 1980; Price et al. 1988). However, in my counselling experience, the couples that make a decision to divorce do not undergo a rational-based, cost-benefits evaluation of preference between two persons. It is a much more complex decision situated in human life dilemmas. It is basically a "no-win" choice, is stressful, and has a severe effect on the future life path of both parties involved.

The writer suggests that divorce is a psychological process of disenchantment rather than a process of weighing of costs and benefits. Bohannon's concept of "emotional divorce" captures the important psychological process of disillusionment and detachment (Bohannon 1970). Guerin vividly describes the process of disappointment due to unmet expectations and calls it "expectation-to-alienation progression" (Guerin *et al.* 1987, 134). In the course of this progression, different layers of intra-psychic forces of as well as beliefs, feelings, perceptions and behaviours are out of alignment, as those involved attempt to make meaning of the threats to the relationship. The discrepancy between expectations and experience within the marriage leads to a sense of dissonance that calls for a reappraisal and redefinition of what is going on in the interactive process of the marriage to construct meaning and explore implications.

Married persons are embedded in layers of systemic forces, arising from their own marital system, their family system, the kinship system, and various systems in their social network. These systems constantly interact with the internal process systems within each spouse, influencing the nature of the experiences and the meaning each gives to these experiences. When relationship tensions arise, these awaken sequences of meaning-constructing processes interacting within each spouse and the family relational systems, which are also affected by the larger social system and by prevailing cultural beliefs and values.

Subscribing to this conceptual perspective suggests divorce may be an interactive uncoupling process with the following characteristics:

1. Divorce is basically a dynamic process of marital disenchantment.
2. The divorce decision is a maturation of various systemic forces within the relational context.
3. The maturation of the various systemic forces could be indicative of the disruption of the attachment bond, arising from a violation of self-identity and the core belief system.

Methodology

A qualitative approach in the form of an in-depth interview (Jorgensen 1989; Merton *et al.* 1990) was employed in this study of four women, to explore and understand how and why Chinese women made divorce decisions. An open-ended, long interview design (McCracken 1988) was used in this research. The research purpose was to study the crucial elements in the uncoupling process and how the incremental progression towards "the point of no return" leads to the decision to divorce. The study was conducted in a service setting, so that the research was grounded in practice with continuous analysis drawing from and linking research data, clinical experience and literature references, somewhat like an induction-deduction spiral process.

The demographic data of the respondents are displayed in the following table:

Table 1. Description of Respondents' Profile

	Wendy	Anna	Jenny	Janet
Age	34	39	42	39
Religion	None	None	Catholic	Protestant
Occupation before divorce	Clerical	Housewife	Housewife	Accountant
Occupation after divorce	Housewife	Housewife	Housewife	Accountant
Type of accommodation before & after divorce	PHU	Private flat	Private flat	Flat
Years of marriage	11	18	16	19
Pre-marital counselling	No	No	No	No
Duration of courtship	6 mos.	3 yrs	2 yrs	2 yrs
No. of children	2	1	2	2
Age of children	3 & 9	16	11 & 8	14 & 17
Date of filing the divorce/ obtaining the decree	June 96	Apr 97	July 96	Jan 97

The study focused on a homogeneous non-probability sample of divorced women. To concentrate on an intensive "thick" description, as proposed by Geertz (1973), a sample of four cases was selected. The background of the women ranged from working class to upper-middle class. All of them are middle-aged, ranging from thirty-four to forty-two years old. It is believed that the older a person grows, the less the tendency for compulsiveness in decision-making. As a result, there is likelihood that the women would approach divorce struggles with more maturity and complexity. The sample consists of Chinese women who filed petitions for divorce within two years prior to this study. The time frame is specifically designed to offer more accurate recollection of experiences. In addition, all women selected are divorced and have children, for it is believed that the struggles in a divorce decision would be even more intense when women have to consider the welfare of the children, and the divorce decision would be more complex and difficult.

The interviewees also come from a variety of religious backgrounds. There is a common belief that divorce is prohibited in religions like Christianity. Reference to people with and without religious beliefs could suggest some constraints. The duration of courtship also ranges from a very short period of six months to a fair duration of three years. Such background details reflect marriages following a short acquaintance as well as fairly long courtships before marriage.

A Brief Overview of the Four Cases

Wendy's case: A Competent Woman Who Yearns for Protection

Wendy did not seek counselling until her elder daughter was truanting and had emotional problems at school. When Wendy approached the worker for assistance, she was determined to divorce her husband. However, her husband was reluctant to see the family break up. He lived with the hope that his wife would not actualize the idea, which she had held for many years.

Wendy had contemplated divorce soon after the first year of marriage. She was disappointed that her husband could not take the lead in the family. In Wendy's eyes, her husband was timid, incompetent and procrastinated in making decisions and fulfilling tasks. Thus, Wendy was forced to shoulder most of the family burdens. She buried her discontentment and became hot tempered. At the same time, Wendy's husband indulged in gambling and changed jobs frequently.

In the third year of marriage, her husband was found to incur a huge debt behind Wendy's back. It was a big blow to Wendy. Her marital satisfaction slide to zero. The event attacked her sense of inner security, which was her main goal in getting married, to find someone to offer shelter and protection. In the following two years, her husband's monthly salary was very unstable to the extent that there was often no money available. Wendy was totally disappointed. She experienced gradual emotional detachment. Every now and then, she thought of divorce.

Wendy made a firm decision to get a divorce soon after the second child was born. The relationship was so conflictual that the couple separated. When her husband refused to take action to apply for a divorce, she believed it was the final proof that he avoided responsibility. Wendy was utterly disappointed with her marriage and acted on her divorce decision. Uncoupling counselling and mediation service was provided.

Anna's Case: Marriage to a Philanderer

Anna married a rich businessman who was to provide her with an enjoyable and comfortable life. She was only sixteen years old when she married. She described her husband as a philanderer who was skilful at winning the heart of a girl. She consented to marry him because he promised to change after marriage.

Anna had the first idea to divorce soon after marriage, when she became pregnant and married life was chaotic. A year later, Anna discovered her husband had had casual sex with other women. Protesting in vain, she learnt to accept that casual sex was perhaps inevitable for a businessman. Nevertheless, Anna carried a sense of insecurity through the years.

Anna claimed she had high level of marital satisfaction, with slight ups and downs for the initial seven and eight years. However, when her father-in-law passed away, Anna was shocked to realize she was basically excluded as an "outsider" in her husband's family. She was also disappointed that her husband did nothing to help her understand his family. These negative experiences were offset by a positive one. In that year, Anna's husband faced a financial crisis in his business. Anna supported her husband in overcoming these hurdles. Marital satisfaction then seemed to have reached a peak.

Their marriage experienced a steep downward slope soon afterwards, for Anna accidentally discovered her husband had a steady extramarital affair for more than ten years. All the trust, hope and faith in the marriage were shattered overnight. Very soon, a second financial crisis occurred in the husband's business. The crisis reunited the couple.

Four years later, Anna' husband was found to be in a relationship with a woman again. Anna was in great despair. She experienced gradual emotional detachment after this blow. The couple was caught in intense conflict. In one outburst, her husband clearly told her that he found nothing wrong in having affairs, as long as he did not leave Anna. Anna's hope and respect for her husband was totally shattered. She made a firm decision to divorce him.

Jenny's case: An Overworked Housewife Who Earned only Blame

Jenny married at twenty-six, after a two-year courtship. The marriage was smooth and satisfactory until the first child was born. There were hidden conflicts with her mother-in-law regarding the child-care arrangement. Finally, she gave up her job in order to take care of the child. The in-law conflicts laid the seeds of marital discontent.

Soon after the second child was born, Jenny's husband started a part-time degree course at university. He was under pressure from his studies. As a result, Jenny was extremely overworked. She vented her feelings a lot to her husband, expecting emotional support and closeness. Oftentimes, her husband tried to solve the problems by giving advice or withdrawing in silence. The couple experienced a further downhill slide in marital satisfaction.

Four years later, Jenny discovered that her husband had an extramarital affair. Jenny was too shocked to accept the reality. She then had the first idea of divorce. But she tried to rationalize and to save the marriage by working hard. Jenny was heartbroken when she found her husband was still acquainted with the third party two years later. This hurt was made worse in that, instead of support and consolation, she was blamed by her mother-in-law for not serving her husband well and driving him to extramarital affairs. In the following years, the marriage was full of turmoil. Jenny's husband shifted from withdrawal to hot temper. Their relationship was increasingly conflictual. After a particularly heated argument, Jenny felt the marriage was dead and decided on a divorce.

Janet's case: A Sad Story of Prolonged Separation

Janet married when she was twenty years old, after three years of courtship. The first child was born one year after marriage. The second child was born two years later. Her marriage remained stable and satisfactory.

Janet's marriage experienced abrupt changes when her husband changed jobs to work in mainland China ten years after marriage. Janet's husband worked most of the time in the Mainland. His time at home was short and irregular. Janet suffered from the prolonged separation and lived like a single parent. She had great adjustment difficulties in the following three years. Her husband also had difficulties adjusting to his loneliness and cultural alienation working in China.

When Janet was more adjusted, she suddenly found her husband showed much emotional closeness to her in the following year. She was so satisfied that her marriage was rising to the peak of her marital experiences. However, she was then shocked to discover her husband had a woman in China who had had a child. The discovery was a great blow to Janet. She could not accept that her husband had two families and two women at the same time. She then had the first idea of divorce. The news of Janet's husband's extramarital affair was soon spread far and wide by a relative. In a reactive manner, Janet raised the idea of divorce with husband. Her husband did not agree or object. He acted passively. Janet was overwhelmed by a sense of hurt and betrayal and acted very fast. After the couple had signed the divorce petition at the law firms, both of them cried bitterly and embraced each other. Janet waited for her husband to beg her to reverse the decision. However, he remained passive and silent. Janet acted on the first impulse to divorce him and did not experience an emotional detachment process. Thus, she was emotionally disturbed long after the legal proceedings were completed.

Divorce Decision as a Process

All the cases showed a roughly downhill slope in marital satisfaction, even though certain significant events may have generated a slightly uphill effect. It was a surprise that dissatisfaction in marriage, which invoked the client's first idea of divorce or separation, could have lasted for a long period of up to ten years. The first idea of divorce could be an alarm signal or "cry for help". After the first idea of divorce emerged, there was a stage when some attempts were made to restore the relationship. If this showed little effect, emotional divorce occurred around this stage. During this period of emotional detachment, there are often preparations for divorce, such as psychological contemplation of life after divorce and a search for information about legal rights and legal proceedings. When the escalation of negative interaction reaches a threshold, the decision to divorce becomes firm, and legal action follows soon after.

The Uniqueness of Divorce Decisions

The divorce decision is never a sudden resolution that just happens overnight. Rather, the decision is a gradual process, with fluctuations, changes and turbulence. A divorce decision is distinct from other daily human decisions, and unique in many ways. Firstly, the divorce decision is virtually a "no-win" situation, and no positively anticipated goal exists. Secondly, the divorce decision is unique, for it is an act situated in a life crisis, as the consequences of the divorce have a significant bearing on a person's future life. Thirdly, divorce is a decision that results in the breakdown of an intimate relationship. Inevitably, there are strong elements of stress and emotions embedded in divorce decision-making. Self-identity is threatened when the intimate relationship falls apart. It explains why the separation process can be so painful. Consequently, normative and affective dimensions rather than pure rational intellectual dimensions should be considered in the understanding of divorce decisions. Fourthly, a decision that affects a person's long-term well-being, as well of those closely related, cannot rest on reason alone.

So, how does the process of deciding to divorce evolve? In this study, the author searched for clues in the pathway that leads to the "point of no return" in coming to this decision.

Danger Signs in Reaching the "Point of No Return"

From the cross-comparison of the first three cases, a pattern of a four-stage divorce decision process was indicated: the idea of divorce, the move to emotional divorce, the firm decision together with preliminary preparations, and then legal action.

1. Marital Reappraisal in "Marital Distress Zone"

In our case studies, both Anna and Wendy felt dissatisfied with their marriages soon after they got married. However, they stayed in the marriage for more than ten years, confirming that marital dissatisfaction may not lead directly to marital instability (Gottman 1994; Lewis & Spanier 1979; Kayser 1993).

In the women's struggles, how do they come to the time of deciding they have reached "the point of no return"? A review of their progression from expectation to disenchantment indicates that a prevailing consciousness of *expectations unfulfilled* and a subjective sense of *entitlement of love unachievable* through the marriage seems to determine the starting point of the momentum for a critical re-evaluation of the relationship. This appraisal focuses particularly on the "marital distress zone" which constitutes the period of marital readjustment from the first idea of divorce to the actual breakdown of the marriage. This is the period when the dissatisfied wives underwent a series of revisions of expectations and activities to salvage the relationship, which proved to be in vain and brought about great distress (see Figure 3).

Across the cases there was an active reappraisal of meaning and reconstruction of meaning of the experience in the marital distress zone. Jenny asked herself what marriage was for. What was the point of working so hard at the marriage? Anna asked if the man she married had integrity and basic respectable morality. Whether a man who has affairs with another married woman is worthy of a good wife? Wendy was alarmed to find her husband had heavy debts. She asked what kind of future she would face if she kept living with this man.

2. Significant Event as Punctuation

Almost all the women mentioned a series of significant events when the idea of divorce emerged. In all cases, the author found that the thread of dissatisfaction was linked by events. For Wendy, these included her husband's gambling activities, frequent job changes, and the big blow of the discovery of a huge debt he had incurred. For Anna and Jenny, the series of events related to their husbands' affairs, which, together with in-law tensions, contributed to a decline in satisfaction. Janet tolerated separation and adjustment difficulties of her husband's prolonged absence working in China, until confronted with having to live in a polygamous marital arrangement. These significant events seem to serve as punctuation points in the couples' married lives (see Figure 4).

From the women's narrative accounts, the meaning they made of the significant events in the marriage is more important than the event itself. The handling of expectations and disappointments is a process of continually interpreting and reinterpreting reality as they experienced it. In this process, attempts are made to readjust between ideals and reality, and to reformulate realistic expectations more harmonious with the constraints of reality. When the reality falls only slightly short of the ideal expectation, it is easier to make a minor readjustment. When the reality is found to have too great a discrepancy with the expectation, the person experiences cognitive dissonance. Perhaps the psychological process of the handling of expectations and disappointments can be illustrated by the following diagrams.

Those couples that are flexible and positive with a rich repertoire of personal resources are able to reformulate and readjust their expectations (see Figure 1, Scenario 1). Those couples that hold to a static view of the loving relationship are likely to fail to work together to modify ideals and reality in a dynamic manner. In the end, they suffer from meaning vacuum and cognitive dissonance. To ease their imbalance, they can either resort to changing the partner or to denying the reality (see Figure 2, Scenario 2). These behaviours are revealed by the four women. These behaviours are also common in the marital counselling process. The research helps to enlighten us about the meaning of these clinical processes.

Interpreting Meaning of Significant Event: Scenario 1

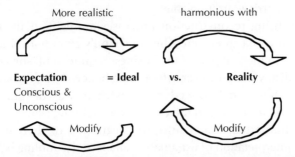

Figure 1. Significant Events Triggers Psychological Process of Reformulating Expectations

Interpreting Meaning of Significant Event: Scenario 2

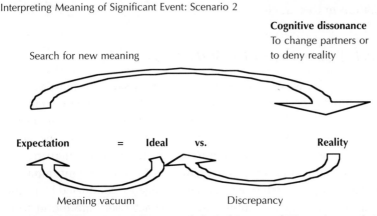

Figure 2. Significant Event Triggers Psychological Process of Disappointment in Failure of Reformulating Expectation

Note: **Expectation = ideal** suggests that a person's ideal state is generally derived from expectation.

3. Construction of Meaning as the Key to Disappointment

Marital expectations are continuously shaped and reshaped according to changing life circumstances. The negative construction of the meaning of an event elicits a negative behavioural response. The positive or negative responses from the partner confirm or disconfirm the negative construction of meaning of events. The healthy marriage with a realistic assignment of meaning and positive dyadic interaction enables the marriage to remain in the upper level of satisfaction. In contrast, negative construction of meaning added to negative dyadic interaction renders lower and lower satisfaction. The dissatisfied spouse, struggling with disappointment after disappointment, repeatedly experiences a decline in marital satisfaction to a lower level until she reaches the threshold and considers her marriage irretrievable.

These meaning reconstruction processes are evident in the four women. When Anna interpreted her husband's extramarital affair as casual sex and an integral part of the business requirement, she was calm in facing his disloyalty. However, when Anna believed her husband took advantage of her and betrayed her trust, she was desperate and disillusioned. Their interaction then grew worse, although she had known about the extramarital affairs since the beginning of their marriage. Likewise, the interpretation of extramarital affairs and gambling behaviour of the husbands by the wives were significant in the decline in marital satisfaction and the increase in negative interaction. Detailed data analysis can be found in my dissertation (Fok 1999). Space does not allow further elaboration in this article.

4. Global Characterization of the Partner

In the study, the wives refer to their efforts to save the marriage and tolerate unmet expectations. The relationships fluctuated with some ebb and flow in satisfaction, in tensions and in stress, until the interactive pattern grew to an explosive point of destructive outbursts. During the period of intense negative interaction, communication turned to bickering, hostility, mind reading, exchange of insults and intimidation. In the laboratory research of emotional intelligence conducted by Daniel Goleman (1995), such communication characteristics are found to be predictors of divorce. This is confirmed by the clinical work of Gottman (1994). Following a period of intense negative interaction, dissatisfied spouses are observed as describing their partners with globally negative characteristics. For instance, Anna said: "I never scolded him before. This time I really scolded him. I told him, 'you are shameless, completely without integrity, you are a scoundrel!'" Wendy said: "I hated him ... He is indecisive, a coward. He lacks incentive and energy. He is incompetent". Jenny said: "Inside my heart, I concluded such a bad guy is not worth my attachment ..." Janet said: "He appeared to be very caring and loving to me ... I felt nauseated when he called and said he was thinking of me ... He is a fake! A sham! I want to vomit mentioning him ... I hated him. He has cheated me, irresponsible; in sum, he is awful, unbearable".

This negative global characterization, which is unequivocal and comprehensive, can be perceived as a signpost of a crucial developmental stage of the marital breakdown. Such an understanding helps the counsellor in two aspects. The counsellor can track the expression of this negative characterization as an assessment tool of the stage of development of marital disintegration. It also offers intervention possibilities. This characteristic can be explained as a psychological dissonance reaction to validate the client's pain and facilitate redefinition to regain his or her balance of life experiences. Putting this in context can ease toxic fixation and open up space for spiritual forgiveness and reconstruction of the relationship.

5. The Reverse of Attachment Process

In this study, the wives were vigilant, active and alert to the ups and downs in their relationships. Their attempts to "save" their marriages are those generally resorted to by many wives in Hong Kong. In their attempts to change the husband, the wife reaches out with advice and suggestions, the husband withdraws, the wife tries harder, the husband retreats further, and the couple engages in the classic dance of pursuer-distancer which, repetitive and redundant, leads nowhere. The ways in which wives assume the maternal role and "parent" the spouse, by advising, reasoning and teaching, paradoxically obscure their position as the attractive sexual and affectionate partner and replace this with that of the stern parent.

Writing on love and attachment, Robert Weiss (1985) postulates that idealization and identification with the partner, through developing trust and belief in the partner, developing mutuality, complementarity and attachment, contributes to the growth of intimacy and the development of a dyadic couple identity. A reversal of the attachment process seriously puts intimate relationships at risk. In the life course of a marriage, significant events, life stresses and disappointments in expectations can lead to the disruption of these relational elements. In this study, these trends are reflected in the wives' narratives, which graphically illustrate their tendency to emphasize the negative aspects of the partner's character, thus disrupting idealization and identification with the partner. Trust is undermined by events perceived as acts of betrayal. Changes in shared beliefs, values and goals, together with lifestyle differences, lead to distancing and the dilution of mutuality. The reverse of the attachment process occurs, resulting in detachment and diminishment in emotional exchange. The stories of the four wives clearly illustrate these processes.

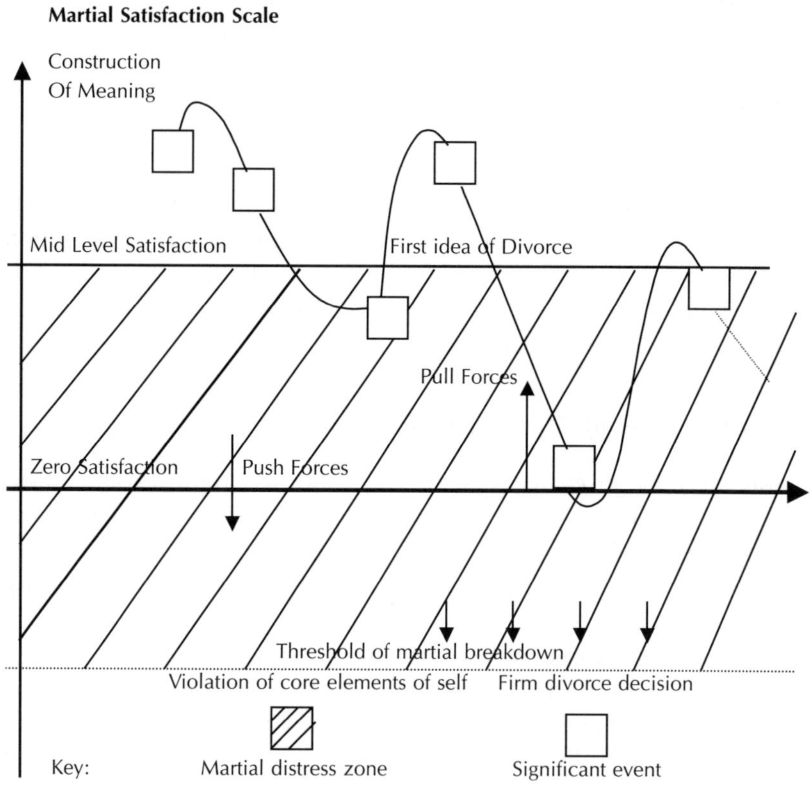

Martial Satisfaction Scale

Figure 3. Developmental Process of Marital Dissolution: Towards Making the Decision to Divorce

Figure 3 helps to illustrate how the divorced women reach the point of no return in the chaotic pathway of divorce decision. The shaded area constitutes the "marital distress zone" portraying the developmental process starting with the first idea of divorce to a firm divorce decision, which will be materialized by legal action. Inside this "marital distress zone", the couple's relationship, though at risk of marital breakdown, is able to endure for quite a lengthy period. The uphill and downhill experience of marital satisfaction is punctuated by significant life events in the marriage. The meaning made of each significant event could lead to a better or worse couple interactive cycle. The interactive cycle is also affected by the pushes and pulls of life circumstances, family developmental stress, such as the birth of a child, loss of a job, mid-life crisis, support or rejection from the extended family, and the social script about gender and divorce. How does the ups and downs divorce decision pathway finally reach the "point of no return"?

Reaching the Point of No Return

How does a person reach the point of deciding that a relationship is irretrievable, and all the energy to salvage the relationship dissipates? This is an experience of total disenchantment. When the author examined the narrative data again and again, a common theme of violation of the core elements of the self preceded the firm decision to divorce.

Violation of Self-identity

For instance, Jenny made a last-ditch effort to discuss with her husband their marital relationship after repeated blows of extramarital affairs. She felt greatly insulted. The theme of her self-esteem being violated was cumulative. Even though Jenny was still worried about the unknown future and the stigma of divorce, she decided to divorce her husband. For Jenny, the hardship and the betrayal were secondary in her divorce decision. The primary force was a violation of her self-esteem and self-identity.

Violation of Core Beliefs and Values

Anna is a person with high moral values and clear principles. She also expected her husband to be a person with integrity. To Anna, extramarital acquaintance implies disruption of another intact family. It transgressed her moral principles. Her belief that her husband should be a person with integrity was deeply violated. Subsequently, she was determined to make a clean break with the person whom she no longer respected.

Janet could not accept a polygamous marriage in any circumstances. Her husband was confronted by an absolute either-or situation. He either chose to leave the third party or to leave her. In reality, her husband treated Janet even better after he started cohabiting with a woman in the Mainland. In expectation of emotional support and affectionate exchange, Janet was more satisfied than at the beginning of their regular physical separation. The only impasse was that Janet's husband refused to make a choice to leave the other woman. Janet could not accept a polygamous marriage. She determined to get a divorce when her core value about intimate relationships was violated.

Violation of Life Theme

Seeking security and protection in life is a prominent life theme for Wendy. She had experienced the trauma of rape. After that, she was extremely fearful that her family could do nothing to protect her. She did not wait for her first boyfriend, whom she would have loved to marry. Instead, Wendy chose to marry her husband, whom she did not love so much. The reason was she was in need of shelter and protection. Her husband looked "tame" and "good-natured". These qualities gave her a sense of security. But her life theme was violated by her husband's gambling and incurring debts without her knowledge. Wendy pointed out that economic stress was not the core reason for their marital breakdown. Wendy expressed the view that if her husband could stick to a low-paid job that ensured family stability, she was confident she could overcome the financial hardship. What troubled her more was the risk-taking behaviour of husband, which disrupted her sense of security and stability.

In sum, a subjective sense of violation of core beliefs, values, principles, life themes and self-identity, experienced as so devastating to require a new reconstruction of self identity and one's world view, took these dissatisfied wives to the threshold of the decision to divorce.

Divorce Decision Therapy derived from Research and Clinical Practice

From this exploration of the divorce process, some research tenets emerge to guide therapeutic work. Findings from the study indicate that the divorce decision process correlates with a downward trend in marital satisfaction, reflecting a disenchantment process, which is punctuated by significant events. Each spouse subjectively makes meaning of these events from underlying assumptions and expectations of marriage. Spouses with a dynamic view of love experience more space for readjustment between expectation and reality. Those with a static view of love have less room for manoeuvre, leading to disappointment and accumulated resentment.

This marital reappraisal is also shaped by any negative elements in the couple's dyadic interaction, dysfunctional conflict resolution pattern, by stress from family developmental issues, and sometimes by inertia, apathy, impulse of the involved parties, which push towards divorce. The stigma of divorce, insecurity about an unknown future, concern for children and anxiety about ability to cope outside marriage serve to dissuade some people from a divorce decision. Amid the push and pull movement of the decision to divorce, the threshold of a firm decision is reached when the marriage is experienced as leading to the violation of the core elements of self, such as self-identity, core beliefs and life themes.

Systemic analysis of a couple's interactive dynamics:
As affected by expectation and reality readjustments in marital life

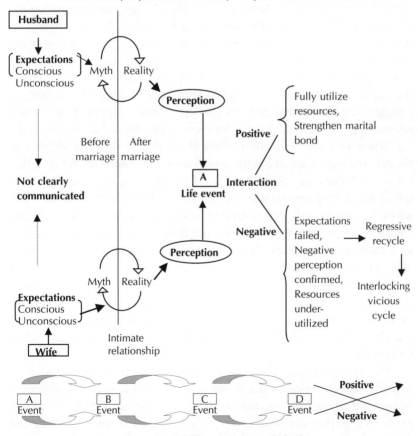

Figure 4. Readjustments in Marital Life

The decision to divorce is a unique human dilemma, as it is intrinsically embedded in risks potentials, has serious implications for future living, implies disintegration of an attachment bond, and is a "no-win" situation. Taking hardship and family life stress as inevitable in life, it seems that hidden expectations, subjective interpretations of the spouse's behaviour, and problematical interactive patterns were conducive to disillusionment. However, successful modification of expectations, more empathic acceptance of behaviour and intentions, and re-establishment of more gratifying interactive patterns, might rekindle the fire of hope and love. Figure 4 helps to illustrate these ideas more fully.

The Practice of Divorce Decision Therapy

The study examines the uncoupling process, but those who are struggling to resolve whether their relationship is retrievable are also simultaneously overwhelmed by the painful process of having to decide whether to divorce. In response to this dilemma, an approach in divorce decision therapy has been developed to test out whether it might be viable for working with Chinese clients. The intervention proposed is derived from the clients' and the worker's insights arising from coping with separation struggles, and from the author's clinical practice. The findings of this research significantly aid the development of this divorce decision therapy

When spouses enter counselling about the decision of whether to divorce, often they are still at the point when "one wants in and the other wants out". The entry point for divorce decision therapy is to start with the ambivalent party. In general, the ambivalent party wants to leave, whereas the other party is motivated to save the marriage. The turbulent emotion of the latter would diffuse the focus of the work. It is wise first to firmly engage the ambivalent party. The foremost task is to allow space and room for the party's ambivalence. Any slight sign of "judgement" or "lecture" will push the ambivalent party away towards a rash decision. It is essential to contract with the client to find "time" and "space" for decision counselling so that he or she will not have regrets in retrospect. It is vital to prevent all parties, including the counsellor, from being pulled by circumstances.

Signs of emotional divorce as indicated from this study are recurrent negative constructions of the meaning of family life events, ambivalent reappraisal of core beliefs, any occurrence of last-ditch efforts at repair, explosive outbursts, low levels of energy, trust and hope in the relationship, as well as any negative global characterization of the partner.

These help to guide the pacing of our work. The more the clients show the above signs, the more they are approaching the threshold. The therapist has to be gentle and tactful to decelerate any further downward trends. Tactful restraint of push forces towards divorce and promotion of healthy pull forces towards marriage are preliminary moves in the divorce decision therapy.

In working with someone who is struggling with the dilemma of staying or leaving the marriage, divorce decision therapy needs to address three levels of exploration and intervention. From the research, we can see that the maturation of the divorce decision develops from a chain of significant events over time. Marital satisfaction tends to deteriorate as unresolved toxic events accumulate. Therefore, it is essential to trace the historical dimension of the marital relationship. Secondly, the interpretation of the significant events serves as punctuation of the uphill slope or downhill slope of marital satisfaction. As a result, the couple interaction is largely affected by such interpretation. The positive or negative interaction can uplift or further undermine the already weakened relationship. Therefore, the level of internal psychological process and interactive process are to be worked out to trace, stabilize and readjust the divorce decision-making process. The author has attempted the intervention method in training workshops. The trainees in the field found the therapy method quite different from other conventional divorce therapy and affirmed the method as helpful and appropriate.

Historical Level

It is crucial to help a client explore and understand the marital problems from a historical perspective. The counsellor has to help the client to track the development of marital disappointment, especially the downhill slope of marital satisfaction. Through tracking, one can identify any significant event which functions as a punctuation point in the marital history. The subjective construction of the meaning of the event has to be decoded, for it may have triggered unresolved marital disappointment. Through deliberating over the unresolved event, the client and the counsellor can reconstruct the meaning of the event. The reconstruction of the meaning of past toxic events through facilitating communication between the couple in the counselling room is crucial in relieving them from grudges and misunderstanding.

From the historical perspective, the contextual issues of family lifecycle stress, such as the birth of a child and a mid-life crisis, can be addressed. Stress from the marriage can be externalized. Externalization of stress can serve to form a united front for the couple in that they can see events as facing a common adversity. Any carry-over effects of rules, beliefs and experiences from the family of origin, when relevant, may have to be recognized and resolved.

The same event can be re-experienced through uncovering additional perspectives from each other. From the writer's clinical practice experience, the same event reinterpreted with new perspectives will help couples promote empathy and mutual acceptance of differences. Past events detoxified sometimes help couples rekindle buried affection for each other.

The Interactive Level

At the point when one partner is contemplating separation, it is nevertheless helpful to attempt to tune in to any positive interactive resources within the marriage that could revitalize existing energy. This could include promoting positive experiences, developing alternative coping strategies, sharing and identifying perspectives on values and beliefs, reaffirming the significance of what is important to both of them in their lives together, at the same time working through unproductive conflict patterns towards a more collaborative stance.

The promotion of positive interaction serves as a powerful resource to enable the couple to meet the challenges at the point of considering a decision to divorce, whether the marriage continues or not. These need to be activated at the same time as attempts at a reduction of negative destructive interactive patterns. Attempts to subdue conflicts could release the rich potentials of two unique persons to cope with the dilemmas and difficulties of their situation. These shifts at the interactive level facilitate the couple's review of their relationship in an atmosphere of mutual respect and willingness to hear the other's points of view.

The Level of Internal Processes

By the time a spouse is considering divorce, he or she is likely to feel desperate after many efforts and much frustration in handling marital problems. In seeking counselling, the client is tired of pseudo-comfort, easy reassurance and positive encouragement towards reconciliation. It is important for the counsellor to keep an open mind and a listening ear. It is unwise to give advice or instruction right at the beginning after only preliminary data collection. However, it is useful to explore the client's feelings and subjective perception around presenting problems and issues of concern. In the divorce decision dilemma, the clients are usually highly anxious, full of uncertainties and sensitive to blame. They raise doubts and blame themselves internally, although they may behave defensively outside. When they are given sufficient space for self-exploration free from anxieties, they will loosen up and be able to focus on real heartfelt concerns. In this way, clients are given a chance to discover the themes in the development of their subjective construction of meaning, and create space necessary for alternative understanding of the life events to emerge.

Very often, through tracing a coherent theme, the counsellor helps the clients to unearth hidden expectations as well as their inner yearnings as a couple. There are universal yearnings behind the daily expectations such as: "Do I have an important place in your heart?" "Do I feel needed?" "Do I feel I belong?" When these have been acknowledged and validated, each spouse is more willing to accept limitations, "let go" or modify unrealistic expectations. The author has tried to develop clinical guidelines for divorce decision therapy to assist the practice.

With assessment of the above levels of the marital and separation problems, appropriate intervention can be planned accordingly. If the client wants to give him or herself a last chance to reconsider the marriage, the therapist can suggest marital counselling for both parties to consider commitment to rebuild the marriage. If the client is firm with the divorce decision, the counsellor provides uncoupling counselling or introduces mediation service.

What of the Husband's Experience?

This discussion was prompted by questions, and raises more questions. What of the husband's experience within the marriage? The wives reviewed the events and experiences that were distressing, and recalled attempts to readjust expectations and salvage the relationship, but the husbands could also have experienced expectations unfulfilled and the subjective sense of love unachieved, and attempted to readjust their expectations. From the wives' accounts, the husbands' distancing through working longer hours, working away from Hong Kong, or taking up further studies could be their way of reducing conflict. Their outbursts of temper may reflect distress. The better times within the fluctuations in satisfaction in the marriage could be when both spouses took a proactive stance to revitalize the relationship. It was a matter of some regret that the retrospective nature of the study two years after divorce made contact with these husbands impossible. This certainly is an area for further research.

The Moral and Spiritual Dimensions of Relationship Breakdown

All of the women were asked: "What is your source of strength, what helped you through the traumatic experiences?" Perhaps a summary table would help to illustrate the essential source of strength and support of the women in going through the traumatic experiences.

Table 2. Source of Strength and Support in Going Through Traumatic Divorce Experiences

Source of strength/support	Wendy	Janet	Jenny	Anna
Family support	✓	✓	✓	
Religion and faith	✓	✓	✓	
Forgiveness and clear conscience	✓	✓	✓	✓
Friends	✓	✓		✓
Reading books				✓
Support group	Not applicable	Not applicable	✓	Not applicable
Fear of a broken family	✓			

The personal disclosures of all of the women reflected moral and spiritual dimensions in the nature of the breakdown of marital relationships. Facilitating an appropriate apology and rendering forgiveness therapy are essential elements in divorce therapy. In facing despair and shattered dreams, there is a natural desire to search for direction for the ultimate purpose in life. The author believes developing post-divorce counselling with built-in recognition of spiritual elements of a search for meaning of life would be appropriate for the integrative family services being initiated in Hong Kong.

Conclusion

The decision on whether to divorce is a major life choice that affects a person's life and self-image, family relationships and the future of the next generation. Just having to make such a decision, and facing the prospect that an important relationship is no longer tenable, induces guilt, sadness, and a deep sense of failure. The processes that a person undergoes to come to realize that the marriage is irretrievable are likely to have unique features different from those of other forms of decision-making. This small study suggests that, for four Chinese women, a subjective sense of violation of core beliefs, values, life themes and self-identity, requiring a reconstruction of their sense of self and of their world view affected their appraisal of their marriage and triggered the decision for divorce. It could be that, for other groups (Mainland wives of Hong Kong husbands) in other contexts (the very rich or the very poor), struggles may reflect other dimensions. The most obvious query arising from this discussion would be: What could have been the pathways of the four husbands in reaching the point of divorce? Because of increasing divorce rates in Hong Kong, our search for further indicators of the process of uncoupling is ever more pressing, as we strive to avoid the premature decision to divorce in the distress of relational breakdown, as in the case of Janet who regretted the divorce even at the lawyer's office but waited in vain for her husband's retraction.

References

Albrecht S.L. and Kunz P.R. (1980). The decision to divorce: A social exchange perspective. *Journal of Divorce*, 3 (4): 319–37.
Bohannon P. (1970). The six stations of divorce. In Bohannon P. (Ed.) *Divorce and after: An analysis of the emotional and social problems of divorce*. New York: Doubleday, pp. 29–55.
Donovan R.L. and Jackson B.L. (1990). Deciding to divorce: A process guided by social exchange, attachment, cognitive dissonance theories. *Journal of Divorce* 13 (4): 23–35.
Duck. S. (Ed.) (1982). *Dissolving personal relationships*. New York: Academic Press.
Edwards J.N. and Saunders J.M. (1981). Coming apart: A model of marital dissolution decision. *Journal of Marriage and the Family*, 43 (2): 379–89.
Geertz C. (1973). *The Interpretation of Culture*. New York: Basic Books.
Goleman D. (1995). *Emotional intelligence*. London: Bantam Books.
Gottman J.M. (1994). *What predicts divorce? The relationship between marital processes and marital outcomes*. Mahwah, NJ: Lawrence Erlbaum Associates.
Guerin P.J., Fay L., Burden S.L. and Kautto J.G. (1987). *The evaluation and treatment of marital conflict*. New York: Basic Books.
Jorgensen D.L. (1989). *Participant observation: A methodology for human studies*. Newbury Park, CA: Sage.
Kalb M. (1983). The conception of the alternative and the decision to divorce. *American Journal of Psychotherapy*, 37 (3): 346–56.

Kayser K. (1993). *When love dies: The process of marital disaffection.* New York: Guilford Press.

Lewis R.A. and Spanier G.B. (1979). Theorizing about the quality and stability of marriage. In Burr W.R. *et al.* (Eds.) *Contemporary theories about the family, research based theories.* Volume. 1. New York: Free Press.

McCracken G. (1988). *The long interview.* Newbury Park, CA: Sage.

Merton R.K., Fishe M. and Kendall P.L. (1990). *The focused interview: A manual of problems and procedures.* 2nd Edition. New York: Free Press.

Price S.J. and Mckenry P.C. (1988). *Divorce.* Newbury Park, CA: Sage.

Weiss R.S. (1985). *Marital separation.* New York: Basic Books.

7

Rediscovery of the "Self": Culturally Sensitive Intervention for Chinese Divorced Women

CECILIA L. W. CHAN, SHIRLEY S. L. HUNG, WINNIE W. KUNG

This chapter examines the stress Chinese women experience from being divorced, and discusses the development of empowerment workshops to enable them to recover from the trauma of divorce. The married Chinese woman's sense of self derives from her roles as wife, mother and daughter-in-law. This sense of self is shattered when her role as wife is dissolved through divorce. Empowerment workshops, based on holistic health concepts borrowed from traditional Chinese medicine, promote the re-establishment of the sense of self through rediscovering and reformulating the meaning of life. Adopting an integrated body-mind-spirit approach, the workshops consisted of interventions that facilitate the participants' struggles through their many losses, to let go of anger and shame. This frees their energy and their strengths to find balance and harmony to move forward in life. These workshops were conducted in Hong Kong, Beijing, and Singapore. Pre- and post-tests indicate they were effective in reducing the participants' stress symptoms, in enhancing their positive sense of self and their perspective of the meaning of life, as well as in promoting active coping and increased energy levels.

Divorce in the Chinese Culture

Divorce is a traumatic event for most Chinese women (Kung, Hung, & Chan 2003). A considerable number of these women remain in a state of grief, loss, and despair, feeling abandoned, helpless, and hopeless for prolonged periods after divorce (Yi, Chan & Lam 2002a). In Hong Kong, three main reasons for divorce were noted: extramarital relationships (Young *et al.* 1995), domestic violence, and gambling, but extramarital relationships were the most often cited (Kung *et al.*, 2003). In many cases, the divorce decision is attributed to several causes, such as the husband being physically, sexually, emotionally abusive towards the wife and children, and being financially irresponsible. Another common pattern is that the husband is a compulsive gambler, exposing his family to threats from loan sharks and at the same time being violent towards his family. Many women who are victims of violence and abuse do not bail out of the marriage until their children's safety is affected. Chinese women, in general, are very tolerant towards adverse marital relationships for the sake of the children, hoping that they can grow up with both parents and in a "complete" family. In a study of a women's hotline in Beijing, some women reported enduring violence in the marriage for over ten years (Lam, Chan, Wang, & Liu 2001). Some women would turn a blind eye to the husband's extramarital relationship, hoping to keep the family intact. Chinese women are quite ready to make personal sacrifices for their children, parents-in-law, and husbands. They are often very "selfless".

In fact, selflessness is regarded as a virtue in Chinese culture, and taking care of oneself can be regarded as being "selfish." The cultural expectation of women being "selfless" is strong, because they are expected to be submissive and compliant towards the man (master) of the family, that is, the father, the husband, and son, throughout their life (Yi, Chan, & Lam 2002a). The meaning of life for a woman is determined by her position in the family. The dominance of her roles as wife, mother, and daughter-in-law often suppresses the development of her "self identity". A woman's sense of self may be shattered when her role as a wife is dissolved through divorce (Yi *et al.* 2002a; Hung, Kung, & Chan 2003). There is a strong sense of shame, self-blame, guilt, and loss among Chinese women who cannot stay in a marriage. This could be further aggravated by mothers-in-law and members of the extended family, who can be a source of oppression rather than a source of support (Yi, Chan, & Lam 2002b).

Social isolation and discrimination, as well as the costly and time-consuming judicial process of divorce, can also be sources of frustration for divorcing women (Irving 2002). For many, their financial situation deteriorates and family income decreases, leaving these women feeling disempowered through divorce (Hung 2000). The remarriage rate of divorced Chinese women is low compared to that of Western women

(Hung 2000). Seeing themselves as "a pair of worn shoes" in a "broken marriage", some divorced women become stuck in anger, jealousy, and hatred towards their ex-spouses (Liu & Chan, in press). Some may even develop obsessive blaming habits and subconsciously implant hatred in their children's minds (Chan & Wong 2001).

Children growing up in the shadow of the mother's "wounded self" are often torn between loyalties to both parents (Chan & Wong 2000; Lo et al. 1998). They strongly desire an intimate relationship with the father but at the same time share the mother's dismay at being abandoned by the father. Thus, these children are caught in a double-bind love-hate relationship with their fathers. They hate the father for leaving the family yet desperately long for his approval and love (Lo et al. 1998). The mixed emotions can be confusing to children and may result in a range of behavioural problems (Ayoub, Deutch, & Maraganore 1999; Jekielek 1998).

Societal Changes Further Increasing Complexities

Coping in the aftermath of a divorce has become even more complex, because of changing demographics in the Hong Kong community. The number of registered marriages in Hong Kong declined from 43,560 in 1987 to 31,869 in 2002 (Ming Pao, citing Census and Statistics Department of HKSARG, A20, 21.07.2004). This may be due to a decreasing youthful population and/or to the increasing number of young people in cohabitation, as they turn away from formal marriage. There are also a significant number of people marrying residents in China, whose marriages are not registered in Hong Kong's marriage statistics. In 2002, altogether 10,127 people applied for a certification attesting that they were not married, in order to get married in China or other parts of the world. In addition, the number of registered marriages to residents from mainland China increased from 7,724 in 2002 to 10,185 in 2003. Because of ease of travel and more contact since Hong Kong became a Special Administrative Region of China, this trend is likely to continue. Even now, marriages to mainlanders registered in Hong Kong account for almost one-third of all marriages. The serious social implications inherent in this situation are further exacerbated by a policy that results in mainland resident partners usually taking a few years to obtain residency in Hong Kong, so that in the early years of their marriage these couples experience considerable periods of separation. Conflicts are often reported from among these families, as reflected in a field study in which, of the forty-two female victims of domestic violence referred by the Social Welfare Department, thirty-five were from mainland China.

Despite the decreasing numbers of registered marriages, the incidence of remarriages (after divorce or being widowed) is increasing. The number of registered marriages to people who had been married before increased from 3,400 to 8,354, accounting for 8.3% and 17.2% of the marriages in 1987 and 2002 respectively (*Ming Pao*, citing Census and Statistics Department of HKSARG, A20, 21.07.2004). The social demographics of decreasing marriage rates and increasing divorce and remarriage rates indicate that the social phenomenon of serial monogamy is now emerging in Hong Kong. Moreover, the growth in the number of stepfamilies in itself adds complexity to existing relationships that needs to be taken into account, as new spouses learn to communicate with stepchildren, ex-husbands, and ex-wives. The unfinished business from previous marriages can hinder the development of new sets of relationships.

Coping with Stress and Trauma

To help women of divorce to recover from the trauma of divorce, we have adopted a set of concepts from Eastern philosophy for reconstructing the "self". We use group interventions to enable them to find the means to heal themselves through forgiveness, letting go, maintaining peace of mind, and in being effective single parents (Chan 2001; Lo *et al.* 1998). This is a form of group intervention based on holistic health concepts borrowed from traditional Chinese medicine. The aim is to nurture and strengthen the clients and their social systems so that they can arrive at a homeostasis which balances their emotions and cognition, as well as physical and spiritual needs (Chan 2001; Chan, Chan, & Lou 2001). Just as there can be the concept of a "good death", we are promoting the concept of a "good divorce" (Lo *et al.* 1998; Chan & Wong 2000).

A Good Divorce

May, 45, has been divorced for five years. She has joint custody of the children with her ex-husband. She lives with the children and they visit their father and grandparents' family every other week. She runs her own import-export firm and spends a lot of time volunteering in raising funds for under privileged children in China. She has come to terms with her divorce and feels calm and at peace with it. May shares her experience with other divorced women, suggesting that it is very important to forgive, to look for a new start, to find meaningful involvement such as volunteering, to not overwhelm the children with bitterness and negative emotions, to exercise, and to keep a balanced diet (Lo et al. 1998). May is happy that she has a "good divorce". Her relationship with her ex-husband and his family is cordial, and they still care for each other. She even called her husband to congratulate him when he had a baby daughter with his second wife. Their children feel loved and cared for by both parents. The parent-child relationship was not affected, as the parents discussed with the children the divorce and subsequent arrangements such as joint custody.

However, good divorces are exceptions rather than the rule, especially in Chinese societies. Many women become bitter towards marriage and heterosexual relationships after the divorce. Violence and homicide also occur when the marital breakup is not handled effectively. Many women indulge in self-pity, live in blame and shame, and identify themselves as lifelong victims of divorce. We developed our intervention in order to help divorcées in Hong Kong and China to end their pain and agony, so that they can have the energy to move on with their lives. Although some men also find it hard to adjust to divorce, this chapter focuses on our experience of a body-mind-spirit group intervention with divorced women only.

Divorce: A Shaming and Disempowering Process

Before detailing our proposed intervention for divorced women, we first describe some of the disempowering stress and trauma these women go through during the divorce process in Chinese societies.

Powerlessness in Marriage and Divorce

Sandy grew up in a family full of conflict. Her father was a drug addict and often abused her and her mother. Her father tried to rape her when she was twelve. The mother was timid, and prevented Sandy from telling anyone. She quit school at the age of fourteen. She worked in casual jobs for two years, and was later introduced to a cook in a restaurant. They dated for three months and she decided to get married so that she could leave her parents, whom she hated. A year after Sandy was married, she had a son. After the son was born, her husband began to act strange. He stopped coming home and disappeared from his workplace. At the age of 17, Sandy was left alone at home with a newborn child. She returned to her mother's home and was verbally abused by the father all the time. When her son was two years old, Sandy was introduced to a 54-year-old man who was willing to marry her and promised to take care of her and her child. She got pregnant soon after the second marriage. This man made a lot of sexual demands on her and she lived like a sex slave. She tried to stay calm and tolerated all unreasonable demands for a few years. Eventually, she sought help from a women's shelter after the second husband began to take a sexual interest in their five-year-old daughter. Sandy felt totally powerless and was at a loss what to do.

Sandy's experience is common among those who married early because they want to move out of high-conflict families. However, they usually have children soon after marriage and do not know how to maintain intimate and effective communication with their spouse and children. Many of these marriages end in divorce, or the marriage stays highly conflictual.

Wives who are financially dependent on their husbands often feel a lack of power. This is particularly so if their husbands expect them to be totally submissive and compliant. Even when there is abuse, neglect and violence, they endure it because of financial needs and because they feel that they cannot divorce their husbands and have their children labeled "children in a single-parent family".

The discrimination against divorced women is strong in Asian Chinese societies such as China, Taiwan, Singapore, and Hong Kong. As virginity is regarded as very important, a divorced woman is considered a "used item" that men would not want. A man who is willing to marry a divorced woman, especially if she has children from a previous marriage, is likely to be of lower socio-economic status. Divorced women without earning power may have very little choice but to marry whoever is available. These marriages may end in divorce as well.

Loss of Identity

Katherine was admitted to a psychiatric hospital when she attempted suicide in reaction to her husband's extramarital relationship in China. She was very disturbed and wanted to kill herself by cutting her wrists. She was diagnosed as clinically depressed with a high suicidal risk, and remained in the psychiatric hospital for more than two years. She requested visits from her six-year-old son, but her husband refused. When she was discharged, she discovered that her husband had filed for and obtained a divorce decree. The custody of the son was granted to the husband, as he claimed that Katherine was not mentally fit to take care of the child.

Upon discharge from the hospital, Katherine lived in a halfway house for discharged mental patients. She cried everyday, as the husband refused to let her see her son. Katherine had married her husband in mainland China before she moved to Hong Kong to join him. She had no friends, family members, or relatives in Hong Kong. Everyone knew her as Mrs Wong. While she lived in the halfway house, she no longer had the status of being Mr Wong's wife. This abandonment also removed her social identity and her meaning of life.

Katherine felt that she had no reason to live. She punished herself by not eating properly. She was absorbed in self-pity. She attempted suicide again after failing to see her son. She was then re-admitted to the mental hospital.

Divorced women often live in shame as a result of the loss of identity of being a wife. They are also isolated as if they have a contagious disease (Hung 2002).

Family as a Source of Misery

Monica married a firefighter and had two sons. The mother-in-law lived with them and raised the children. Monica worked as a saleslady of cosmetics with very long working hours. She had to work on weekends and evenings. Her relationship with the mother-in-law was poor. She found her mother-in-law too controlling, whereas the mother-in-law found Monica lazy for not doing housework. Thus, Monica would go out even when she was off work. In times of conflict, the husband would always ask Monica to give in and apologize. Eventually, the mother-in-law persuaded the son to divorce Monica, as she was not a good mother and wife. As a devoted son, the husband believed that divorcing Monica was the only way out of this conflictual situation at home. He later married a woman introduced to him by his mother. Monica did not obtain custody of the children, as the boys had all along been taken care of by the mother-in-law.

Monica was the loser in the power struggle with the mother-in-law. As the only son of a widowed mother, her husband was very emotionally attached to the mother and was exceedingly compliant. Monica felt very frustrated, as her requests for visiting her sons were often denied. She lived in anger and hatred for many years after her divorce.

Feeling overwhelmed, divorced Chinese women tend to blame other parties for the misery of the divorce. The source of misery, however, can come from the women's own family members, and, in many cases, from their own mothers. It is common to find that women who subscribe to traditional values are harsher towards divorced women.

Mandy married a man of whom her mother disapproved. After Mandy had a daughter, the husband vanished because of heavy debts from gambling. Mandy had to return to her mother's house, though it was fully occupied by the families of her siblings. She lived with her daughter in a small temporary structure in the courtyard. Her mother and siblings were abusive towards her. Mandy was scolded every day, and her life was miserable. Her daughter was severely punished for small misdeeds, and she grew up in fear. When she came to our group in Beijing, her daughter was nineteen years old. Living with a depressed, fearful, and often tearful mother and among mean relatives all those years, Mandy's daughter weighed only sixty-five pounds and was four feet three inches tall. Mandy's mother verbally and emotionally abused Mandy and her daughter, because she was still very angry with Mandy for marrying a man of whom she disapproved and for returning home after the divorce, thus casting shame on the whole family.

The misery of many women is rooted in their families' faithful adherence to the traditional Confucian teaching that a woman, once married, should stay in the husband's family for the rest of her life. The husband's family is supposed to give her meaning in life and the status of a good woman. A woman is expected to be selfless and unconditionally tolerant towards all her husband's wrongdoings. The divorce of a daughter is regarded as a disgrace to her family of origin, as she is considered to have been abandoned by her husband for misdeeds which reflect negatively against her upbringing.

Loss of Face for the Women and her Parents

Traditional Chinese communities consider it "wrong" to break up and leave a marriage. Women are expected to endure and stay in the family, no matter what the hardships. If the married daughter returns to the parents' home after divorce, the parents may experience a sense of shame. This belief can be traced to the laws of the Ching Dynasty, which state that only the husband can cast out the wife and not vice versa (Yi *et al.* 2002a).

Mary from Taiwan studied in Britain and married Sam from Singapore. After they moved to Singapore, Mary stayed home and did not go out to work. After five years, Sam wanted a divorce because of an extramarital affair. Mary was very frustrated and asked to return to her parents in Taiwan. Her parents told her that it was best for her to stay in Singapore. Mary recognized that her parents were fearful of a loss of face if she returned, because people in Taiwan were still quite prejudiced against women who divorce. However, she felt that it was very unfair to her for her parents to insist that she try to find a new life in Singapore, where she did not belong.

Mary had thoughts of suicide because of the persuasion from her parents not to return to Taiwan. The traditional teaching on resilience is that one should try to stand up on one's two feet from the place where one falls. A Chinese person is expected to be self-reliant and able to tolerate hardship (Chan & Chan 2001). Mary's family lived in a small village which is still very traditional and where social discrimination against divorced women is strong.

Social Discrimination and the Disempowering Process

From the shame and guilt experienced by these women, their sense of powerlessness, the misery imposed by their own families, and the loss of face experienced by families, one can see that divorce is indeed social degradation for many Chinese women. The extreme circumstance of outright rejection even by members of a woman's family, as in the case of Mandy, is rather unusual. However, social discrimination towards divorced women in Chinese societies is common (Hung 2000). Many divorced women feel isolated and excluded from previous social circles. Their opportunities for employment and for renting a place to live can be seriously compromised.

The judicial process also imposes pressure on women. Women who want to divorce have to go through costly and time-consuming legal procedures in Hong Kong. In Taiwan, divorced fathers are often given custody of the children, because they carry the father's surname. Moreover, if the children stay with the mother who remarries, they will have to go through the adoption process to change their surname to that of the stepfather, because many Chinese men do not want to raise children with another surname.

Marriage and the family are everything to some women. Women of divorce lose their sense of identity after the divorce, as Katherine did. Many felt that they have lost their meaning in life as well. Many of the women of divorce suffer from depression and have to resort to psychiatric treatment.

Sometimes they are regarded as "sexually casual and easy" by men. Other women friends may stop inviting divorced women to their homes or become reluctant to have their husbands interact with them. A few divorced women reported that landlords refused to rent rooms to them because of their marital status. Many divorced women tend to blame the ex-husbands, their family members, their in-laws and other people who discriminate against them.

In interviews with divorced women, it is common to hear heartbreaking stories of betrayal, hurt, guilt, shame, self-blame and blaming of others. Respondents are usually tearful when they describe their pain, bitterness, emotional turmoil and their loss of self. Chan (1999) suggests that the emotional process of divorce reflects five phases, starting with denial, followed by blame and shame, then grief and mourning, a search for refuge and healing, and finally redirection and transformation. Emotions accompanying these phases are often complex and mixed. Women may move back and forth from one phase to another.

We believe that divorce, though traumatic, can be a positively transforming experience. Some divorced women move out of very chaotic marital circumstances and regain peace of mind. Many also establish new life goals after divorce.

Stage Model of Empowerment: Reversing the Disempowering Process

Based on the emotional process of divorce, the authors propose a four-stage model of empowerment of the "self" for divorced and divorcing women. The stages are: loss of self, denial of self, rediscovery of self, and building of the new self. As in other traumatic experiences, divorce may lead to feelings of loss, but it can also give rise to opportunities for growth. Table 1 describes the personal, interpersonal and social aspects of the four phases of the loss and recovery of the "Self" in divorce.

Empowerment Workshops

We believe that, if divorce is properly handled, it can be an effective way to end chaos and misery so that the couple can make a new start instead of being bogged down by a sense of anguish and torment. In order to help Chinese divorced women to move out of their negative emotions and actively build a new life, we have designed an intervention programme in the form of empowerment workshops (Liu & Chan, in press). The workshops were conducted in collaboration with various social service agencies between 1997 and 2001. The following agencies in Hong Kong were involved: Caritas Hong Kong, Hong Kong Young Women's Christian Association, Hong Kong Federation of Women's Centers, Harmony House, Single Parents' Association, and Kwan Fuk (a mutual help group for survivors of domestic violence). Collaborating organizations include HELP (Help Every Lone Parent) of Singapore, as well as the China Women's College, Maple Women's hotline, and the Women's Federation of Beijing.

The empowerment workshops were conducted either in the form of five to six weekly three or four hour sessions or a two full-day weekend workshop. They were called workshops or training courses in order to emphasize the learning aspects of the programme, which tended to be more appealing to Chinese women than the notion of joining a group, given the cultural emphasis on education (Chan, Fan, & Gong 2003). In

Table 1. Loss and Reconstruction of the Self among Divorced Women

Emotional Process	Personal Aspects	Interpersonal Aspects	Societal Aspects
Loss of Self	• Anger • Grief • Out of control • Sense of loss • Helplessness • Fear	• Blaming others • Getting help from friends and family • Having an urge to take action or revenge	• Social stigmatization of divorce • Loss of status rendering the individual a victim
Denial of Self	• Bitterness • Sense of betrayal • Self-pity • Grief • Loneliness • Sadness • Resurging of suppressed anger • Depression	• Distrust • Avoiding new relationships • Loss of capacity to care for children and others	• Lack of resources and information • Loss/changes in status and roles • Discrimination
Rediscovery of Self	• Acknowledgement of loss and grief • Development of ability to handle negative emotions and thoughts • Self-assurance and self-acceptance • Loving oneself • Rebuilding strength	• Letting go and forgiving • Reconciliation with ex-husband and family members • Discovery of joy • Reconnecting to social network and friends	• Normalization • Advocacy for respect or dignity and social resources for divorcees • Advocacy against discrimination towards divorcees • Development of new role identity
Building a New Self	• Relief balanced emotions • Self-appreciation • Development of new roles • Search for meaning in life • Developing new strengths	• Establishing new networks and trust towards men • Helping children to re-establish trust	• Mutual help • Resource mobilization • Advocacy for social justice and anti-discrimination for divorcees

order to help these women to develop a sense of control, we focused on re-establishing the sense of self, rediscovering joy, and reformulating the meaning of life for these women in the empowerment workshop. Chinese are pragmatic and goal-oriented. If these women can generate new meaning in their lives after divorce, they can persevere and recharge their energy to work towards their goals.

The workshops start with some self-help skills to help the participants develop a sense of mastery over their own negative emotions, because most of these divorced women suffered from some symptoms of depression such as insomnia, poor concentration, and a loss of appetite. From our clinical observations of working with over 150 divorced women, we found that around one-third of the workshop participants had been seeing psychiatrists for severe mood swings and suicidal thoughts. In these empowerment workshops, we aim at helping the women to accept the misfortune of their marital breakdown, acknowledge their losses, recognize their own defence mechanisms and move on to create a new life for themselves and their children. Table 2 presents the intervention plan for empowerment integrated with the different phases of the emotional process associated with divorce.

Table 2. Promoting Empowerment for Women of Divorce

Emotional Process	Empowerment Intervention
Loss of Self	• Supportive intervention: Provide self-help skills, shelter, and financial and practical help • Normalization • Problem-solving
Denial of Self	• Emotional expression: Acknowledge bitterness and mixed emotional reactions • Prevention of self-harm • Divorce education
Rediscovery of Self	• Affirming their sense of self • Establish positive self-image and sense of self-efficacy • Love and forgiveness
Building a New Self	• Advocacy, mutual support • Meaning reconstruction • Focus on growth through pain

Carrying out the above intervention plan in a group format has several advantages. Each participant in the group can come to realize that she is not the only one who suffers in a divorce. The realization that "I am not the only one who suffers" and sharing experiences with "others in the same boat" can be quite consoling. In the intervention to promote the rediscovery of self, our team engaged the divorced women in a storytelling process and in a process of reconstructing meaning from these narratives.

The organization and time frame may differ slightly, as mentioned, yet the main themes of the group sessions are often organized as follows:

Session 1   Growth through pain: Normalization of divorce.
Session 2   Letting go and forgiving: Acceptance of loss and determination to move on.
Session 3   Loving yourself: Rediscovery and taking care of self.
Session 4   Transformation and extending the self: Mutual help, volunteering, and social support.
Session 5   Bringing up children in love and forgiveness.

We implemented a creative programme of combining short lectures, group sharing, games, songs, positive self-affirmation exercises, meditation, guided imagery, rituals, physical exercises, acupuncture, hugging, group massage, a homework assignment, and reporting in each session. We ensured that the flow of the sessions was smooth and infused with fun and laughter, so that members can rediscover joy and energy in the process. This positive experience can help them regain a sense of confidence in mastering their own lives. The sessions are designed to be long, in order to create a positive and affirming atmosphere so that the group members can have enough energy to sustain their efforts to change. Long sessions of three to four hours can also allow the group members time for in-depth sharing and reflections on what is most important in their lives. Through these workshops, the sharing of common experiences helps them to control and master their individual hurt. This enables them to develop the ability to grow through the pain of divorce to become persons with broader minds and stouter hearts.

The empowerment workshops aim to address the divorced women's personal, interpersonal, and social needs. Through training in effective emotional expression and communication, the needs of these women and those of their children can be more adequately expressed and attended to, thus minimizing the destructive costs of family conflicts and disintegration. It enhances the women's sense of self-efficacy through more positive self-appraisal and problem-solving skills and promotes their interconnectedness with others and society at large. The workshop also highlights the oppression of Chinese culture on divorced women. The participants are trained to be more assertive and self-confident. Group members are encouraged to love and take care of themselves as well as free themselves from blame and shame through forgiveness. In the following discussion, we highlight some of the important intervention strategies in the workshops and some anecdotes of the participants.

Normalization: Affirmation of Self

Many Chinese women find it hard to accept divorce, because they subscribe to the belief that marriage is for life and divorce is not acceptable. In the workshop, the first message we give to the women is that all marriages end one way or another; some end with the death of the spouse, whereas others end in divorce. Around one-third of the marriages may end in divorce, as the number of divorces is around 13,000 every year in Hong Kong, and registered marriages stands at around 30,000. If divorce is becoming more and more "normal", why do women blame themselves for it and feel ashamed? When Chinese women felt that divorce was not an option, many attempted suicide to end the very painful marital relationship. The suicide rate of women in Chinese societies is, in fact, very high (Phillips, Li, & Zhang 2002). In modern society in which people have the freedom to marry or divorce, women should take advantage of the divorce system in order to free themselves from distressing marital relationships that cannot be remedied.

The realization that divorce is a realistic response to unhappy marriages can be liberating. Divorce can be responsible behaviour, because studies have shown that children living in high-conflict marriages suffer more than do children of divorce (Yeung 1996, 1998). Thus, taking action and divorcing a husband who is abusive is actually responsible behaviour in the best interests of all parties concerned. Normalization can help remove the guilt, reduce the self-blame and shame as well as instill peace of mind among women who need to develop self-belief and a sense of self-confidence.

After the first day of the workshop, Mandy began to wear a smile on her face. She became more relaxed about being a divorcée. On the second day, she wrote a letter of forgiveness to her ex-husband, her mother, and her siblings. She was willing to start a new life and made a decision to take charge of her own life. Mandy's daughter, Susan, gained ten pounds in one month after her mother attended the two-day workshop. Susan's supervisor at the supermarket commented that Susan was more cheerful and talkative after her mother had attended the workshop. As Mandy became more relaxed and less depressed, Susan also turned a new page in her life. Because of more physical and emotional strength, Susan took evening classes to continue her education.

Letting Go and Forgiving: Liberating the Self

The Chinese character for "anger" is composed of two parts: the part "slave" is above the part "heart". We help the workshop participants to appreciate that anger, jealousy, and hatred is physically and emotionally consuming. In anger, we become slaves of our own heart. The participants are asked to write letters of forgiveness to their ex-husbands so that they can forgive them and put aside the hurt from the marital turmoil. Without forgiveness, the trauma of divorce will remain a lifelong burden on the women. However, with forgiveness and appreciation, the women can be freed. They can love themselves more and turn a new page in their lives.

The following is a letter of forgiveness written by a participant in a workshop in Singapore:

> I forgive you for not satisfying my needs, for abandoning us ten years ago. I hated you for being disloyal to the marital vows but I am now ready to forgive you. You have your own family now and I am living happily with my own children. You have missed a lot of fun and joy that we now have. I forgive you and set you free. By so doing, I am also setting myself free. I am going to live as a free and happy person. I shall not let the divorce experience affect me anymore. By forgiving you, I am also helping the children to learn to be accommodating, persevering, resilient, and forgiving as well.

Some of them have written letters of a different sort:

> I cannot forgive you yet, but I know that I have to let go of you. I cannot change the reality and the trauma that you have caused us, but I can let go of the grudges that bothered me for so long. You are an irresponsible father and we shall no longer live in your shadow. Your children are going to grow up as loving, caring, responsible adults who know how to love themselves and other people.

The letter of forgiveness is very powerful. The group members appreciate that the act of forgiving is not for the sake of others but to free themselves from bitterness. They can then learn to be unconditionally loving and forgiving to themselves and their children, as well as the people around them. With such emotional accommodation, they feel a greater sense of mastery over their own lives. They will not stay as "victims" of divorce but instead become "survivors" of trauma, including divorce and other misfortunes in life. The Taoist philosophy of letting go and accepting the unpredictable is often used in the discussion.

Forgiveness is helpful to the children, too. Children often feel torn by their parents in a difficult divorce. The children may blame themselves for not behaving as they should, because they are sometimes held responsible for causing the parents' conflicts. They may also feel confused, as they wish both parents to be loving and caring, even as they experience them to be hot-tempered and unpredictable. The loyalty dilemma of siding with the victim of violence (mothers, in most cases) while desiring affection from the father can be hurtful to the children. Unless the mother is willing to truly forgive and let go, the couple cannot cooperate and communicate effectively as responsible parents. Forgiveness sets the children free as well.

Transforming the Self: From Trauma into Personal Growth

The workshop adopted an integrated body-mind-spirit approach with strong emphasis on acceptance of the misfortunes in life as normal and natural (Chan, Chow, & Ho 2002). Spirituality here is defined as a sense of meaning in life and relationship with the transcendent or the universe. The ability to accept unpredictability in life and persevere in suffering is perceived as a kind of transcendence and some form of spirituality in Chinese culture. The participants were also encouraged to be more aware of their spirituality as they are helped to develop a sense of peace through breathing techniques, physical exercises, social support, resilience training, and group support, which in turn enhances their motivation for attitude and lifestyle changes. Stories of outstanding role models such as Jessie Yu, who has taken on the leadership role in advocating for single parents, are shared in order to energize the participants. Jessie's emergence from being a modest and reserved woman to an outspoken leader is described in the next section. Success stories can be liberating, because these women are inclined to think that, if another person can be transformed from the experience of divorce, they can, too.

After Sarah came to our workshop for divorced women in Beijing, she realized that she had locked herself in anger and hatred for over two decades after she left her abusive husband. Having disappointed her mother, she punished herself by not forgiving herself for the divorce, just like her mother. Unconsciously, she passed onto her daughter values of distrust and hatred toward men. After the two-day workshop, she decided that she was not going to live as a victim of the divorce. She wanted to turn over a new leaf in her life. She was determined to take charge of her life and to live happily from then on. Her change of attitude affected her daughter Amy, who became much happier as the mother was freed from hatred and bitterness. Six months later, Sarah was laid off her job. She then worked as a full-time volunteer at a women's hotline service to help other women. Amy began to date. Sarah supported Amy in her search for a romantic relationship, as she felt that the parents' marital problems should not affect the daughter's life choices.

Two years later, Sarah's flat was demolished and she had to relocate to another part of the city, but she found a job in her old neighbourhood. Every day she had to ride a bicycle for one-and-a-half hours to go to the bus terminus and then ride the bus for an hour to work, which totaled five hours on the road daily. It was very trying, especially the bike ride, considering the extreme temperatures in Beijing. Sarah indicated that, if she had not attended the empowerment workshop, she would be telling herself every day how miserable her life had been and it would be better that she died. Now that she had taken charge of her own life, she was able to appreciate the beauty of the city and the five hours went by quickly. She said: "It is simply a state of mind. The training workshop changed me. I look at life differently now".

Sarah was able to move out of remorse after twenty years of self-denial. She realized that, by focusing on her personal growth and counting her blessings, the whole world looked different. Her transformation is a result of watching the videotape of Jessie Yu of Hong Kong. Jessie was transformed from a victim of violence to an advocate for the rights of single parents. Sarah felt liberated as she came to realize that the divorce experience could nurture growth of resilience, perseverance, compassion and new meaning of life.

Service to Others: Finding a New Self

Being able to help others is an important component of survivorship.

The satisfaction of being able to help others gives meaning to one's suffering. Although these divorced women cannot change what happened in their own marriages, by helping others to prevent a divorce or ease the pain of going through a divorce, they derive great satisfaction that at the same time is therapeutic to them. In the helping process, they become more convinced about the importance of letting go, of forgiving, gaining respect, and self-care.

Jessie was abused by her husband for ten years, until she decided to divorce him. After the divorce, she worked part-time to support herself and her children while continuing her secondary school education in the evenings. Later, she pursued higher education in social work and formed an organization for single parents with the help of a professor from the City University of Hong Kong. Elected the chairperson of the organization, she started advocating for the rights of single parents, for both men and women. She had changed from a shy, withdrawn woman with low self-esteem to a passionate leader with vision and foresight. Jessie provided the leadership behind a strong single-parent movement in Hong Kong. She is a good role model of how divorce can be a transforming experience for women.

Many other women of divorce who participated in our groups become active volunteers in women's mutual help organizations and social service groups. They participate as peer counsellors in women's telephone hot-line services, provide home-care support as well as contribute to collective advocacy for the rights of women after divorce.

Dolly devoted herself wholly to helping her husband establish his business in a toy factory. When her husband's business had financial difficulties, Dolly borrowed money from her own family to help with the cash flow. She worked day and night at the factory until the business turned around and was doing well. Then she found that her husband was filing for divorce. All of the assets in the factory were transferred out and the business was sold without her knowledge. Dolly was severely depressed and suicidal. After attending the empowerment workshop, she became a volunteer for the hotline service at the women's centre. She heard stories of other women who were severely abused physically and sexually by their husbands, and of unreasonable treatment by their mothers-in-law. She learnt about available social services and support for women such as women's shelters and crisis centres. She found her own problem relatively trivial compared to those of others. She was able to refer women to services that she had found helpful. She discovered new meaning in her life and said: "the divorce has given me a new life. In the past, I was just a housewife who only cared about serving my husband. Now I can help other women and make a difference in their lives. I am proud of my personal growth through this trauma".

Traditional Chinese Values and Intervention

Chinese culture emphasizes the importance of the family, respect for hierarchy in interpersonal relationships, solidarity and harmony, modesty and contentment, and perseverance through hardship and suffering (Yang 1995). The notions of centrality of family over one's life, filial piety, continuation of family name, keeping harmony and the "face" of the family, and the inferior status of women all contribute in shaping the perceptions of marriage and divorce in Chinese societies (Kung et al. 2003).

In the workshops, we help the participants to differentiate between what is beneficial in Chinese culture and what is not. It becomes easier for them to forgive themselves and others when they can appreciate that the ex-husbands, ex-in-laws, relatives, and people who discriminate against them are also oppressed by the dominant patriarchal culture. They can then decide whether or not to continue feeling guilty for disappointing their parents, accepting excessive filial obligations, and respecting the will of unreasonable members of the family. Participants reported that conflicts with in-laws and members of the extended family are one of the common causes of marital disputes and divorce in Chinese societies (Cheung & Chan 2002). An understanding of the influence of cultural imperatives can free the participants from excessive anger and feelings of being oppressed, as they come to appreciate the domination and the detrimental effects of our patriarchal past on Chinese women.

According to traditional Chinese values, individuals are not supposed to disclose family problems to outsiders, in order to protect the family from losing "face". Such an attitude prevents people from seeking help, as they may feel guilty disclosing family secrets or washing dirty linen in public. Open conflicts and confrontations are also not tolerated in more traditional Chinese families. Over-emphasis on harmony often suppresses the expression of disagreement and grievances (Cheung 2000). In contrast, the group experience of finding other women in the same boat and experiencing very similar stresses under unjust social systems can be healing to the participants. They can cry and laugh together, sing and share their joy as a group. They feel that others easily understand them.

In conducting the workshops, we are aware that our therapeutic interventions have to take into account the culture and social context of the couples in divorce. We help the participants to attain a sense of balance and harmony in the midst of the chaos of the long divorce process. We also tend to be more task-focused, solution-oriented and pragmatic instead of concentrating on their negative emotions, recognizing that emotional expressions of the Chinese are often subdued due to their socialization.

Most importantly, we try to acknowledge the conflicts between traditional and modern expectations on marital and divorce relationships, and help the women make more realistic decisions. For example, despite some lawyers' efforts to ensure that individuals' rights are protected in the negotiation process during divorce, some women still feel uneasy or guilty asking for some form of compensation and protection. Some even make "no claim" for maintenance, or just ask for a token of one dollar for alimony, in order to denounce the relationship and their dependency. Such acts often ignore their own needs and those of their children. Helping these women learn to take care of their own needs and those of their children is emphasized in the workshop. However, transforming attitudes inherited from a clan-based collective system in traditional China which existed for thousands of years to an individual-based legal conception of justice and fair play is neither easy nor straightforward (Ma 2000).

A non-confrontational and problem-solving approach, which stresses agreement and appreciation of differences, is found to be very effective. Normalizing divorce and promoting the maintenance of a cordial relationship with the ex-spouse is also helpful. We help the divorcées to realize that being divorced is not the end of the world, nor is it the end of the relationship with the ex-spouse. Although the couple can no longer live as husband and wife, they can still be in an amicable relationship. In any case, they have to perform the role of responsible co-parents. A significant number of couples do perform the co-parents' role effectively after divorce. Good divorces can happen if couples work together for their interests and their children's best interest. Parents can be helped to affirm their lifelong commitment as parents to their children (Chan & Wong 2000).

Through the therapeutic process of the group, the participants are helped to express their own thoughts and feelings and to appreciate others' view points. This process helps them to appreciate their own needs, explore various meanings of their experiences, find new perspectives and new possibilities, and begin to reconstruct their sense of self. The notions of forgiving and letting go are really important to these women. They can unlock their hatred, free themselves from obsessive thoughts of victimization and revenge, and start anew. Thus, through the empowerment group, we help the divorced women to transform a previously hostile and destructive relationship with their ex-spouses into cordial partnerships, each working towards the benefit of all parties concerned, including their own benefit, that of their ex-spouses, and, most importantly, that of their children.

Intervention Outcome Assessments

For an evaluation of the programme, the participants filled out a questionnaire before and after the workshop. Research data and the participants' personal reports showed that, following participation in the workshops, these women experienced fewer stress symptoms, a better sense of well-being, greater confidence, a stronger sense of self, a clearer sense of meaning in life, and higher energy (Chan, Chan, & Lou 2001). The effects of a workshop, whether conducted over five weeks or a two-day weekend, were similar. A systematic outcome assessment by Chan found that there was significant reduction of stress, an increase of energy, and growth in positive empowerment. Table 3 provides a summary of the findings of a study of sixty-seven divorced women before and after the group intervention. Follow-up assessments, six months and one year later, found that participants' growth and changes were maintained (Chan 1999).

On a scale of one to ten (one being very low, ten being very high) the outcome measures of perceived stress, self-reported level of energy and competence showed statistically significant alterations in a desirable direction. Perceived stress went down. Physical and psychological energy as well as life satisfaction were raised. The women's sense of competence also increased significantly.

Table 3. Empowerment Intervention: Outcome Findings of Stress, Energy and Competence Among Women of Divorce

Intervention Outcome	Mean before Intervention	Mean after Intervention	F Value
Stress			
Relationship with ex-spouse	6.60	5.32	13.46**
Practical problems	5.42	5.05	4.33*
Child-rearing stress	6.48	5.45	15.92**
Financial difficulties	6.16	5.43	14.07**
Role and emotional disturbances	6.25	5.52	8.63**
Interpersonal relations	5.86	4.86	10.46**
Energy			
Physical energy	5.04	6.49	25.83**
Psychological energy	5.40	6.87	21.16**
Life satisfaction	5.74	7.06	34.62**
Competence			
Emotional management	5.51	6.77	26.46**
Positive self-identity	6.53	7.86	24.30**
Sense of mastery	5.70	7.32	38.25**
Parental competence	7.02	8.16	17.62**
Social support	6.95	8.11	21.31**

Mean score in scale ranges from 1 to 10.
Significance levels: * $p < .05$, ** $p < .01$

Summary

Throughout our workshops, we find that it is important to help the divorced women to realize the importance of rediscovering their *self*. Helping them re-establish a sense of self is of utmost importance, because it is only through reconstructing the meaning of what they have been through that these women find new strengths. The creation of new hopes and dreams also provides energy for the women to move on with their lives. We find that the divorced women who come to our workshop could move from a submissive, passive, avoidance coping style towards a much more active and effective one. They become more confident and capable in problem-solving. It is important for social workers or counsellors to focus on the strengths and resilience of the clients instead of on their psychopathology and weaknesses in the group process.

The promotion of mutual help among the women is also crucial, especially as the majority of them will not remarry. We note that some of these women have gained a new sense of peace of mind through the influence of the empowerment workshop, and some even became advocates for women's rights. The effectiveness of this intervention approach in helping divorced women in various Chinese societies to regain their sense of self and take charge of their own future was evident. However, we are also aware that further research and more refinement of the model are needed. Like traditional Chinese medicine that combines a number of herbs in the preparation, we need to search out more specifically the elements and processes that work for these women as they move towards healing and health.

References

Ayoub C., Deutch R. and Maraganore A. (1999). Emotional distress in children of high-conflict divorce: The impact of marital conflict and violence. *Family and Conciliation Courts Review, 37*(3), 297–315.

Bacon B. and McKenzie B. (2001). *Best practices in parent information and education programs after separation and divorce.* Ottawa, ON: Family Mediation Canada.

Chan C.L.W. (2001). *An Eastern body-mind-spirit approach: A training manual with one-second techniques.* Resource Paper Series: No. 43, Hong Kong: Department of Social Work and Social Administration, University of Hong Kong.

Chan C.L.W. and Chan E.K.L. (2001). Enhancing resilience and family health in the Asian context. *Special Issue of Asian Families in Crisis: Resilience, Choices and Self-Determination, Asia Pacific Journal of Social Work, 11*, 5–17.

Chan C.L.W., Chan Y. and Lou V.W.Q. (2001). Evaluating an empowerment group for divorced Chinese women in Hong Kong. *Research on Social Work Practice, 12*(4), 558–69.

Chan C.L.W., Fan F.W. and Gong R.Y. (Eds.) (2003). *The body-mind-spirit integrative health approach: Group counseling theory and application.* Beijing: Ethic Publishing House. (In Chinese).

Chan C.L.W. and Wong C.K. (2000). *A fulfilling single parenthood.* Hong Kong: Zero to One Publishing Ltd. (In Chinese).

Chan Y. (1999). *Empowerment intervention with divorced single mothers.* M.Phil. Dissertation, Department of Social Work and Social Administration, University of Hong Kong.

Cheung G. and Chan C.L.W. (2002). The Satir Model and cultural sensitivity: A Hong Kong reflection. *Contemporary Family Therapy: An International Journal, 24*(1), 199–215.

Hung S.L. (2000). The economic impact of divorce — poverty of divorced women and their children. In *Proceedings of 2nd Asia Regional Conference on Social Security: Social Security amidst Economic Uncertainties in Asia, Challenges and Responses.* Hong Kong: Hong Kong Council of Social Services and Social Welfare Department.

Hung S.L. (2002). *Meaning of divorce, a feminist analysis of the narrative accounts of*

Chinese divorced women in Hong Kong. Ph.D. Dissertation. Hong Kong: The University of Hong Kong.

Hung S.L., Kung W.W. and Chan C.L.W. (2003). Women coping with divorce in the unique sociocultural context of Hong Kong. *Journal of Family Social Work,* 7(3), 1–22.

Irving H. (Ed.) (2002). *Family mediation: theory and practice with Chinese families.* Hong Kong: Hong Kong University Press

Jekielek S.M. (l998). Parental conflict, marital disruption and children's emotional well-being. *Social Forces,* 76(3), 905–35.

Kung W.W., Hung S.L. and Chan C.L. (2003). How the socio-cultural context shapes women's divorce experience in Hong Kong. *Journal of Comparative Family Studies,* 7(3), 33–50.

Lam D., Chan C.L.W., Wang S.J. and Liu M. (Eds.) (2001). *Women's issues and social change: Reflections from the Beijing women's hotline research.* Beijing: China Social Science Press. (In Chinese).

Law C.K., Chan C.L.W., Young K., Ko G., Wong Y.C., Mehram T., Chang K.C. and Li L. (1995). *Contemporary Hong Kong families in transition.* Hong Kong: Hong Kong Women's Foundation and Department of Social Work and Social Administration, University of Hong Kong, Monograph Series, No. 21.

Liu M. and Chan C. (in press). *Working manual for empowerment group for single mothers.* Beijing: Chinese Academy of Social Sciences Press. (In Chinese)

Lo W.F., Chan Y., Chan C.L.W., Hung S.L., Wong F.L. and Tsang K.H. (Eds.) (1998). *Empowerment training manual for divorced women.* Resource Paper Series No. 33, the Department of Social Work and Social Administration, the University of Hong Kong.

Ma Y.N. (2000). The science of marriage and family law in China in the twentieth century. *Social Sciences in China,* 3, 72–88. (In Chinese).

Phillips M.R., Li X.Y. and Zhang Y. (2002). Suicide rates in China, 1995–99. *Lancet,* 359, 835–40.

Yang K.A. (1995). *Taoism and health.* Heilongjiang: Heilongjiang Xinhua Books. (In Chinese).

Yi S.G., Chan C.L.W. and Lam C.W. (2002a) "Independence" and divorce: A quantitative and qualitative analysis. *Jiangsu Social Sciences,* May, 77–85. (In Chinese).

Yi S.G., Chan C.L.W. and Lam C.W. (2002b). *Study on the support network for divorced women in China: A qualitative and quantitative analysis.* Paper presented at the First International Symposium on "Chinese Women and their Network Capital", June 20–21, 2002, The University of Hong Kong.

Yeung K.C. (1998). *The dynamics of interparental conflict and adolescents' behavior problems.* Ph.D. Thesis, Department of Social Work and Social Administration, The University of Hong Kong.

Yeung K.C. (1996). Focus group study on adolescents' responses to interparental conflicts, *Asian Journal of Counselling,* 4(1): 43–53.

Young K., Chau B., Li C.K., Tai L., Yim P.L. and Wong Y.C. (1995). *Study on marriages affected by extramarital affairs.* Hong Kong: Caritas Family Service and the University of Hong Kong.

8

Ambivalent Exit and Ambiguous Entry: Ten Hong Kong Men's Perception of Spousal Relationships in and Out of Marriage

ROGER WAI-HONG KWAN

In this study, divorced men were found to have exited from marriage reluctantly, despite the difficulties in their spousal relationships. They went along with the wife's divorce decision, having previously adopted means like working long hours, brooding, and engaging in extramarital relationships to deal with their unhappiness. An ambivalent exit from one marriage may or may not lead to clear entry into another marriage for the divorced men, even though in Hong Kong they have an advantage over their counterparts, the divorced women, in the marriage market. Their consequential ambiguity about entry — marrying again — probably reflects their commitment to any children from the former marriage, and financial considerations rather than personal inclination. Whether they have custody of the children is another motivation for quick entry. However, their adjustment and recovery from the failed marriage also directly affects their remarriage prospects.

Introduction

As the divorce rate has been rising in recent years, there is increased attention to the vulnerability of marriage and family institutions in Hong Kong. However, we do not as yet have an adequate understanding of the parties involved, in particular, the perspective of the divorced men. A knowledge gap remains, although fatherhood studies from overseas offer some indications of certain aspects of their situation (Dowd 2000; Marsiglio, Amato, Day, & Lamb 2000; Amato 1999; Lamb 1997; Dongen, Finking, & Jacobs 1995). In Hong Kong, there has been some murmuring against continuing child support from non-custodial divorced fathers, though in general the male voices in divorce have been barely heard. The men, sometimes considered "deadbeat dads", are unwilling to be studied (Bourmil & Friedman 1996: 11). Their evasiveness, which constitutes a methodological hurdle for a researcher on divorce, has itself been a subject of study (Garfinkel, McLanahan Meyer, & Seltzer 1998). As early studies were based mainly on clinical populations, fatherhood literature tended to embrace a deficit perspective (Blankenhorn 1995). However, later research with more positive clinical paradigms developed normative-adaptive perspectives (Visher & Visher 1991) and generative fathering possibilities (Hawkins & Dollahite 1997).

The purpose of this study is to understand how the divorced men assess the spousal relationship before and after separation. It may affect the way they perceive remarriage, which in turn has a possible bearing on the care of the children from the first marriage.

The key questions for this study are:

- How did the divorced men perceive the spousal relationship in the context of marriage and divorce?
- How did they see remarriage and forming a stepfamily as a consequence of the previous experience?

Why is a study of divorced men's perception of the former spousal relationship important? First, such perception might have a bearing on men's co-parenting behaviour, namely, their compliance with the divorce settlement. The post-separation behaviour of the non-custodial divorced men has been subject to scrutiny in the last decade, as it raises issues of public policy (Carling, Duncan, & Edwards 2002; Ganong & Coleman 1999; Greif 1997; Marsiglio 1995). It affects not only the child's welfare (King & Heard 1999; Popenoe 1996) but has wider implications on government finance to the custodial mothers (Boumil & Friedman 1996) and on service provision (Hetherington 2002). Secondly, it is important in providing some indicators of the effects on remarriage and development of stepfamilies. Such perception of a former marital union was found to be a significant factor affecting remarriage consideration (Chiu & Kwan 1997; Booth & Edwards 1992). Besides the decision for remarriage, such perception would likely shape the men's relationships within stepfamilies (Coleman, Ganong, & Fine 2000; Buehler & Ryan 1994; Ihinger-Tallman & Pasley 1987; Spanier & Glick 1980).

A Study of Divorced Men's Perceptions In and Out of Marriage

The data for discussion in this chapter are drawn from a study on divorced men who have at least one child. They may be non-custodial, non-resident, or custodial, thus resident, fathers. The presence of the children highlights the role of the ex-wife as a co-parent. Exit refers to divorce or leaving the marriage for the men — how they experience the separation. Entry is the simile for marriage after divorce — starting a new marital relationship with a woman other than the former wife. Therefore, re-entry describes remarrying the former wife, which is beyond the scope of this paper.

A qualitative approach is used, based on the rationale that data regarding divorced men are not widely and readily available. Also, their voices are not heard either because they are reluctant to express their viewpoints or they might find it unhelpful to say anything. The sensitive nature of such data renders it more appropriate to use snowball sampling. The sample is not restricted to clinical cases or welfare clients. Some of the divorced men were identified through staff from two types of welfare organizations. They were clients of divorce mediation services or family life education services, and their friends and acquaintances. In the last two years, I interviewed ten divorced men, three of them having remarried by the time we met. They each had one to two children from three to eighteen years of age. Former wives of the divorced men and the wives of the remarried men were also interviewed (Ragin & Becker 1992). A semi-structured interview guide was drafted, and data were collected through meeting with these divorced men (Gubrium & Holstein 2002). The interviews, on average, lasted for seventy minutes. All interviews were audiotaped and transcribed. The data were then coded and categorized (Emerson, Fretz, & Shaw 1995). Patterns and themes were identified (Silverman 2000; Miller & Fredericks 1996; Feldman 1995).

A non-random, maximum variation sampling approach was used (Patton 1990). This provided a wider range of divorced men for examination. The inclusion of these men was nonetheless subject to their availability and readiness for interview. Some dimensions of interest were their divorced and remarried status, age and educational attainment, socio-economic status, and having at least a child under their care. The sampling might alternatively be considered criterion sampling (Patton 1990), as these divorced men met such criteria. Given the small size of the sample, the divorced men in this study are by no means representative of the population.

The focus of this study was on the divorced men's experiences of separation that might influence their perceptions about spousal relationships. The construct of interdependence was adopted as the conceptual framework, which is based on systems theory. The family is seen as a system with its subsystems interlocking to maintain equilibrium. When dysfunction sets in so that some subsystems are separated, the changed system has to find ways to regain balance. However, feedback continues to be exchanged between the separated parts. Seen in this light, the divorced men and women, though separated, are interdependent as co-parents in a family. The use of the interdependence concept to examine the post-separation spousal relationship is rather unusual but seems appropriate from the men's description of their experience.

Table 1. Demographic Characteristics of the Divorced Men in this Study

Case Name	1. Al	2. Ben	3. Chad	4. Dan	5. Ed
Age	40	41	37	28	39
Education	Junior secondary	Secondary graduate	University graduate	Post-secondary	Post-secondary
Employment	Semi-skilled	Jr. Management	Professional	Technical	Managerial
Monthly Income (HK$)	10,000	17,000	40,000	15,000	35,000
Child support	Not applicable	Not applicable	8000	7000	Not applicable
Children & age	Son/6	Daughter/9	Daughter/13	Son/3	Daughters 11/9
Visitation	Father custody	Father custody	Irregular	Irregular	Father custody
Status	Remarried	Remarried	Remarried	Single with girl friend	Single with girl friend

Case Name	6. Frank	7. Glen	8. Hon	9. Ian	10. Jay
Age	42	52	46	38	43
Education	Post-graduate	Primary	College graduate	Secondary graduate	Junior secondary
Employment	Professional	Unskilled	Professional	Semi-skilled	Business/ self-employed
Monthly Income (HK$)	70,000	3000	20000	13000	Varied
Child support	15,000	Minimal	4600	NA	NA
Children & age	Son/5	Daughters 18/16	Daughter/14	Daughter/5	Two teenage children
Visitation	Every day	Every day	Every day	Father custody	Mother custody
Status	Single with girlfriend	Single	Single	Single	Cohabiting

Table 2. Brief Profiles of the Ten Divorced Men in the Study

Spousal Relationship in Marriage	Marital Break-up	Spousal Relationship out of Marriage	Perceptions of Remarriage and a Second Family
Al, 40 Spouse aged 21 was colleague, acquainted for one year and cohabited for three. Wife came from a big family (not given attention) and was attached to him. She moved in with him because he lived with his mother only. (A marriage of convenience.)	Young wife ran away. After having a child, she became depressed and moody. Things did not work out, even though the couple moved away from the mother-in-law. Left son (6) in his care.	Urgent need to have a mother for the child. "I wanted to have a companion. I was used to married life ..."	Remarried — "a mother for the child". "Having a companion by my side, life would be richer". Explained mutuality in marital expectations. "She chose me because she felt I had such a need, not having a wife and the child not having a mother. She was single and had no relatives. Her parents died a long time ago, so she had no one. She also wanted to have a companion. We were middle-aged, so it was about time (to form a family)". Satisfied with personality of second wife. Concern: "She did not have a baby, so somehow she lacked affection", too demanding of child.
Ben, 41 First marriage at 24, then ex-wife's family emmigrated overseas. Second marriage at 32, with Mainland woman aged 24, who had a daughter. He agreed to marry her "as her parents were not greedy."	Couple had little planning for their future but lots of friction. The marriage lasted two years, meeting the legal requirement. Second marriage lasted two years, found no appeal in wife, and did not see her her regularly. Physical separation did not help to reduce conflict.	Contemplating remarriage for companionship when old. Marriage at a distance did not "benefit him", and he felt he rushed into it. Found consolation in colleague who became his confidante.	Third marriage to former colleague acquainted with for over a decade. Had a lot to share with third wife, who was also divorced and had a daughter. The third wife was the person involved in extramarital affair in his second marriage.

Table 2. Brief Profiles of the Ten Divorced Men in the Study (*Continued*)

Spousal Relationship in Marriage	Marital Break-up	Spousal Relationship out of Marriage	Perceptions of Remarriage and a Second Family
Chad, 37 Marriage was conflict-ridden and stressful to both. Some acts of violence. Stormy home environment drove him out.	Break-up due to personality differences. Perceived ex-wife as busy and unromantic. Sought consolation in affair with colleague. Ammunition for final blow to already wrecked marriage. Wife initiated divorce.	Daughter 13, pivotal in post-separation spousal relationship. Paid child support, dissatisfied at having to pay to ex-wife. Visited as much as possible. Harboured guilt about leaving daughter with incomplete family. Family of origin helped develop sense of commitment. Wanted to but could not form intimate relationship with daughter.	Remarried his affair partner. No plans for children. Claims daughter is his priority.
Dan, 28 There were unending conflicts over minor issues, such as money, time availability at home. Worked long hours in evening and over weekends.	Wife petitioned for divorce over his suspected extramarital affair. Divorce proceedings lengthy, as couple fought over properties he inherited. Had to give in to avoid publicity. Bitter about separation. Wants nothing to do with ex-wife.	Son 3, link for divorced couple. Mother had custody. Father looked after son in case of need. Took one month off work when ex-wife went away, to care for son in paternal grandparent's home. Not sure if his compliance brought about ex-wife's cooperation.	Has steady girlfriend. Does not want to establish another family yet. Finance a consideration. Would like to look after his son.

Table 2. Brief Profiles of the Ten Divorced Men in the Study (Continued)

Spousal Relationship in Marriage	Marital Break-up	Spousal Relationship out of Marriage	Perceptions of Remarriage and a Second Family
Ed, 39 The couple grew apart. Wife was a homemaker while he was advancing in career, doing part-time graduate studies. Wife suffering and recovering from mental illness.	Divorce long anticipated, as he was psychologically ready, pending wife's mental state in order to enforce legal separation. Having an extramarital relationship.	Concerned about the daughters. Ex-wife moved out of family home for their benefit, and grandparents supervised domestic helper. He was busy at work.	No plans for remarriage. Saw no need for the time being. Stable relationship with girlfriend.
Frank, 42 Considered "Marriage what everybody did, just like having children". Vague idea of what he had to offer in marriage. "When others got married, I got married, Wanted to have child while she was willing". Marriage punctuated by conflicts, though no physical violence.	Break-up due to two incompatible individuals. Viewpoints about life and life goals so different. Wished affinity would be determined by destiny. Wife initiated divorce and he agreed.	Separation painful. Living on own demanding. Minimal contact with ex-wife. Affection for son (5); visits every evening and weekends. Enjoys freedom, fewer obligations. Since divorce, improved in productivity, happiness, concentration, and use of time. Daily living is not convenient.	Now has lady friend. Remarriage: "will only marry someone I feel good with". Cautious about commitment. Priority is welfare of the child.
Glen, 52 No affection towards wife, due to personality differences. Wanted to maintain marriage for the sake of the children. Sees no need for divorce.	Wife initiated divorce on grounds of his alleged extramarital affair. He claimed to have close friends including female but no such affairs. The misunderstanding could not be resolved.	Unemployed for last few years. Held temporary jobs on and off. Took over domestic role. Care for daughters' (18 and 16) daily living, meal preparation, laundry, house cleaning. Keeps household going. Ex-wife works full-time and studies part-time.	Does not intend to marry again, limited employability, age and health are prohibitive factors. Close relationship with daughters.

Table 2. Brief Profiles of the Ten Divorced Men in the Study (Continued)

Spousal Relationship in Marriage	Marital Break-up	Spousal Relationship out of Marriage	Perceptions of Remarriage and a Second Family
Hon, 46 Did not want separation and not aware of any problems with marriage. Did not agree with wife's claim of incompatible personality.	An extended negotiation prior to taking divorce procedure. Despite legal and physical separation not technically leaving home; still returns home for laundry and evening meal.	Finding it extremely hard being on his own; loneliness, "having no one to talk to", feeling deprived of domestic comfort, missing seeing his daughter.	Has no plan for remarriage due to age (having limited choice), financial constraints, and attachment to child.
Ian, 38 Felt committed to marriage, having purchased and decorated the matrimonial property. Devoted to wife and daughter. Felt slightly inferior to wife in career development.	Attributed tension to wife wanting a "break and good time" as she had extramarital relations with a colleague younger than she was. All three of them were in the same field and the affair was well known.	Maintaining wishful thinking that the wife would change her mind and return to him. Taking different measures to attempt to rectify the wrecked marriage. Feeling torn and pained, not wanting to let go.	Making all concessions in order to lure the ex-wife back. No plans for remarriage due to vague hope that ex-wife could get tired of the game with boyfriend soon. Physical and emotional exhaustion plus role strains.
Jay, 43 First marriage at age 24 due to pre-marital sex and girlfriend's suspected pregnancy. Felt physically attracted to ex-wife.	Did not want divorce but wanted to keep the family with two children and the extramarital person at the same time. The ex-wife initiated divorce, and he accepted it reluctantly.	Having given up former family, he moved in with extramarital person who was helpful with his business. He felt he found true love in the woman.	He did not formally marry the girlfriend though they were socially known to be a couple living together. He cohabited with her and the stepdaughter, looking after her when co-habitant was away from Hong Kong.

Applying the paired images of *exit* (as affected by their experience within the spousal relationship and their experience of the divorce process), and *entry* (as affected by the experience outside the spousal relationship and the perceptions regarding remarriage), a variety of patterns emerge.

Table 3.   Exit and Entry

	Exit from first marriage	*Entry* to remarriage
Case One, Al Marriage of convenience	Helpless exit, young ex-wife ran away; left with custody of child.	Actively seeking entry for child and himself for practical considerations. Remarried.
Case Two, Ben Marriage of convenience	Confused about repeated exits; two brief but difficult marriages.	Lengthy assurance before commitment. Third marriage to ex-colleague, who was extramarital partner in second marriage.
Case Three, Chad Conflictual marriage	Equivocal exit, despite conflictual stressful marriage. Extramarital involvement.	Quick entry. Committed to child. No plans for another child. Claimed financial constraints. Remarried.
Case Four, Dan Conflictual marriage	Entangled exit, fight over properties, extramarital liaison.	Cautious over entry. Taking a wait-and-see option about another marriage. Has girlfriend.
Case Five, Ed Distancing marriage, drifting apart	Planned exit. Wife left home. Grandparents supervise domestic arrangements for two children.	Not necessary to have entry. Fairly pleased with status quo.
Case Six, Frank Distancing marriage due to incompatibility	Reticent exit, painful aftermath, then relief and freedom.	Guarded prospects for entry; will not make mistake again. Child as priority.
Case Seven, Glen Distancing marriage; fading affection	Procrastinated and reluctant exit. Complicated procedures involving public housing.	Not considering entry due to age, poor job prospects, and commitment to children.
Case Eight, Hon Continuing attachment to ex-wife	Wanting to delay exit; unprepared and reluctant to let go.	Sees no possibility of entry, as emotionally not having exited.
Case Nine, Ian Continuing attachment to ex-wife	Torn and reluctant exit; retaining wishful thinking of reunion	No idea of entry. Wants to revive first marriage.
Case Ten, Jay Wanted co-existence of marital & extramrital relationships	Passive and disconcerted over exit; Initially had unrealistic expectations.	No formal entry. Cohabitation. Wants to revive first marriage. Later, enjoyed alternative family life.

Ambivalent Exit

The divorced men showed the dilemma they were in about continuing or leaving marriage. They were probably *ill prepared for marriage*. They could hardly articulate what marriage would involve. One respondent claimed marriage was supposedly for everyone, and having a family and children was something everyone would have. Two of the remarried men (Ben and Jay) rushed into the first marriage when fairly young, probably due to the physical attraction of the women. Of these ten marriages, those of Al, Ben, Chad, and Dan were no longer viable; two were marriages of convenience, in which one wife had run away, and the other remained in the Mainland; and two were highly conflictual, so that life at home was described as hostile and stressful. For Ed, Frank and Glen, their marriages reflected gradual distancing, drifting apart, incompatibility, and fading affection. Nevertheless, they had reservations over relinquishing the relationship. The last three men, Hon, Ian and Jay, expressed various degrees of attachment to their former spouses, and two were highly ambivalent about what they perceived as an enforced exit from their marriages.

The divorced men further found that staying married and leaving marriage were equally demanding. The frequent conflicts and tension within marriage culminated in divorce. They divorced for different reasons, generally explained as personality clash. The incompatibility in thinking and lifestyle of the couple brought about different ways to cope. These men did not know quite how to manage tensions in the marriage. Either they took an escape route by becoming involved in a relationship with another woman, or they waited until the ex-wife made the decision about discontinuing the relationship. A couple of the men found new confidantes or girlfriends while married. This male way of coping triggered the divorce process.

Separation was highly stressful for the men. Being left on their own, having to manage the daily tasks of living, having to move away from the habitual accommodation, being devoid of the comfort afforded by family life was experienced as very difficult for them. The separation from the children appeared to have had an obvious effect on some of these men. The adjustment was demanding and at times painful (Stone 2001). These difficulties put them off other commitments, except those established during the marriage. The post-separation adjustment shaped their views about remarriage (Kruk 1994).

The divorced men in this study regarded the former spousal relationship with ambivalence. The end of marriage did not terminate the spousal relationship, *because of the child*. Various forms of co-parenting emerged; one father assumed high levels of daily care (Glen); others made frequent, daily visits (Frank and Hon). One offered occasional care when needed (Dan) or made contact whenever possible (Chad), and four divorced men (Al, Ben, Ed and Ian) were left with the custody of the child. Two of them remained single. The non-custodial fathers (Chad, Dan, Frank, Glen and Hon) chose to rely on the former wives or others for childcare. They were clearly convinced that the children would be better off if they were looked after by the birth mother or mother figures, so that during the divorce proceedings they did not challenge custody being awarded to the mothers. Contrary to some popular beliefs, some divorced men did not evade their responsibilities to their children. Indeed, they felt they had not done enough for the children. They expressed guilt towards the children for failing to maintain a normal dual-parent family. In Ian's thinking, the daughter provided hope for the ex-wife to come back. Seen in such light, the dependent children helped to draw the estranged parents together. These divorced men did communicate with the former wives about the children, having entrusted the welfare of the children to them. Reluctantly, they kept contact with the former wife, even though some of these contacts might be minimal.

The boundary between the men and their former wives was drawn fairly clearly, at least in one aspect. Because the ex-wives were gainfully employed, these men resented having to pay child support to them, though it was virtually impossible not to pay. Moreover, the perceived fairness of the divorce settlement positively affected the divorced men's perceptions about their spousal relationships (Lin 2000). The *financial contribution* the divorced men made to the former wife was also relevant in shaping their perceptions of remarriage.

Ambiguous Entry

The divorced men's perception of remarriage was coloured by their experience in and out of the spousal relationship as well as the divorce and separation process.

All of the men said that their priority for the future was to try to *secure the welfare of the child*. This for some may reflect the affectional bond between father and child (Snarey 1993); it also reflects the cultural expectation of men's filial duty to ensure family continuity and is thus a socially approved sentiment. The children therefore played a central role in the divorced men's post-separation heterosexual relationships.

Understandably, the presence of a child maintained co-parental ties: although the men might not enjoy having any contact with the ex-wife, they were aware that they had to cooperate as co-parents for the sake of the children. The concept of interdependence and reciprocity is applicable here, in that the divorced fathers and mothers managed to redefine their boundary and keep the family going. Furthermore, the children presented some responsibilities for the divorced men in finance and time. The burden of keeping two separate households meant that the divorced men had to consider remarriage carefully. Reservations about remarriage arose partly because they had to look after the children financially (Sweeney 1997). The remarriage plan or the childbearing plan if they were remarried could be deferred partially due to economic considerations. They are cautious over the expenses required in having children with the second wife.

The men's *need for companionship* is indicated in the post-separation involvement. Three of the ten divorced men did not have a girlfriend at the time of the study. They were attached to either the ex-wife (Ian) or the children (Glen and Hon). Three divorced men had remarried, and the others had a relationship with a regular partner. For them, there were advantages and disadvantages to marrying again. Some of the divorced men felt the sense of stigma attached to divorce (for instance, Ben). At the same time, they yearned for a companion to establish a normal lifestyle for themselves as well as for their children (as in Al's case). Jay was actually looking after his cohabiter's daughter. There was no mention of his own two teenage children. They were with their mother in Hong Kong, and Jay never contacted them. He might have looked after the cohabiter's daughter as his own, for compensation. Entry into another marital relationship means exit from the single state, or single fatherhood. They were still learning that whether or not marriage was satisfying would depend on the efforts on both sides. However, a few divorced men did find a congenial partner who seemed to be compatible and supportive. To them, entry was natural and spontaneous. The divorced man (Al) having child custody clearly demonstrated the practical functionality of having a mother for the child. It might be indicative of the inadequacy of the divorced man in childcare.

The men were generally reticent about *personal and emotional need fulfilment* for themselves through remarriage, and about what their concerns over this might be. One informant (Jay) observed that he enjoyed the "quiet and peaceful family life, looking after his partner's daughter mostly on his own". He gave up his two children from the former marriage and did not see them after divorce. He devoted his time and effort to the adolescent stepdaughter and developed a harmonious relationship with her, much to the partner's satisfaction. He and the partner never went through legal marriage. Another informant (Ben) found in his third wife someone with whom he could share his worries and pleasure. After all, they had been acquainted for over a decade before getting married.

Such views of the divorced men who have remarried confirmed what Ganong and Coleman (1994) postulated about reasons to remarry. They included, for the men, help in raising children, response to social pressure, relief from loneliness, the need for a regular sexual partner, the need to take care of someone and be taken care of, re-establishing domesticity, and a regular home life.

The men desired to have family life, but they learned to be cautious before making another commitment. Men tend to have more economic resources than women do, and they are in a better position than women in the marriage market. They can more easily find a partner. Whether they are willing to commit to another relationship is a complex question.

Marriage, Divorce, and Remarriage

This chapter examines the experiences and perceptions of some divorced men about their remarriage considerations. The way they reflect upon whether to revisit marriage depends on how they have managed the divorce and its aftermath (Madden-Derdich & Leonard 2000; Madden-Derdich, Leonard, & Christopher 1999; Goetting 1982). The relevant issues to consider are the implications of the first marriage and the divorce experience on their view of and decision about remarriage.

Before any discussion of remarriage, it would be useful to apply the concept of the marriage market. This refers to the availability of potential partners for the marriage-seekers. In the marriage market, male marriage-seekers tend to have an advantage over female ones (Gurak & Dean 1979). Given similar educational and income levels, men and women in the same age bracket do not have the same options in mate selection. Men have far more choices than women, because men can find a partner who is much younger than they are. In the process of looking for a prospective marriage partner, men and women fare differently. Given the relative advantage for the men in the marriage market, divorced men can supposedly find a mate easily. This factor may affect their perception of past and future marriage.

The Divorce Experience

In this study, the handful of divorced men seemed to be reluctant to formally separate from the family. They had conflicts with the wives, but they stonewalled the demands of the wives. Gottman (1998) described this as the negative affect reciprocity model: if one partner is affectively negative, the spouse is subsequently much more likely to be negative than he or she usually would be. This could be further complicated by two other processes. One is reciprocation in kind, anger being met with anger. The other is escalation, whereby anger is met with stronger negative feelings like belligerence or contempt. Home life thus became conflict ridden and stressful. They then responded to the wives by withdrawing, or seeking consolation elsewhere. Eventually, it was the wives who took the initiative to petition for divorce (Sweeney 2002).

On the whole, the men found the separation painful. They paid a price financially and emotionally. As a couple of divorced men said, living on their own was extremely inconvenient, besides being economically burdensome. Leaving the child was traumatic for the divorced men. Emotionally, they might be close to the children. Nonetheless, for most of these divorced men, leaving the children with the ex-wives appeared to be the best option (Sunjoo 1986). They could barely cope with the childcare responsibilities on their own. They all considered it important to work full-time, and the children were best placed with the mother if possible. Practically, they felt they could not cope with having full-time employment and child care responsibilities at the same time. Besides the practical consideration, this may reflect the Chinese men's culturally conditioned gender perspective that child care is women's work, further reinforced by the belief that children are better off cared for by the mother.

The Chinese families in Hong Kong subscribe to a fairly clear sex-role differentiation between men and women. In the patriarchal tradition, men enjoyed tremendous power in the family, having unquestioned right as head of the family. Chinese families were also known for their hierarchical ordering of family members (Goodwin & Tang 1996). Childcare indeed has never been the forte of men in the family, in either the Chinese or Western context. Although modern fathers are observed to be somewhat more involved in child care, critics remain doubtful "whether men have really changed" (Haywood & Mac an Ghaill 2003).

In some cases, the divorced men took an escape route from the marriage through extramarital involvement. They did not attempt to address the issues raised in the marital conflicts. They claimed that the marriage had failed on the grounds of incompatibility. They then found solace in another woman's arms. Emotionally, some of the men may have already divorced their former wives before the legal divorce.

The Post-Separation Spousal Relationship

The children drew the divorced men and their former wives together. Without the children, the former spouses would have little in common. Although local statistics on custody decisions from the judiciary are not available, my impression is that the trend seems to be that the mothers took on custody of the child and the fathers were responsible for child financial support. The divorced men could exercise their right to visitation, making regular visits to the children.

Child support is a highly sensitive issue for all the parties concerned. The single mothers having to look after the children are rendered financially restricted if not poverty stricken. Some of them may resort to public assistance and bear the stigma with dignity. To the divorced men, child-support payment presents an equally frustrating problem. The initial question is whether the amount of child support granted the ex-wives could be seen to be fair. One divorced man complained that his hard-earned monthly income was given over to his ex-wife with the assistance of the court. To him, it was inequitable for the ex-wife to spend his money, supposedly for the children. Such bad feelings on his part reflect the intrinsic nature of the child- support arrangement. It is possible also that, through this complaint, the divorced men were displaying their continuing resentment against their former wives. They resented having to pay child support to the former wives, who decided on the way the money was spent. This meant that the women could exercise discretion in the use of the payment but the men could not.

The men felt they had no sense of control over the use of the money, which should specifically be for the children. They either paid or did not pay. The deciding factor was the welfare of the child, a priority for all the fathers. One respondent felt torn; he did not see why he should financially support his able-bodied ex-wife, but the children would suffer if he stopped payment.

Indeed, child support could be used as a tool to manoeuvre the former spousal relationship. The ex-wives allowed the fathers' flexible schedules for child visitation, and they reciprocated with steady child-support payments.

Future Spousal Relationships in Remarriage

The divorced men in this study are observed to need nurturing from women. They cannot really manage without women as their companion, sexual partner, caretaker in daily living, and child-minder. Their ambivalence in separation and their involvement in extramarital relationships are testimony to this. Remarriage, that is, entry again to marital commitment, is deferred until the men have recovered emotionally from the trauma of divorce. They also have to work out their finances, in particular in regards to their commitment to the children. They made a promise to take care of the children in the divorce settlement, so they try to honour the pledge. The children are important for them; some men have had a close bond with them since they were young. In some ways, the promise reflects the fathers' sense of guilt for leaving them in a divorced family.

Another contributing factor affecting the men's perception of remarriage is the way they assess the child's need for a mother. The sense of urgency for such a woman was obvious. From this perspective, it was more for practical considerations that the divorced men remarried. From the few illustrations of divorced men, a variety of coping methods can be discerned. Two of the remarried men married the partner in the extramarital affair. One divorced man remarried allegedly for a substitute mother for his son. The others claimed they had no remarriage plans. All were guarded in expressing their lack of intention to have another child.

In short, some opaque patterns emerge from the descriptions of the divorced men's perception of spousal relationship. Their reluctant exit could be explained by their fear of the loss of domestic comfort in married life and contact with their children. The post-separation spousal relationship hinges on their attitude towards the children. Besides affective ties with the children, there is an element of guilt and sense of duty to maintain the father-child relationship. Such ties seem to be the only thing left that draws the former spouses together. Remarriage prospects might be good, but whether the divorced men rush in depends on financial considerations and their attachment to the ex-wife and the children. When the divorced men have custody of the child, they would feel the need to remarry to rebuild a home for the children.

Comparing Other Research and Literature

Some of the divorced men in this small Hong Kong study appear to reflect Kruk's findings (1994) on men's adjustment to separation. Kruk surveyed eighty non-custodial divorced men, half of them disengaged from their children. He found the majority of these men went through a grieving process during divorce, which was related to the loss of their children. The loss of children was most salient of the post-separation losses for the men. The coping responses of these divorced men differed. Some worked through the grief but others did not. Some of them developed a relationship with the children even though they were not necessarily attached to them before the divorce. Most fathers who were attached to the children before the marriage broke up had difficulty managing the post-separation grief.

On how the divorced men perceived the former spousal relationship, Arditti and Kelly (1994) surveyed 225 divorced fathers and found seven predictors of the perceived quality of the co-parental relationship. They included a) satisfaction with custody arrangements, b) the number of topics that the former spouses discussed, c) the fathers' educational level, d) the number of children, e) satisfaction with the property settlement, f) pre-divorce close relationships with the children, and g) assumed blame for the marital break-up. Our situation reflects Arditti and Kelly's perspectives. However, these predictors can be reorganized. In Hong Kong, the way the divorced men assessed the former spousal relationship depended on their perceived fairness of the divorce settlement, a conflict-free co-parental relationship, the pre-separation father-child bond, the degree of assumption of responsibility towards the children, and the men's socio-economic status.

Gottman's lines of argument are particularly salient in explaining the divorced men's ambivalence in the midst of separation. He maintains that men generally are inadequately prepared for forming a family when they get married, compared with their wives. Men do not know how to articulate their feelings. The men would do better if they were willing to follow the wives. Gottman (1998) used a multi-method approach in collecting data on marital and family interaction. He noted the dramatic differential socialization of emotion for each sex. While highlighting huge individual differences, he concluded that cross-sex relationships like marriages would work to the extent that men could accept influence from women. To explain his findings, he noted that the wife generally presents the concerns in marital interaction and gets the couple to look at these issues, whereas the husband may deny or may not even be aware of them.

Following on his hypothesis of differential socialization of emotion for males and females, Gottman's suggestion to improve the situation at home sounds reasonable and relevant in the Hong Kong situation. There is an obvious gender difference in the home- and family-building experience between males and females in our culture. The Chinese male is socialized to achieve outside the home, with little emphasis on his role at home besides being the wage earner and disciplinarian. In marriage, he encounters in his wife an expert in the emotional and practical aspects of creating a home, because the Chinese female is traditionally groomed to be the caregiver in the family. Taking up Gottman's proposition, it could be argued that the man who can allow himself to be socialized through his marriage could emerge with a greater sense of fulfillment than merely upholding his assigned position of authority within the Chinese family system. Space does not permit this cultural conditioning to be thoroughly examined here. Nonetheless, the Chinese male's socialization certainly plays an important part in shaping him for marriage and parenthood in our society, which still has a patriarchal base.

Rethinking Men's Perspectives and Needs in Spousal Relationships

These observations have been developed after examining some divorced men's views about the post-separation spousal relationship and the perspectives of remarriage. Appreciating how some of these men perceived the spousal relationship, I get the sense that most of the divorced men rely heavily on women in building a family, in looking after the children, and in maintaining a nurturing home environment. This study reveals the divorced men's reliance on the former wives for child care. They basically surrendered custody, delegating the child care responsibility to the ex-wives, despite their affective bond with the children and the cultural imperative to maintain family continuity. Complementing this, the divorced mothers, even though they were also gainfully employed, accepted the importance of mother care in assuming the care-taking role.

The men took time to regain self-confidence from their failed marriages, in which conflicts with the ex-wives were rife. After separation, they found it demanding to manage daily care on their own. The bond with the child was a double-edged tool, helping to keep former spousal interaction while motivating the divorced men to look for suitable partners. Few men in this study appeared to be well equipped for marriage and family. They could not cope with marriage and family life, given the socialization and possibly some personal tendencies. They have to learn to communicate and to empathize with their partners in order to facilitate any future relationships they may be entering.

The findings have service implications. We may have to gain a better understanding of divorced men and their experience of stress, loss and depression. Their needs may be overlooked, as they tend to present a strong posture, hiding their vulnerability. Social work practitioners may have to find ways to approach these clients. The use of mediation is to be encouraged and publicized as an alternative form of dispute resolution in domestic settings, through which the men could participate and experience some control of the divorce outcome. At this time of fast-paced change, Hong Kong needs to develop more constructive ways of feeling and thinking about the uncoupling process for the separating parties, and of preparations and affirmation of those striving to build second families. An aspect of this is to review and revise some of our practices in gender socialization so that the acculturation process takes into account an appreciation of gender differences. Parents, schools, the media, professional groups, and the public have much to contribute in partnership to moderate societal expectations of gender roles in interpersonal relationships.

References

Amato P.R. (1999). Nonresident fathers and children's well being: A meta-analysis. *Journal of Marriage and the Family, 61*(3), 557–74.

Arditti J.A. and Kelly M. (1994). Fathers' perspectives of their co-parental relationships post divorce: Implications for family practice and legal reform. *Family Relations: 43*(1), 61–73.

Blankenhorn D. (1995). *Fatherless America: Confronting our most urgent social problem.* New York: Basic Books.

Booth A. and Edwards J.N. (1992). Starting over: Why remarriages are more unstable. *Journal of Family Issues, 13*(2), 179–94.

Boumil M.M. and Friedman J. (1996). *Deadbeat dads: A national child support scandal.* Westport, CN: Praeger.

Byrd A.J. and Smith R.M. (1988). A qualitative analysis of the decision to remarry using Gilligan's Ethic of Care. *Journal of Divorce, 11*(3/4), 87–102.

Buehler C. and Ryan C. (1994). Former-spouse relations and non-custodial father involvement during marital and family transitions: A closer look at remarriage following divorce. In K. Pasley and M. Ihinger-Tallman (Eds.) *Stepparenting: Issues in theory research and practice.* Westport, CN: Greenwood.

Carling A.H., Duncan S. and Edwards R. (2002). *Analyzing families: Morality and rationality in policy and practice.* New York: Routledge.

Chiu H.K.T. and Kwan R.W.H. (1997). *Decision on remarriage: Research report on a preliminary study of remarried families and remarriage consideration of single parents in Hong Kong.* Hong Kong: Christian Family Service Center.

Coleman M., Ganong L.H. and Fine M.A. (2000). Reinvestigating remarriage: Another decade of progress. *Journal of Marriage and the Family, 62*(4), 1288–1307.

Cuzzort R.P. and King E.W. (1995). *Twentieth-century social thought.* Fort Worth, TX: Harcourt Brace College Publishers.

DeVault M.L. (1999). *Liberating method: Feminism and social research.* Philadelphia, PA: Temple University Press.

Dongen M.C., Finking G.A. and Jacobs M.J. (Eds.) (1995). *Changing fatherhood: An interdisciplinary perspective.* Amsterdam: Thesis publishers.

Dowd N.E. (2000). *Redefining fatherhood.* New York: New York University Press.

Emerson R.E., Fretz R.I. and Shaw L.L. (1995). *Writing ethnographic field notes.* Chicago, IL: The University of Chicago Press.

Feldman M.S. (1995). *Strategies for interpreting qualitative data.* Thousand Oaks, CA: Sage.

Ganong L.H. and Coleman M. (1994). *Remarried family relationships.* Thousand Oaks, CA: Sage.

Ganong L.H. and Coleman M. (1999). *Changing families, changing responsibilities: Family obligations following divorce and remarriage.* Mahwah, NJ: Lawrence Erlbaum.

Garfinkel I., McLanahan S.S., Meyer D.R. and Seltzer J.A. (Eds.) (1998). *Fathers under fire: The revolution in child support enforcement.* New York: Russell Sage Foundation.

Goetting A. (1982). The six stations of remarriage: Developmental task of remarriage after a divorce. *Family Relations, 31*, 213–22.

Goodwin R. and Tang C.S. (1996). Chinese personal relationships. In M. H. Bond (Ed.) *The handbook of Chinese psychology.* Hong Kong: Oxford University Press.

Gottman J.M. (1998). Toward a process model of men in marriages and families. In A. Booth and A. Crouter (Eds.) *Men in families: when do they get involved? What difference does it make?* Mahwah, NJ: Lawrence Erlbaum.

Greif G.L. (1997). *Out of touch: When parents and children lose contact after divorce.* New York: Oxford University Press.

Gubrium J.F. and Holstein J.A. (2002). *Handbook of interview research: Context & method.* Thousand Oaks, CA: Sage.

Gurak D.T. and Dean G. (1979). The remarriage market: Factors influencing the selection of second husbands. *Journal of Divorce, 3*(2), 161–73.

Hammersley M. (1992). *What's wrong with ethnography? Methodological Explorations.* London: Routledge.

Hawkins J.A. and Dollahite D.C. (Eds.) (1997). *Generative fathering: Beyond deficit perspectives*. Thousand Oaks, CA: Sage.

Haywood C. and Macan Ghaill M. (2003). *Men and masculinities: Theory, research, and social practice*. Buckingham: Open University Press.

Hetherington E.M. (2002). Marriage and divorce American style. *The American Prospect, 13*(7), 62–4.

Ihinger-Tallman M. and Pasley K. (1987). *Remarriage*. Newbury Park, CA: Sage.

King V. and Heard H.E. (1999). Nonresident father visitation, parental conflict, and mother's satisfaction: What's best for child well being? *Journal of Marriage and the Family, 61*(2), 385–97.

Kruk E. (1994). The disengaged non-custodial father: Implications for social work practice with the divorced family. *Social Work, 39*(1), 15–26.

Lamb M.E. (1997). *The role of the father in child development*. New York: Wiley.

Lin I.F. (2000). Perceived fairness and compliance with child support obligations. *Journal of Marriage and the Family, 62*(2), 388–99.

Madden-Derdich D.A., Leonard S.A. and Christopher F. (1999). Boundary ambiguity and co-parental conflict after divorce: An empirical test of a family systems model of the divorce process. *Journal of marriage and the family, 61*(3), 588–98.

Madden-Derdich D.A. and Leonard S.A. (2000). Parental role identity and fathers' involvement in co-parental interaction after divorce: Fathers' perspectives. *Family Relations, 49*(3), 311–9.

Marsiglio W. (Ed.) (1995). *Fatherhood: Contemporary theory, research, and social policy*. Thousand Oaks, CA: Sage.

Marsiglio W., Amato P., Day R.D. and Lamb M.E. (2000). Scholarship on fatherhood in the 1990s and beyond. *Journal of Marriage and the Family, 62*(4), 1173–92.

Miller S.I. and Fredericks M. (1996). *Qualitative research methods: Social epistemology and practical inquiry*. New York: Lang.

Patton M.Q. (1990). *Qualitative evaluation and research methods*. Newbury Park, CA: Sage.

Popenoe D. (1996). *Life without father: Compelling new evidence that fatherhood and marriage are indispensable for the good of children and society*. New York: Free Press.

Ragin C.C. and Becker H.S. (Eds.) (1992). *What is a case?: Exploring the foundations of social inquiry*. Cambridge: Cambridge University Press.

Scull C.S. (Ed.) (1992). *Fathers, sons, and daughters: Exploring fatherhood, renewing the bond*. Los Angeles, CA: J. P. Tarcher.

Silverman D. (2000). *Doing qualitative research: A practical handbook*. London: Sage.

Snarey J.R. (1993). *How fathers care for the next generation: A four-decade study*. Cambridge, MA: Harvard University Press.

Sunjoo O. (1986). Remarried men and remarried women: How are they different? *Journal of Divorce, 9*(4), 107–13.

Spanier G.B. and Glick P.C. (1980). Paths to remarriage. *Journal of Divorce, 3*(3), 283–98.

Stone G. (2001). Father postdivorce well-being: An exploratory model. *The Journal of Genetic Psychology, 162*(4), 460–78.

Sweeney M.M. (1997). Remarriage of women and men after divorce: The role of socioeconomic prospects. *Journal of family issues, 18*(5), 479–502.

Sweeney M.M. (2002). Remarriage and the nature of divorce: Does it matter which spouse chose to leave? *Journal of family issues: 23*(3), 410–40.

Visher E.B. and Visher J.S. (1990). Dynamics of successful stepfamilies. *Journal of Divorce & Remarriage, 14*(1), 3–12.

Walker A.J. (2000). Who is responsible for responsible fathering? *Journal of Marriage and the Family, 62* (2), 563–70.

Wallace R.A. and Wolf A. (1999). *Contemporary sociological theory: Expanding the classical tradition*. Mahwah, NJ: Prentice Hall.

Warshak R.A. (1992). *The custody revolution: The father factor and the motherhood mystique*. New York: Poseidon Press.

Weston C.A. and Macklin E.D. (1990). The relationship between former spousal contact and re-marital satisfaction in stepfather families. *Journal of Divorce and Remarriage, 14*, 25–47.

Willig C. (2001). *Introducing qualitative research in psychology: Adventures in theory and method*. Buckingham: Open University Press.

9

The Making of a Second Spring:
The Experiences of Remarried Persons
in Hong Kong

LIANNE YAU-YEE TAI

This qualitative study explores the experiences of remarried people in Hong Kong. The findings reveal that, although remarriage could be a preference or a way out for divorced persons, the choices and chances for remarriage were limited, the presence of children being the most significant limiting factor. In fact, children occupied an essential position in the self-spouse-child triangle. Patterns of this triangle that emerged include the torn-between-two-loved-ones, the remarriage challenger and the remarriage smoother. However, although old hurts were not obliterated, they were not baggage of the past marriage but had served as a valuable lesson for remarried persons in handling the new relationship. The informants also showed a strong will to make their remarriage last. At the societal level, the general social attitude toward remarriage was perceived as more liberal nowadays. Yet, not all informants felt well accepted by the spouse's extended family or by society. Faced with the stresses and challenges of remarried life, all the informants in this study demonstrated a high degree of ability to cope and grow.

Introduction

Similar to data in many developed countries, statistical data in Hong Kong showed a marked rise in the remarriage rate over the past twenty years, despite a drop in the marriage rate (Census and Statistics Department,

2002). It is postulated that the increase in remarriages is a consequence of the sharp increase in divorce over the same period. Table 1 speaks for itself.

Table 1. Trends in Marriage, Divorce and Remarriage in Hong Kong

	1981	2001	Rise/fall
No. of registered marriages	50,756	32,825	-35.3%
No. of first marriages of one party and remarriages of other party	1,891	5,416	+189.6%
No. of remarriages of both parties	305	1,857	+508.9%
No. of divorces	2,060	13,425	+551.7%
Marriage rate[1]			
All men	49.7	32.9	-33.9%
All women	56.9	27.2	-52.1%
Divorced men/widowers	23.9	40.1	+67.8%
Divorced women/widows	5.4	11.7	+116.7%

[1]The number of marriages per 1000 unmarried men or women aged sixteen and over.

The rising trend of divorce and subsequent remarriage calls for attention from the community to the challenges facing remarried couples and their families. Yet, despite an increased body of research in the area of remarriages in the past decade, little has been done about the process of meeting the challenges of remarriage (Coleman, Ganong & Fine, 2000). Local resources on related topics, in particular, are meagre (Lam-Chan, 1999; Tai, 1998).

This study attempts to furnish local material on remarriage and to throw light on the experiences of remarried persons in Hong Kong. Certainly, the challenges they face are closely tied with cultural traditions and values about marriage and family that are particular to our socio-cultural context.

Remarriage in the Cultural Context

There are various sayings that reflect Chinese values towards marriage, one of which is "staying with one partner from the beginning to the end" (從一而終). Yet, it seems that fidelity applies only to women, and thus the saying really means "staying with one husband from the beginning to the end". Although, traditionally, it was common for men to have "three wives and four concubines" (三妻四妾), proper women were not expected to have more than one husband. It was not until 1971 that monogamy was stated in the law as the only form of legal marriage for both men and women in Hong Kong. The value of fidelity in women has undoubtedly contributed to less social acceptance of remarriage for the female than for the male. A widower remarrying is said to be "reconstructing the broken string" (續弦), which is a positive act, but the term "marrying a second time" (翻頭嫁) carries a negative connotation of the woman, who is viewed as "worn shoes" (Lam-Chan, 1999). The child brought into the second marriage by a woman is called "greasy oil bottle" (油瓶), denoting a carrier of grease "which will never be washed away because the shame and filth of the remarried mother will cast on her child forever" (Lam-Chan, 1999: 80). According to some traditional stories, the term "greasy oil bottle" may have come from the similar sounding term "sick" (有病), which indicates a negative view of the child. No such term is applied to a remarried man's child.

In addition, the image of stepparents has not been positive. The stepmother is referred to as "a female who comes after" (後娘), which denotes an inferior status, and in colloquial Cantonese the term even carries the meaning of a female beast (Lam-Chan, 1999). The negative image of a wicked woman who is cruel to her stepchildren (刻薄) has been reinforced by some old Chinese films. Stepfathers are seen as dangerous people who may abuse their stepchildren, and more specifically, sexually abuse their stepdaughters. Even to the present day, whenever there is news about child abuse by stepfathers, the word "stepfather" is usually prominent. The negative image of stepparents not only affects the stepparents but also the remarried biological parents, who may worry that their children will be subject to risk of abuse.

In contemporary Hong Kong, we do see a change in attitudes towards marriage and remarriage. The traditional value of having a lifelong marriage seems to be no longer prevalent among youth, as indicated by the findings of some local surveys (Yeung & Kwong, 1998). The degrading terms denoting members of remarried families are also no longer commonly or overtly used. However, certain traditional views are inevitably brought home to us through socialization and are subtly influencing our perception of remarriages. A negative stereotyping of remarriage, especially for women, still exists (Lam-Chan, 1999; Tai, 1998).

The Chinese often refer to menopause as "a second spring", probably because, at this stage of life, a woman has acquired "tremendous life experience and wisdom that will allow her to fully blossom into who she is" (Ni, 2003). This term is also suitable for denoting remarriage, which can be likened to "a second spring" by its implication of a new beginning for those who have gone through vast experiences of happiness and pain in married life and have gained much insight and wisdom to cope and grow. Instead of being held back by the negative stereotype that our culture brings, the remarried person may experience a rebirth in a positive light. In the following sections, we tap into the experience of the remarried person in the making of the second spring.

A Study of the Remarriage Experience

The present article is based on a small qualitative study of eight remarried persons in Hong Kong, conducted in 1998. The study employed McCracken's (1988) open-ended long interview method to tap in depth the experiences of remarried persons. To avoid encountering too wide a divergence in experiences that might sacrifice the uncovering of meaningful common themes, only those who were in their second marriage, whose previous marriage ended in divorce and who had children below twenty-one years of age from the previous marriage were recruited as informants through a non-probability purposive convenience sampling method. For the purpose of this study, marriage was not necessarily taken in the legal sense. Hence couples who were not legally registered for marriage but who presented themselves socially as husband and wife were also considered married.

All potential informants of this study were identified through the personal network of the researcher's friends and colleagues. Other methods, such as publicity at family life education programs for remarried couples, yielded no results. It was intended that an equal number of remarried men and women be included in the study, but, due to difficulties in recruitment, the researcher decided to take in all suitable persons willing to participate in the study and did not insist on a balanced sample in sex. Eight remarried persons, six women and two men, eventually participated in the study; hence, it must be noted that the experiences uncovered may contain a bias of the female views. Among the informants, there were two couples in which both husbands and wives had been previously divorced. There was one informant whose second husband was previously widowed. The spouses of the remaining three informants were first-time married persons. All except one had custody of their own birth children from the previous marriage. Four had stepchildren living together in the family. Four of them had had children with the second spouse. The average age of the informants was forty-three. The median length of remarriage was two-and-a-half years, the longest being seventeen years and the shortest being only three months. All of them were ethnic Chinese residing in Hong Kong. All except one of the spouses were also ethnic Chinese. (For the family composition of the informants, refer to Table 2.)

Table 2. The Remarried Informants and their Families

Informant	Marital status of spouse	Length of remarriage	CFM	CSM	SC	NRC	Remarks
Mrs Koo	2nd (W)	17 years	2	1	2		
Mrs Lee	1st	14 years	1	1		1	Both 1st & 2nd husbands non-Chinese
Mrs Mok	1st	3 years	1	2			
Mrs Ng	1st	10 years	2	1			
Mr Siu	2nd (D)	2 years			2*	2	Couple
Mrs Siu	2nd (D)	2 years	2				* Mr Siu's SC = Mrs Siu's CFM
Mr Tin	2nd (D)	3 months	2		2*		Couple
Mrs Tin	2nd (D)	3 months	2		2**		* Mr Tin's SC = Mrs Tin's CFM ** Mrs Tin's SC = Mr Tin's CFM

Key: 1st: Spouse first married
2nd (W): Spouse previously widowed
2nd (D): Spouse previously divorced
CFM: Child from first marriage
CSM: Child from second marriage
SC: Stepchild
NRC: Child from first marriage not residing with the remarried family

All eight interviews were conducted at places of the informants' choice that allowed private conversation. The average time of interviews was one-and-a-half hours, the shortest being one hour and the longest being almost two-and-a-half hours. All interviews were audiotaped and then fully transcribed verbatim.

Many prominent themes emerged from the retelling of the remarriage experience. They are presented and discussed with respect to the choices and chances of remarriage, the self-spouse-child triangle, the past and present marriages, and the views of others in the community. The review of how the informants have coped and experienced growth from meeting the many challenges is discussed.

The Making of a Second Spring

Choices and Chances of Remarriage

The making of a second spring had various meanings to the informants of this study in their decision to remarry. For some, remarriage was a choice of their own and a choice for the better; for others, remarriage was not so much a matter of choice.

Remarriage as a preference

Some of the informants considered remarriage a choice over single parenthood. Mrs Lee for example, preferred not to stay single after leaving her first husband. Remarriage came as a natural course when she met a suitable new partner.

> In my mind, I had always felt that I would not raise my daughter all by myself on a long-term basis. I did not have this concept at all. I felt it was sad and pitiful to be all alone (孤苦伶仃). (Mrs Lee)

Several other informants expressed the same preference for remarriage and felt that divorce and single parenthood were more difficult to go through. For some of them, it seemed that being married was at least socially more proper, invited less discrimination, and brought about less embarrassment than staying divorced.

For Mrs Mok, who did not have a strong preference for a particular kind of life, her decision to divorce and to remarry were matters of her choice for the better.

> Psychologically, I had accepted the possibility that I might remain single for the rest of my life. At the same time, I was very ready for another relationship. ... I also had the feeling that if I had the chance, my second would be better than my first. So to me, remarriage is just a natural course. (Mrs Mok)

It was definitely Mrs Mok's choice to marry Mr Mok, her second husband, and she was obviously happy. Yet, Mrs Mok realized that she could have the freedom to choose what she preferred, because she had the financial resources.

Remarriage as a way out

For the informants who did not have as many personal resources as Mrs Mok did, remarriage seemed to be more of a practical way out than a preference. Mrs Siu, whose first husband had another woman, considered her remarriage to be an inevitable course, as she did not have the personal resources required for independent living.

> If I could choose my path again, I would continue my education and seek self-enrichment, so that I do not need to be dependent on others. The fact is that I did not continue my studies, so I have to depend on another person to provide for me. If I have good education and get a job, marriage is not that important. Now, it is a must that I remarry. (Mrs Siu)

Although Mrs Siu had received secondary education and was by no means unable to work, it seemed that her previous life as a *"tai-tai"* in a wealthy family had made it difficult for her to adapt to independent living.

Apart from personal resources such as education and earning ability, some informants felt that the availability of social resources could make a difference in a divorced person's choice. Mrs Ng had this to say:

> It would be good if services like refuges and government assistance were available to divorced people. I did not know about such resources at that time. Because of all those practical problems and strong emotions, it was really very difficult to be divorced. If I did not remarry, I had to face a lot of problems. I could not possibly solve those problems by myself. (Mrs Ng)

Remarriage as a divorce accelerator

The data of this study showed that the temporal sequence between remarriage and divorce was not necessarily clear. For more than half of the informants, divorce and remarriage in fact overlapped. In a sense, the process of divorce had been hastened by the start of a new relationship. The chance of remarriage had made it possible for Mrs Siu to break away from her empty first marriage. For her husband, Mr Siu, who had also been separated at that time, the new relationship had accelerated the formal procedures for divorcing his first wife. Mrs Lee, who came to know her second husband after she left her first husband, had once considered reconciliation upon her first husband's request but had then given up when Mr Lee proposed to her. Mr and Mrs Tin were both unhappy in their first marriages, but it was after they had started their extramarital affair with each other that they began to think seriously about divorce.

To the informants who experienced such overlap between two relationships, it was basically a personal choice of one partner over another. However, from the social and moral perspective, such an overlap may have serious implications. For example, Mr Siu believed that his family's objection to his remarriage was in some way related to the fact that he had not formally divorced his first wife at that time. Mr and Mrs Tin had to bear enormous pressure for causing the termination of their first marriages. Mrs Tin told of her feelings during the overlapping period:

> At that time, I was very confused (迷惘). I did not know where I was. It was just a mess (混亂). I was not able to calm down sufficiently to evaluate my marriage. It was just like I was in a lost world (迷失的境界). There was much moral pressure on me. It seemed that I had destroyed the marriage and had caused the children to suffer. The pressure was really great. ... After all, I had to take considerable responsibility for the end of my first marriage. (Mrs Tin)

Limitations in choices and chances

No matter whether the remarriage was considered a preference or a practical way out, most of the informants felt that the choices and chances for remarriage in Hong Kong were in fact limited. The presence of children seemed to be the most significant limiting factor. As Mr Tin stated:

> A divorced man is still very attractive if he has good education, a good job, and is middle-aged. The problem comes if he has children. When a girl wants to develop a relationship with him, there would then be more obstacles. ... Conversely, if I am a single man selecting a marriage partner, whether she is previously married is not important. But if she has children, then I have to think seriously. (Mr Tin)

Several other informants echoed Mr Tin's view. Mrs Koo, for example, felt that the only choice for a woman with children was probably to marry a man with children:

> It was really difficult to remarry and at the same time be a stepmother. I do not mean that women should not remarry. Perhaps it would be better if they do not choose men with children. But, if you don't choose those with children, what qualification do you have that enables you to remarry? (但是如果不選擇那些有兒有女的，你又有什麼資格去再婚呢?) Very often, those who are willing to marry previously married persons are themselves previously married. (Mrs Koo)

Mrs Lee also felt that her daughter had limited her choice for remarriage. Having an American ex-husband had been an additional limitation. It was understandable why she felt she had to grab the opportunity when it came:

> If this was my first marriage, I could still afford the time to choose a better husband. But when it was the second time, I would not wait to see if there would be another one. I liked this person, and he was willing to marry me, so I accepted. I would not waste time. I would need to grab the opportunity (把握時機) and would not waste any more of my time. (Mrs Lee)

Discussion

The considerations made when going into a first marriage may be different from those made for a second marriage, and the feelings involved may be different. Although some researchers (Hunt, 1977, cited in Garfield, 1980; Kvanli and Jennings, 1987) found that the courtship before remarriage is often taken as a time of caution, and the partners tend to hold off commitments to make sure that they are making the right decision, the informants of this study were ready to grasp the opportunity when it came. Be it for emotional or practical reasons, they all considered married life to be preferable to life as a divorced person. For some of them, however, it was not so much a real choice, as they realized that their paths could be different if they had more resources in money, education, or community support. Also, bringing children into another marriage was acknowledged as the most significant factor in limiting choices, for both men and women.

Wu (1994), applying social exchange theory to examine the broad determinants of the remarriage process in desirability, eligibility, barriers, and market constraints, highlighted the remarried persons' initial estimate of the cost/benefit balance prior to the decision to remarry. He found that structural barriers such as religious affiliation do affect remarriage behaviour and that there are more constraints in the remarriage market for women than for men. It seems that the informants in this study were well aware that choices and chances for remarriage are limited in Hong Kong society, where previously married persons, especially women, are considered "worn shoes" and children brought into the remarriage are called "greasy oil bottles". Given the constraints in the remarriage market, they inevitably had to adjust their expectations accordingly in their choice of a remarriage partner.

The Self-spouse-child Triangle

From a systems perspective, remarried persons live in an intricate network of relationships in the family, the smallest unit of relationship not a dyad but a triangle. The self-spouse-child triangle is the basic unit that makes up the stepfamily. A few prominent patterns of this triangle emerged from the analysis of the interviews. These patterns were interrelated and by no means mutually exclusive.

Torn between two loved ones

Remarried persons are the intimate partners of their second spouses as well as the biological parents of their children from the previous marriage. The informants of this study, with the exception of Mr Siu, who was not residing with his own children, felt torn between their spouses and their children when the new family was formed. Mrs Siu spoke of how her younger daughter and her husband competed for her time and attention at the beginning of her remarriage:

> My younger daughter wanted me to cuddle her while watching television. Mr Siu then came to sit with us. After a while, he asked my daughter to go and do something else. As my daughter had to be in bed by nine o'clock, she felt that my husband had sent her away so she could not stay close to me for a little while longer. I dared not say anything and did not know what to do. Sometimes, after dinner, Mr Siu proposed having a chat or going for a walk with me. However, I wanted to be close to my daughter before she went to bed. ... I was most unhappy during that adjustment period. Now it is much better. (Mrs Siu)

Certainly, stress and coping change over time. For Mrs Siu, it took all three parties in the triangle quite some time to gradually work out an equilibrium, which may still further adjust with time.

Being positioned between one's spouse and one's child, the remarried person often sees a responsibility in smoothing the relationship between the two. Mrs Mok made a conscious effort to create opportunities for her husband to get closer to her son Mickey, and for her to step back to allow for the strengthening of the stepfather-stepson subsystem:

> When we got married, and when we had our first child together, we recognized that we should make a conscious effort for Mr Mok to spend more time with Mickey. Sometimes he

would purposefully take Mickey out and drive him to the Peak
to buy ice cream, or take him to a movie, and I would not go
with them. (Mrs Mok)

The remarried person also performed a smoothing role by saying
good things about the spouse in front of the child, and vice versa. One
informant said:

> My son minds his stepfather's behaviour very much, and often
> complains that he is unfair. Yet I comfort him and say: "Your
> stepfather is not like that. Don't be silly. It is not so. Is there
> any misunderstanding?" I cover my conscience to say such
> things. I explain this and explain that because I don't want my
> son to have prejudice against his stepfather. (Mrs Koo)

The remarriage challenger

For some informants, the position of being torn between two loved ones
could arise from conflicts over stepparenting, and could damage the
marital relationship. Mrs Tin spoke of her difficulty in reaction to her
husband's stepparenting style:

> Sometimes we do not handle child discipline in the same way.
> I am softer and Mr Tin is firmer. It is not a problem when he
> is firm with his kids, because they are used to it. However,
> when he is firm with my son, I am not used to it, and so I
> jump up to protect my son. When I do this, he thinks that I
> don't love him enough and that I am not putting him in first
> place. This hurts him severely. This situation is the most
> difficult for me. I am squeezed in a gap between them (在一
> 個夾縫裡面). My husband is not happy; my son is not happy.
> … I am stuck between their conflict (變了磨心), and this affects
> my relationship with my husband. (Mrs Tin)

The negative effect of such a scenario in the marital relationship was
confirmed by Mr Tin, who described the handling of his stepson as the
biggest source of conflict between the couple. Though difficulties in the
step-relationship remained, the couple, through insights gained from
religious teaching, coped with the challenge by examining their priorities:

> In my prayers, God tells me to learn to be a good wife. … If
> our hearts are not together, our family will disintegrate. It is
> no use for me to protect my son if there is no family. …

> Therefore I give priority to the relationship with my husband.
> For the time being, I cannot love my son with all my heart.
> This is not easy, and my religious belief helps me to overcome
> much of my psychological block. (Mrs Tin)

Some other informants, like Mrs Lee and Mrs Mok, echoed the Tins'
emphasis on the marital relationship by bringing up the need for couple
time. This is especially relevant, because remarried couples do not have
the luxury of enjoying a honeymoon period without their children
around.

Though arguments between couples on matters of child discipline
may happen in any family, the fact that the marriage is a second one
seemed to have made the marital relationship more vulnerable for some
informants. Also, although coping in remarriage may be less of a problem
when children are young, the cumulative stress of children reaching their
teens can present a challenge to the remarried family (Crosbie-Burnett,
1989). As stated by Mrs Lee:

> Difficulty in our marriage arose when my daughter reached her
> teenage years. She gives us a lot of trouble. As you know, the
> teenage period is a difficult one. It makes my husband feel that
> she hurts our marital relationship. Well, our relationship is
> fine, just that we often argue because of my daughter. ... My
> husband has been very accepting of her but she is disturbing
> our routine. ... He did not have this child, but she gives him
> so much trouble. I worry that our marriage may be jeopardized
> because of this. (Mrs Lee)

In Mrs Lee's case, regrets about taking the child into the second
marriage occurred at stressful moments.

The remarriage smoother

It is noted from this study that children watched over their biological
parents closely, and that the bond between the children and their
biological parents had an important place in the self-spouse-child triangle.
Some of them made an effort to maintain a satisfactory step-relationship
for the sake of their biological parents and contributed to the smoothing
of the remarriage relationship. Some actively acted as "smoothers"
between their biological and stepparents and even as protectors of their
biological parents when the latter were in conflict with their stepparents:

My daughter treats her stepfather as "mother's other half". ...
She says that my husband is in fact very good to me, and asks
me not to be unhappy about him. When he gives me a bunch
of flowers, I often think that he is in fact sending somebody
else flowers and just leaves some for me. My daughter would
say, "You shouldn't care whether he buys the flowers for a
'chicken' or a 'duck'. Why does he have to buy one more bunch
for you? That's because he is thinking of you." (Mrs Siu)

When I quarrelled with my husband, both of my children
warned him not to fight with me. ... My daughter also said to
me, "Mama, you'd better not fight with him, or else he would
be happy about making you irritated." (Mrs Koo)

Discussion

Whereas a first marriage begins with a dyadic relationship, a remarriage
starts with an instant family (Lloyd, 1990; Roberts & Price, 1987). The
remarried couple has to integrate their children from a previous marriage
into the structure of the new family and adjust to several relationships
right from the beginning (Atwood & Zerbersky, 1995; Berger, 1998).
There is also a blending of relationships that includes blood relationships
as well as step-relationships in the remarried family (Bray, 1999; Coleman
& Ganong, 1997; Lamanna, 2000). Yet, the formation of an instant family
structure does not come with instant love among the new family members
(Bray, 1993; Dainton, 1993; Visher & Visher, 1978). The implications of
these characteristics of the remarried family for the dynamics of the self-
spouse-triangle are well illustrated by the patterns identified in this study.
As biological parents to their children, the remarried informants were very
much involved in the relationship between their children and spouses.
They not only frequently assumed a smoothing role in the step-
relationship but were also often torn between them. Notwithstanding the
intensity of their involvement in the triangle, a number of informants
realized the need to make a special effort to strengthen the couple
boundary and find time for "a world of two". However, although some
informants conscientiously made private time with their spouses, this was
possible only when supportive resources, such as a maid or their own
family of origin, were available to look after the children. Couples who
may not have such resources will have to identify other mechanisms to
protect their marital relationship.

In this study, the role of children in the marital relationship was
found to be significant. A strong challenge to the remarried couple's
relationship sometimes arose when arguments concerning the children

occurred. This corresponds well with the findings in other studies that identify the difficulty in dealing with stepchildren as a major factor destabilizing remarriages (Dahl, Cowgill & Asmundsson, 1987; Pasley, Koch & Ihinger-Tallman, 1993; White & Booth, 1985). How the biological custodial parent and the stepparent together work out ways to meet the challenge of the presence of children in the remarried family, and how the biological custodial parent defines the parenting role of the ex-spouse and the present spouse, are thus crucial parts of the remarried relationship (Bray, Berger & Boethel, 1995; Grizzle, 1999). Children were also found to be close observers of their biological parents. In this sense, they were in fact active participants in the remarried couple's relationship.

The Past and the Present

The experience of having gone through a first marriage and its dissolution is an essential part of remarried persons' personal history. In this section, I discuss how the remarried informants in this study integrated this piece of their history into the second marriage.

Baggage of the past

Most of the informants said that they currently either had no contact with their ex-spouses at all or maintained minimal contact with them only on matters relating to their children. Past hurts and feelings, however, still affected some of them, as expressed by Mrs Tin:

> You are like a person who has suffered burns. Today, you may be leading a happy and healthy life, but the scar from the burns will not disappear. The scar does not necessarily affect you now, but you may have to pay the price such as bearing an emotional and spiritual burden (代價包括感情的包袱，心靈的包袱). (Mrs Tin)

For Mrs Siu, the experience of a previous failed marriage seemed to have reduced her confidence in durable relationships. Her previous husband's extramarital affair had been a great shock to her and had made her realize that nothing on earth was predictable.

For most of the informants, this baggage of the past seemed to have more impact on the handling of their children than on the remarried couple's relationship. Mrs Lee, for example, still had hard feelings towards her ex-spouse and was not ready to let her daughter meet him:

> No, I have not thought of letting my daughter meet her father. Firstly, I feel that the situation is embarrassing. Secondly, I don't want to meet him myself. I don't want to be reminded of the unhappy things that happened in the past. ... I said to her, "I don't mind what you do when you grow up, but now, I would not deliberately take you to see him. I don't feel the need". (Mrs Lee)

No matter what kind of residual feelings the informants had about their past, most of them considered their ex-spouse merely a link with their children, and some of them had been cautious not to put their current family at risk:

> Now I just consider my ex-husband my children's father, so I respect him. If he needs my help, say, financially, I would help him. Otherwise, I would not do anything. I must protect my present family and be at my present husband's side. (Mrs Siu)

Not again

The remarried informants of this study presented their second marriages as more stable than their first ones were. Most of them, except Mr and Mrs Siu, who had not yet legally registered for marriage, indicated that they were ready to see the current marriage last. Mr and Mrs Tin, for example, showed that their confidence in their marriage had not been shattered by their previous marital failure, especially as they had found faith in their common religion. Mrs Mok stated that she had a more satisfactory relationship with her second husband than with her first. Mrs Lee considered her marital relationship to be good. She did not want to experience another failure and was ready to "sacrifice anything to make this marriage a better one". It seems that, after having gone through a failed marriage, many of the informants had come to treasure the current marriage more. Some informants, though, did not consider their second marriage happy but were still prepared to stay in it. Mrs Koo explained why she did not leave this marriage when her relationship with her second husband went extremely bad some years ago:

> If I had married this same husband in a first marriage, I think I would have the courage to seek a divorce immediately. But this was already my second marriage, so I did not want to fail again. I had to uphold my sense of self-respect. Another reason for my staying in the marriage was that we had a son. I did not want to hurt one more child. ... My first marriage was

already bad; my second is worse. If I marry for the third time,
wow, I dare not think about it! (Mrs Koo)

A point to note from Mrs Koo's account is the influence of the mutual
child on her second marriage. The same happened to Mrs Ng, who had
once contemplated divorce from her second husband but then gave up
the idea when she thought about the welfare of their mutual child. A
similar picture was presented in Wineberg's (1992) study, in which the
birth of a mutual child was found to be favourable to marital stability
in the first ten years of remarriage. It seems that, having observed their
children suffer from the trauma of the previous divorce, the remarried
informants were reluctant to have the history repeated. It also seems that
this determination to maintain the marriage had helped them endure
long enough to pass through the most frustrating period in their marital
life and to see some improvement.

In contrast to the other informants, Mrs Siu seemed to be less sure
about her second marriage, though she enjoyed and treasured the present
relationship. She just hoped to maintain it as long as she could:

> What is sweet about my remarriage is that Mr Siu sometimes
> makes me very happy. However, there is also a bitter side. I
> am uncertain about the future. I just live from day to day (過
> 一日得一日). The reason is that Mr Siu still has girlfriends. (Mrs
> Siu)

Learning from past experiences

In comparing their first and second marriages, most of the informants
reported that they experienced some change in themselves or in the way
they dealt with their current marriage. For Mrs Tin, this change had
occurred through a process of self-reflection:

> I have gone through a reflection on why my first marriage
> failed and how I can make this marriage succeed. The first
> marriage failed not only because there was a shift of love. Love
> doesn't shift by itself. There must be some reason for the crack
> to exist. If there is no crack, you can't place a grain of sand
> inside. So, I looked back to examine the past, and to see where
> I am now. (Mrs Tin)

Self-reflection and evaluation were also evident in the experiences of
most other informants. Several consequences of this process have been
identified as follows.

More accommodating

Mrs Mok noted that much change had occurred in her attitude towards her first and second husbands:

> I was too demanding of my ex-husband and of myself. In retrospect, I think I was unreasonable. ... When it comes to my second marriage, I certainly became conscious that I could not expect everything to be perfect. ... I have also learned to accept the other's differences and accommodate him. (Mrs Mok)

Some other informants, like Mrs Siu and Mrs Tin, also reported a similar shift to a less demanding, less rigid, and more accommodating mode. They were more able to respect their spouse as an individual and to accept individual differences in style. Such a shift seems to have indicated growth to a more mature way of dealing with intimate relationships and a better understanding of human nature.

Better communication

Another common change reported by the informants, including Mrs Lee, Mrs Mok, and Mr and Mrs Tin, was better communication with the spouse in the second marriage. This included mutual sharing as well as mutual problem-solving. Although conflicts in couple relationships were inescapable, the informants stressed the need for open communication and on not avoiding an argument. This was how Mrs Lee evaluated her communication with her ex-husband, which gave her insight into how she should change for the better:

> It is very important for us to frankly tell each other how we feel. If we don't speak out, we won't be able to understand each other, and we might explode. ... I did not speak my feeling in my first marriage. When negative feelings accumulated and eventually exploded, I just turned away and left the marriage. (Mrs Lee)

More self-protective

Having gone through disappointments in the first marriage and continuous disappointments in the second marriage, Mrs Ng and Mrs Siu seemed to have lost confidence in men and had come to a stage at which they felt it more important to protect themselves than to rely on their spouses. Mrs Ng, whose first husband was a drug addict and her second a gambler, had this to say:

Both men were a burden to me. Women must be self-reliant and not dependent on men. ... Don't trust the man completely and don't give out so much (別放那麼盡). You have to protect yourself and your children, so that when he changes in whatever way, you can still get what you should get. You must be on guard (防人之心不可無). (Mrs Ng)

Do more of what works

Learning from the past did not only mean a shift in one's way of dealing with the marital relationship. It also meant a transfer of effective strategies used in the first marriage to the second marriage. Generalizing his understanding of women, and applying his experience from his first marriage, Mr Siu stated:

I would apply my experience in relating to my first wife to my present marriage. ... For example, when there is an argument, resolve it as soon as possible and don't leave it overnight. To prevent her nagging all night, make an effort to please her. Usually women feel better when they have the upper hand. (Mr Siu)

Discussion

One characteristic of remarriage is the history of a previous marital relationship. This experience has become part of the remarried person's current self, and, in one way or another, part of the current family. The adjustment to remarriage thus involves not only the recoupling tasks of building trust and mutual accommodation but also the individual tasks of giving up old hurt and grievances and resolving unfinished business from the past (Berger, 1998; Kvanli & Jennings, 1987). Current relationships with ex-spouses may also create difficulties in establishing boundaries around the remarriage, especially when the children in the stepfamilies still have regular contact with their non-custodial parents (Ganong & Coleman, 1994; Gold, Bubenzer & West, 1993; Knox & Zusman, 2001). For most of the informants of this study, the presence of their ex-spouses did not obviously affect their remarriage relationship. Yet, past hurt had not been completely erased, and sometimes the children may even be stuck in the unresolved conflict between the remarried persons and their ex-spouses.

The divorce rate of remarriages has consistently been reported to be moderately higher than that of first marriages (Booth & Edwards, 1992; Ceglian & Gardner, 1999; Cherlin, 1992; Stets, 1993), seemingly indicating that remarriages are more vulnerable. Some studies, however, suggest that remarriage is not inevitably associated with less marital happiness or a lower quality of marital relationship, and in some cases, it is even associated with less conflict (Glenn, 1981; Hobart, 1989; Ihinger-Tallman & Pasley, 1997; MacDonald & Demaris, 1995; Stets, 1993; Vehemer *et al.*, 1989). The data of this study supported the latter findings, in that the informants' experience of a failed marriage had helped them handle their remarriage better. Though not necessarily very satisfied with the present relationship, most of the informants did treasure their second marriage and had a strong will to make it last. Their responses echoed Levin's (1997: 125) view that the remarried person's "strong motivation to 'succeed' and to avoid a new 'failure' can be likened to starting a *project*".

Revising Cultural Perspectives — In the Eyes of Others

Blessings of social support

According to Lamanna (2000: 496), the rising rate of divorce and remarriage has led to "greater cultural tolerance of stepfamilies". Most of the remarried informants in this study felt that remarriage was no longer uncommon in present-day Hong Kong and claimed that they had not experienced any outright social discrimination. As Mr Siu put it:

> Remarriage is a natural product of this era. People now have more choices and chances. The social context is also more favourable now. ... In feudal societies, divorce and remarriage were seen as shameful (不名譽). Now in a place as civilized and westernized as Hong Kong, divorce and remarriage are considered intelligent choices (明智的選擇) for marriage partners who have lived in pain for long periods. (Mr Siu)

Despite the perceived change in social attitude towards remarriage, all of the informants did, in one way or another, feel that the acceptance was only partial. Some sensed that there was gossip behind their backs, and some felt that people were more sensitive to problems in remarried families. This has created tension in their remarried life. That is why Mrs Lee preferred to hide her marital history from her colleagues and from her daughter's teachers:

I have not told my daughter's teacher about my remarried status. I think it is better that they don't know unless the child has a problem. As both my daughters are psychologically healthy, it is better not to let the teachers consciously pick on their problems. I admit that being a remarried person, I have sometimes acted a bit stealthily (閃縮). The reason is that I don't know whether other people will have any prejudice against me. ... I don't want this to affect how others perceive me. I don't want them to gossip. I don't want them to embarrass me. (Mrs Lee)

Mrs Lee's feeling was completely different in another social environment. She felt much more comfortable with her remarried status when she visited her in-laws in America, because she felt the people there were more liberal. Considering the vast difference in her feeling, it was clear that her experience as a remarried person was very much a product of the social context.

For Mr and Mrs Tin, who were fervent Christians, the church was the most significant social environment in their lives. In contrast to the common belief that divorce and remarriage are strongly opposed by the church, Mr and Mrs Tin's story showed that the church could in fact be a great support to a remarried couple by treating the remarriage issue in a flexible way:

Remarriage is basically not allowed in the Bible unless your spouse has passed away. Otherwise, it is not encouraged and is considered a sin. Before we got married, we had asked the pastors how they viewed the matter. According to them, this issue is in fact very controversial. It depends firstly on whether you are still in your first marriage when you start to believe in God. Secondly, it depends on whether the remarriage is constructive and whether it brings hope, that is, whether you regret your past and have the sincerity to build a new family. Thirdly, it depends on whether the previous marriage can still be saved. In our case, when we started to believe in God, both of our first marriages had already terminated. Our remarriage did in fact bring about hope and not damage. Also, Mr Tin's ex-wife had remarried at the time of our marriage. Although my ex-husband had not remarried, he was not willing to live with me again, so there was also no chance for us to reconcile. (Mrs Tin)

According to both Mr and Mrs Tin, the accepting attitude of the church greatly supported them in facing the psychological pressure brought about by their remarried status and in building confidence in their new life.

Acceptance of the extended family

Marriage is almost never considered just a matter of two persons but a matter of the whole extended family. In Chinese societies, marriage banquets are usually held in the name of the couple's parents. Although "the mandate given by parents" (父母之命) no longer applies in contemporary Hong Kong, parental approval of one's marriage is still considered essential. The acceptance and support of the extended family definitely makes it easier for the remarried couple to cope with the many demands of the stepfamily. As Mrs Tin stated:

> Mr Tin's mother is very nice to me. His sister goes to the same church as we do. She gave us much support during the difficult times of our relationship. ... His family is nice to my kids. My mother-in-law often praises them. She sometimes cooks their favourite food for them. She gives every child the same birthday lai-see. I think it is very good already. (Mrs Tin)

Rejection shown by the extended family, however, may become an additional challenge to the remarried couple's relationship. Mrs Mok considered her in-laws' negative attitude towards her the most bitter part of her remarriage. In fact, after almost three years, his family was still unwilling to meet her, and she unwilling to meet them:

> His family members were really against our relationship ... When they knew that he was having a relationship with a divorced woman, and what's more, a divorced woman with a son, they were devastated. ... His mother could not accept it, and she forbade him to see me. ... She not only gave him pressure but also made phone calls to my home and my office to scold me. ... I finally had to tell Mr Mok that I also wanted him to choose between his family and me. I really could not have gone on like this. (Mrs Mok)

Mr Mok eventually made the decision to stay with Mrs Mok and had to bear the pain of distancing himself from his family. Fortunately, Mrs Mok felt that the situation had not adversely affected the marital relationship, as they were open and honest in communicating their feelings with each other.

As for Mrs Ng, the rejection that she felt was subtle. Although her relationship with Mr Ng's family was harmonious on the surface, her hard feelings and anger were directed towards her husband, who had tried to hide her marital history from his family. It was some years after her remarriage that she could not stand the situation and told his family the truth herself:

> My husband did not let his family know that I was previously married and had two children. He was a chauvinist and felt that it was a loss of face to let others know that he married a previously married woman … After his family knew about my history, they did not say anything in front of me but made comments when I was not around. I heard that my husband's aunt said, "If I had known that she was previously married and had children, I would not have let him marry her". (Mrs Ng)

Both Mrs Mok and Mr Siu mentioned the matter of "face" (面子), a socially important concept in Chinese families, when they referred to the negative response of the extended family towards remarried persons. Although their unfavourable attitude may not hurt a marital relationship that is sufficiently strong, and may even present a common challenge that draws the couple closer to each other, it may bring about more blaming and hostility in marriages that are already vulnerable.

Discussion

The findings of this study suggest that, though remarriages are more and more common in Hong Kong and are apparently more socially acceptable, remarried couples may still face blatant or subtle rejection, especially from the extended family. It could be that, compared with the situation in North America, the individuation of adult children from their families takes place more slowly in Chinese societies. The influence of one's extended family is very significant even when one reaches adulthood or is married. Negative reactions from the extended family may even be intensified when it concerns face or the family name. In any case, the attitude of the extended family as well as of other people in society does make a great difference in the lives of remarried couples.

Meeting Challenges of a Second Spring: Coping and Growth

The remarried informants in this study had to go through many challenges, not only arising from the intricate network of relationships in the remarried family but also from the attitude in the social context and the demands of social reality. Although some had more pleasant experiences than others did, and some had more confidence in their remarriage than others did, all of them had survived and were willing to share their experiences with other people. In this section, I examine how the informants have coped and experienced growth through the challenging times.

Take it easy

As mentioned, a number of the informants felt that they had become more accommodating of their spouses. It seems that they had also learned to use the same kind of "take-it-easy" strategy in face of other challenges in their remarried life. Apparently, not taking things seriously and not expecting too much (看開點，眼不見就算了，化了) made them more adaptable to a reality that was beyond their control. Take, for example, Mrs Koo, who had led a life as a middle-class *"tai-tai"* in her first marriage but had then become a poor housewife having to work to cover her husband's debt and to take care of several children in her second marriage. She attributed her change to "fate" and tried to accept it as it was:

> When I was first married, I had servants to take my kids home from school; now, I have to act like a servant at home. Before, I was ignorant about child care; now, I have to take care of so many kids. To a certain extent, I accept this as fate (認命). I believe in fate (命運), because my experiences in the first and second marriages are completely opposite. In my first marriage, I was very bad tempered. I hit my ex-husband, and threw things at him. Now, my second husband hit me in return. Before, I hated to see people smoke, and I felt so disgusted when my first husband smoked one or two cigarettes; now, my husband is a chain smoker. I feel it is not fair if I just inhale the smoke from him, so I learned to smoke, too. What I did is now done against me (報應). (Mrs Koo)

Whether or not it was really "fate" as Mrs Koo termed it, apparently, the harshness of the reality had forced her to increase her ability to adapt and made her a different person.

Think positively

Cognition has a significant place in how a person experiences a potentially stressful event (Folkman & Lazarus, 1991). The remarried informants in this study clearly demonstrated that it was helpful to use positive thinking in their appraisal of events. Mrs Mok talked about how she appraised her in-laws' rejection of her and refusal to meet her:

> I often say to myself that it is better the way it is now. At least, I don't have to worry about the expectations of my husband's family — whether I know what to do during festivals, whether I do the right things for them (懂不懂過時過節應做什麼，會不會得失別人). It is better this way. I have fewer problems to handle. (Mrs Mok)

With the support of their religious belief, Mr and Mrs Tin appraised their ability to deal with their challenges in a positive way. The Bible also helped them cognitively and spiritually to cope with their challenges and to look ahead with confidence. As Mrs Tin quoted from the Bible: "Forgetting what is behind and straining toward what is ahead, I press on toward the goal to win the prize for which God has called me heavenward in Christ Jesus" (忘後力前，向著鏢竿直跑).

In addition to calling on insights from the Bible, Mr Tin seemed to have used much positive thinking. Many times in the interview, he said that he was fortunate: it was fortunate that his ex-wife had got married before he did, it was fortunate that his elder son did not show outright rejection of Mrs Tin, it was fortunate that Mrs Tin had two children instead of one so that his poor experience with his stepson could be balanced by his good experience with his stepdaughter ... Perhaps it was this ability to count his blessings that helped him better appreciate his present life.

Do your part; don't care about what others think

In coping with other people's unfavourable attitude towards them, most of the informants felt that, because they could not control what others say or think, it was better for them to do their own part and not care about other people's attitude.

> My mother-in-law and my sister-in-law did not like me at the beginning. They thought that I was lazy and useless. At that time, I felt very sad, but then I came to learn not to care about what they think. If I have done my part (做自己本份), I will

not feel any guilt (問心無愧). "Distance tells the strength of a horse; time tells the heart of a person (路遙知馬力，日久見人心)." (Mrs Ng)

Mrs Siu used a similar strategy to Mrs Ng's to cope with the belief that she was going after her husband's money. She thought that it was most important to do things that she herself felt was right (過得自己). She would then just let others see in the long run (放長雙眼看) that she was not the person they had thought her to be.

Build one's own strength and adaptability

Whereas some cognitive strategies like "take it easy" seemed to be passive ways of coping, some informants had at the same time attempted to actively shape their own lives. For example, when Mrs Ng found that she could not rely on her husband, she went out to work. She felt that it was her effort to build up her strength that enabled her to protect herself and her children.

> It seemed that, because I was dependent, he felt I had no way to escape from his control (飛不動). ... I took a job, although it only paid me $3,000 a month to work for eleven hours a day. I felt that there was nothing that could beat me. Life had been difficult in the past, and I had been able to go through it. (Mrs Ng)

Managing stress

When stress was inevitable, some of the informants found their own ways to deal with it. Mrs Siu said that she went on a trip by herself, so that she could feel free and could learn to be independent. Mrs Koo, who probably could not afford to go on a trip, said that she would retreat to her little haven, the kitchen:

> When I am not happy, I write in my diary at night in the kitchen. The kitchen is my place. Sometimes I read the newspaper, listen to music, smoke a cigarette, or drink some beer in the kitchen. Then I will sleep well. When I open my eyes in the morning, it is another day. (Mrs Koo)

Like Mrs Koo, Mrs Tin liked to write down her thoughts and feelings. It seems that this not only served as an opportunity for self-reflection but also as a means to vent her feelings.

Discussion

In face of the stressful and yet inevitable demands of remarried life, the informants of this study demonstrated their capacity to shape their lives with their coping efforts as well as their amazing potential for growth. The coping strategies reported above reflect careful self-evaluation and self-searching to find adaptive ways of dealing with the various aspects of life. It would seem that the trying experiences they had gone through in the process of marriage, divorce and remarriage have activated learning and growth in many creative ways. These strategies also reflect the influences of their social context, as could be seen from the cultural and religious wisdom contained in them.

Implications for Practice

The findings of this study indicate the importance of understanding the remarriage relationship in the light of the self-spouse-child triangle. Social workers in family practice may need to appreciate the complexity in relationships that remarried family members experience, and to understand presenting problems and situations in different dimensions. The data of this study also point to the active part played by the children in the remarried family relationships. This calls for further research on children in remarried families, and for social workers' sensitivity to the responses and needs of the children, who may often be neglected.

The findings of this study point to the significance of the socio-cultural context in the experience of the remarried couples. When the environment is seen as non-accepting, the remarried family members could experience much stress, and it certainly takes up their energy to have to deal with unfriendly eyes or to hide their family status. Conversely, a conducive environment and adequate social support could facilitate the coping of the remarried families and prompt their potential for growth and development. Although the remarried family type deviates from the norm of first married families, the reality is that it is here to stay. The negative notion of remarriage as an "incomplete institution" (Cherlin, 1978) thus needs to be redefined. Also, social education on the remarried family as a viable family type is necessary to increase the acceptance of remarriage in society.

Whereas many studies of remarriages highlight problems in these families, the findings of this study bring our attention to the possibility of remarriage as a choice for the better, and to the fact that remarriages are not inevitably problematic. In fact, most of the informants went through reflection and evaluation of their experiences in the past marriages and learned to make their second marriage work better. They cherished the current marriage, were determined not to let it fail, and made an active effort to deal with the challenges of remarriage. In the making of a second spring, they had come up with many creative coping strategies, and through the process, they achieved growth and enhanced adaptability in handling their life situations. The hard-learnt adaptive process to work out new roles and establish new relationships also provided the family members, including the children, with rich experiences in family interactions, and perhaps enhanced their appreciation for harmonious family relationships. This suggests that social workers in practice should address the strengths and potentials of remarried persons and their families, and support them in identifying and expanding their coping strategies. Furthermore, they can encourage remarried persons to share their valuable experiences and rich coping strategies with other people in the same boat, or with those planning to get on the boat, so that they can benefit from mutual support.

References

Atwood J.D. and Zebersky R. (1995). Using social construction therapy with the REM family. In C.A. Everett (Ed.) *Understanding stepfamilies: Their structure and dynamics.* New York: The Haworth Press.

Berger R. (1998). *Stepfamilies: A multi-dimensional perspective.* New York: The Haworth Press.

Booth A. and Edwards J. (1992). Starting over: Why remarriages are more unstable. *Journal of Family Issues, 13*(2), 179–94.

Bray J. (1993). Becoming a stepfamily: Developmental issues for new stepfamilies. *The Family Journal: Counseling and Therapy for Couples and Families, 1*(3), 272–5.

Bray J. (1999). From marriage to remarriage and beyond. In E.M. Hetherington (Ed.) *Coping with divorce, single parenting, and remarriage.* Mahwah, NJ: Lawrence Erlbaum Associates.

Bray J.H., Berger S.H. and Boethel C.L. (1995). Role integration and marital adjustment in stepfather families. In K. Pasley and M. Ihinger-Tallman (Eds.) *Stepparenting: Issues in theory, research and practice.* Westport, CT: Praeger.

Ceglian C.P. and Gardner S. (1999). Attachment style: A risk for multiple marriages? *Journal of Divorce and Remarriage, 31*(1/2), 125–40.

Census and Statistics Dept. (2002). *Demographic trends in Hong Kong, 1981–2001.* Hong Kong.

Cherlin A. (1978). Remarriage as an incomplete institution. *American Journal of Sociology, 84,* 634–50.

Cherlin A. (1992). *Marriage, divorce, remarriage.* Cambridge, MA: Harvard University Press.

Coleman M. and Ganong L. (1997). Stepfamilies from the stepfamily's perspective. In I. Levin and M. Sussman (Eds.) *Stepfamilies: History, research, and policy.* New York: The Haworth Press.

Coleman M., Ganong L. and Fine M. (2000). Reinvestigating remarriage: Another decade of progress. *Journal of Marriage and the Family, 62,* 1288–1307.

Crosbie-Burnett M. (1989). Application of family stress theory to remarriage: A model for assessing and helping stepfamilies. *Family Relations, 38,* 323–31.

Dahl A., Cowgill K. and Asmundsson R. (1987). Life in remarriage families. *Social Work, 32,* 40–4.

Dainton M. (1993). The myths and misconceptions of the stepmother identity: Descriptions and prescriptions for identity management. *Family Relations, 42*(1), 93–8.

Folkman S. and Lazarus R.S. (1991). Coping and emotion. In A. Monat and R.S. Lazarus (Eds.) *Stress and coping: An anthology, third edition.* New York: Columbia University Press.

Ganong L.H. and Coleman M. (1994). *Remarried family relationships.* Thousand Oaks, CA: Sage.

Garfield R. (1980). The decision to remarry. *Journal of Divorce, 4*(1), 1–10.

Glenn N. (1981). The well-being of persons remarried after divorce. *Journal of Family Issues, 2,* 61–75.

Gold J.M., Bubenzer D.L. and West J.D. (1993). Differentiation from ex-spouses and stepfamily marital intimacy. *Journal of Divorce and Remarriage, 19*(3/4), 83–95.

Grizzle G.L. (1999). Institutionalization and family unity: An exploratory study of Cherlin's (1978) views. *Journal of Divorce and Remarriage, 30*(3/4), 125–42.

Hobart C. (1989). Experiences of remarried families. *Journal of Divorce, 13*(2), 121–44.

Ihinger-Tallman M. and Pasley K. (1997). Stepfamilies in 1984 and today: A scholarly perspective. In I. Levin and M. Sussman (Eds.) *Stepfamilies: History, research, and policy.* New York: The Haworth Press.

Knox D. and Zusman M.E. (2001). Marrying a man with "baggage": Implications for second wives. *Journal of divorce and remarriage, 35*(3–4), 67–79.

Kvanli J.A. and Jennings G. (1987). Recoupling: Development and establishment of the spousal subsystem in remarriage. *Journal of Divorce, 10*(1/2), 183–203.

Lam-Chan G.L.T. (1999). *Parenting in stepfamilies: Social attitudes, parental perceptions and parenting behaviors in Hong Kong.* Aldershot: Ashgate.

Lamanna M.A. (2000). *Marriages and families: Making choices in a diverse society.* Belmont, CA: Wadsworth.

Levin I. (1997). Stepfamily as project. In I. Levin and M. Sussman (Eds.) *Stepfamilies: History, research, and policy.* New York: The Haworth Press.

Lloyd D.R. (1990). *The social world of remarried families.* Ann Arbor, MI: University Microfilms International.

MacDonald W.L. and DeMaris A. (1995). Remarriage, stepchildren and marital conflict: Challenges to the incomplete institutionalization hypothesis. *Journal of Marriage and the Family, 57*(2), 387-98.

McCracken G. (1998). *The long interview.* Newbury Park, CA: Sage.

Ni M. (2003). Enjoy your "second spring" during menopause. *Points: The acupuncture.com newsletter, 1*(1), cover article.

Pasley K., Koch M.G. and Ihinger-Tallman M. (1993). Problems in remarriage: An exploratory study of intact and terminated remarriages. *Journal of Divorce and Remarriage, 20*(1/2), 63-83.

Roberts T.W. and Price S.J. (1987). Instant families: Divorced mothers marry never-married men. *Journal of Divorce, 11*(1), 71-92.

Stets J.E. (1993). The link between past and present intimate relationships. *Journal of Family Issues, 14*(2), 236-60.

Tai L.Y.Y. (1998). *A study of the experiences of remarried persons in Hong Kong.* M. Soc.Sc. Dissertation, the University of Hong Kong.

Vehemer E., Coleman M., Ganong L. and Cooper H. (1989). Marital satisfaction in remarriage: A meta-analysis. *Journal of Marriage and the Family, 51 (3)*, 713-25.

Visher E. and Visher J. (1978). Common problems of stepparents and their spouses. *American Journal of Orthopsychiatry, 48*, 252-62.

White L. and Booth A. (1985). The quality and stability of remarriages: The role of stepchildren. *American Sociological Review, 50*, 689-98.

Wineberg H. (1992). Childbearing and dissolution of the second marriage. *Journal of Marriage and the Family, 54*, 879-87.

Wu Z. (1994). Remarriage in Canada: A social exchange perspective. *Journal of Divorce and Remarriage, 21*(3-4), 191-224.

Yeung C. and Kwong W.M. (1998). A study of attitudes of pre-marital couples toward marriage in Hong Kong. *Hong Kong Journal of Social Work, 32*(1): 71-84.

10

Gender Considerations in Couple Work: Reflections From Social Workers Involved in Marital Counselling

TIMOTHY Y.K. LEUNG, MONICA L.T. NG, YEUNG K.C., IVAN T.Y. YAU

This chapter reports on a study to determine the factors that would encourage partners experiencing difficulties in their marriage to participate in working together on their relationship, through counselling or group or enrichment programmes. Two focus groups were conducted to explore what might be helpful and non-helpful factors promoting participation. Nine social workers with more than five years of relevant working experience participated in these two focus groups. It was found that regulation of emotional communication between the couple and reactivating positive aspects of the relationship were important in the beginning phase. To maintain the couple's continuing participation in the process, reframing the marital problems from individual defects to relationship difficulties, validating the men's strength and contribution in marriage, maintaining a balance of attention between the partners, and focusing discussion on areas of mutual interest contributed to promoting engagement. In addition, it was important for the couple to facilitate the mutual understanding of the underlying positive intention and appreciation of the vulnerabilities of each other in order to enhance cohesion. Non-helpful factors included a loss of neutrality by the worker and an avoidance of dealing with marital conflict directly. The focus groups were also of the opinion that, in helping distressed couples, communication skill training was not as effective as other strategies. Rather, promoting a constant flow of positive interaction was more conducive to marital well-being.

Towards a Companionship Marriage Model

Traditionally, marriage in Chinese society was considered mainly a permanent, lifelong bond between two partners for the purposes of reproduction and the survival of the family unit. It was a common practice, even within the early twentieth century, that marriages were arranged by the elders of the family, in the interest of the extended family. Now, for many Hong Kong people, the major goal of marriage has shifted to that of attaining personal satisfaction and mutual support from each other. In a study on the attitudes of premarital couples toward marriage in Hong Kong, most of the respondents (ninety-eight percent to ninety-nine percent) endorsed the statement that "sharing of love and care" and "mutual help, support and encouragement" were two major reasons for getting married. The third reason for marriage is companionship (Yeung & Kwong 1998). These findings illustrate that the "companionship marriage model" has gained widespread acceptance in Hong Kong.

This shift, together with weakening support for the nuclear family from extended families in Hong Kong, has made the conjugal relationship the major source of support for the partners. For couples experiencing difficulties in resolving conflict, these high expectations and demands for affectional sharing and mutual support could not be achieved through marital interaction.

Demands of a Companionship Marriage — Not Easily Met

Hong Kong has witnessed a sharp increase in divorce in the past two decades, as shown in Table 1.

Table 1. Divorce Decrees — 1995–2001

Year	1995	1996	1997	1998	1999	2000	2001
Decrees	9,404	9,473	10,492	13,129	13,408	13,048	13,425

Source: Census and Statistics Department (2003)

The crude divorce rate has increased from 0.4 per 1000 person in 1981 to 2.0 per 1000 person in 2001 (Census and Statistics Department 2003). Further, marital problems are recorded as the major reason for seeking help from family counselling services in Hong Kong. Difficulty in solving conflicts is one of the major factors leading to relationship deterioration. The Hong Kong Family Welfare Society (2002) surveyed 500 married adults and found that fifteen percent had resorted to violence due to couple conflicts, and twenty-five percent had divorce ideation after conflicts. The figure for couples resorting to violence was higher for those who turned to negative means such as avoidance or quarrelling to deal with their conflicts. This study coincided with existing research findings from overseas that husbands or couples displaying elevated levels of withdrawal during conflicts had deteriorating marital satisfaction (Gottman & Krokoff 1989; Smith, Vivian & O'Leary 1990).

Table 2. Major Problems of Hong Kong Family Welfare Society Counselling Service
2001–02

Nature of problems	No. of Cases	Percentage
Marital	1,559	27.9
Emotional/behavioural/personality	817	14.6
Parenting	902	16.2
Parent-child relationship	357	6.4
Mental problem	292	5.2
Adjustment	292	5.2
Child abuse/spouse abuse/elderly abuse/other family violence	137	2.5
Interpersonal relationships	155	2.8
Child care arrangements	157	2.8
Family relationships	226	4.1
Other	667	12
Total	5,579	100

Marital difficulties (27.9%) were the major reason for seeking counselling service in Hong Kong. Just as in the United States, family therapists also found that "couple problems" (fifty-nine percent) exceeded "whole family problems" (forty-two percent) in their caseload (Simmons and Doherty 1995). A follow-up national survey by Doherty and Simmons (1996) of family therapists showed that these clinicians treated about twice as many couples as they did families. Whisman, Dixon and Johnson's survey on practising family therapists also found that couple problems dominated their work profile (1997).

Differences in Participation: In Counselling, Research, Group and Workshop Attendance

Generally, couples are not willing to seek help with marital difficulties until the problems become unbearable. The vast majority of couples wait until one or both partners, usually the female party in the Hong Kong context, are dissatisfied with the marriage and in some degree of suffering, before seeking outside assistance. In Hong Kong, it is more common for women to seek counselling for marital problems, whereas men tend to be less willing to discuss personal concerns. In Young's study (1993) with a sample of 261 marital cases, 86.2% of the principal clients who initially applied for counselling were wives, and 13.8% were husbands. In this sample, 40.5% of the cases had only one spouse engaged in the counselling process. Of cases with both parties involved in counselling, many were "visitors"; only 16.5 % had both spouses engaged in face-to-face interviews with the social worker for half or more of the counselling time, to work on the relationship. However, the gender of the principal client who initiated counselling services was significantly associated with the partner's participation. The female party was more likely to be involved if her male partner initiated counselling services. In contrast, the male party was less inclined to be involved if the female party initiated the request for services.

Men are less likely to participate in research. In Hong Kong, it has only been possible to engage them in research through personal outreach to small numbers on issues of concern to them, such as domestic violence (陳高凌 2001) and extramarital affairs (Young & Kwan 1995). When domestic violence is concerned, the male partners were motivated to seek services or to attend counselling groups only when their wives left home or threatened divorce. This difficulty of involving men in family matters has also been of concern in the United States (Garfinkel et al. 1998; Gottman 1998).

When family life education group meetings or enrichment workshops are mounted, the authors observe that, usually, it is the wives who first enroll for the husbands and then invite them to attend. Martial enrichment groups in Hong Kong are frequently cancelled due to inadequate enrolment.

Culturally Assigned Self-Perception, and Gender Differences

In a Chinese society such as Hong Kong, there is clear gender differentiation in expectations, responsibilities, role performance and task assignment. This is particularly so in marriage, so that the husband's and wife's experience in the same marriage could be dissimilar. This confirms Bernard's observation that there are two marriages in every marriage, his and hers (1982). This variation in marital experience according to gender is also noted in Hong Kong (Young 1995: 99–103). Consistent findings show that men tend to be more satisfied with their marriage than women are (Bernard 1982; Law et al. 1995; Wong 1995). Regardless of the stage in the family lifecycle, there is greater male satisfaction with the spouse's help at home, and over child care (Rhyne 1981).

Overall, men and women have different conceptions of self-identity. Men tend to emphasize self-other boundaries, whereas women are more concerned with self-other connections. After reviewing the literature, Stets and Hammons (2002: 6–7) observed that:

> Men are oriented more to agency, independence, and autonomy, whereas women are oriented more to communalism, interdependence, and connectedness. Men tend to define the self in terms of individuality, autonomy, and uniqueness. Boundaries between the self and other are delineated. Women define the self more in terms of their configurations of relationships. Self-other boundaries are not as distinct. Essentially, the relation between the self and others tends toward differentiation for men and integration for women.

This seems to be true for Hong Kong. The married Hong Kong man tends to derive his sense of self and status from his achievements outside the home as provider, and inside as a disciplinarian and authority figure. The married Hong Kong woman derives her sense of worth from being integrated into the family network and being central in ensuring the well-being of the family and emotional climate in the home. In this context, as wife and mother, she is sensitive to changing emotional nuances and to relational tensions in the marriage and the family. She takes on and is culturally assigned the responsibility to do something about what goes on inside the family.

The Concept of Face

The men's perspective is of expecting their wives to give them face by showing concern and respect for their capacity to be responsible for the family. It is postulated that men would believe they have lost face if their wives sought outside help to deal with couple and family problems, as this reflects their inadequacy and loss of authority. Chan (2001) used this concept of "losing face" to explain men's reluctance to seek help, especially on family matters.

Li (1999) found that men tend to be more willing to self-disclose about their ability and performance, whereas those with a high tendency to protect "face" would be less likely to disclose what they perceive to be immoral acts. Many men regard seeking help from a counselling service as an admission that their partners consider them unable to solve their own problems. This will be an attack on their self-image and potency. They therefore avoid confronting difficulties in their marriage, presenting a front of a higher tolerance of relational tensions.

Counselling usually involves clients' disclosure of their vulnerabilities, or even acts that they may consider indecent, inappropriate or even immoral, in front of a counsellor, who is a stranger and an outsider to the family. Such exposure is more difficult for men whose upbringing socializes them to be self-reliant, self-sufficient and self-protective. Help-seeking is directly in conflict with these values acquired through socialization (Nadler et al. 1984). Hence, it is a common clinical observation that men are reluctant to come for marital counselling. The situation is even worse when their behaviour is perceived as immoral, such as betrayal due to extramarital affairs, or as irresponsible through gambling and creating huge debts for the family.

Gender Differences in Health, due to Marital Conflict

Hong Kong has little relevant data relating to the effects of marital tension on health, and in this regard it is necessary to rely on studies from other countries to provide some indicators of gender differences.

Couples having relationship problems are more prone to have anxiety, depression, suicidal notions, or substance abuse. They are more likely to have both acute and chronic medical problems and disabilities, such as impaired immunological functioning, high blood pressure, and health-risk behaviours such as susceptibility to sexually transmitted diseases and accident-proneness (Bloom, Asher & White 1978; Kiecolt-Glaser et al. 1987; Burman & Margolin 1992). Further, the children of distressed marriages have a higher chance of having anxiety, depression, behaviour problems, and impaired physical health (Gottman 1994).

Married individuals are healthier than unmarried ones (House et al. 1988). Nevertheless, marital conflict is associated with poorer health (Burman & Margolin 1992; Kiecolt-Glaser et al. 1988). Marital interaction studies suggest possible mechanisms that may account for these links. For example, hostile behaviour during marital conflict results in alterations in immunological (Kiecolt-Glaser *et al.* 1993, 1997), endocrine (Kiecolt-Glaser *et al.* 1997), and cardiovascular functioning (Ewart *et al.* 1991). In general, marital conflict has a more significant health effect on females (Gottman & Levenson 1992; Kiecolt-Glaser *et al.* 1993, 1996, 1997; Malarkey *et al.* 1994).

Fincham, Beach, Harold and Osborne (1997) discovered that relationship functioning was a more important predictor of depressive symptoms in women than in men, for recently married couples. Specifically, they found that, for women, the temporal path was from initial marital dissatisfaction to later depressed mood. They found the converse to be true for men. The husband's path moved from depressed mood in the initial stage to later marital dissatisfaction.

Methodology

As most of the literature on marital work is based on overseas studies, an exploratory study was conducted to find out from social workers their views and understanding of men's and women's differences in dealing with seeking help as regards their marriage. We explored experienced workers' suggestions on how men could be encouraged to involve themselves in marital therapy or marital enrichment workshops. What are the helpful factors and non-helpful variables in encouraging participation in counselling and marital workshops? Also, what strategies could be adopted that could interest both husbands and wives in attending marital enrichment programmes?

Networking was used to generate a purposeful sample. The participants were found through the snowball technique. The criteria for selecting the participants included social workers with more than five years' experience in martial counselling and/or marital enrichment programmes. The first focused group was made up of five female social workers with over ten years of counselling experience. At the end of this focus group discussion, the participants were asked to recommend a male social worker for the study. The second focus group was made up of four male social workers with a range of five to over twenty years of experience in marital counselling. The focus group meetings were scheduled for about two hours. Most of the data collected were derived from focus group discussions. This was supplemented by individual contacts with some participants, for clarification and elaboration on particular aspects that they had contributed. (For details of the guidelines for the focus group, please refer to Appendix 1.)

Findings and Analysis

Taking the Initiative for Counselling/Marital Enrichment Programmes

There was a common observation by all participants of the focus groups that women took the initiative in seeking marital counselling. Even for marital enrichment workshops, it was common for wives to enroll for husbands first and then inform their husbands. Men seem to have a higher tolerance for relationship problems. Hence, they seldom sought counselling services unless there were major disruptions in relationships. One female focus group participant stated: "Men tended to take the initiative if there are major incidents such as wives leaving home after outbursts of violence at home or prolonged gambling problems of the husband, which had left the family in dire financial circumstances". This was echoed by an observation from the male focus group that men tended to come for counselling services as a last resort. One male participant observed that women with more power through having personal, economic or family resources so that they could leave the marriage if the relationship worsened, were more likely to motivate husbands to seek help.

Beginning Sessions: Interesting Couples in Attending Counselling Together

Strategies to reach out to the partners to encourage them to participate in counselling were debated. In this situation, ways and means had to be worked out with the wife to invite the husband to come. If the wife had difficulty involving the husband and sought the support of social worker, the focus group suggested one possible strategy. After getting initial agreement from the wife, the female worker could contact the husband and say: "Your wife is seeking counselling services to deal with her emotional problems. As you are an important person who has a great deal of understanding of her, you are invited for an interview to share your understanding and provide information so that the social worker can help your wife better". This approach suggests a positive stance, validates his importance in the relationship, and makes explicit that he has something essential to contribute which would be helpful to his wife.

Emotion Regulation Especially at Beginning Sessions

The women may have to be briefed about the purpose of the first joint interview. Some may be encouraged not to blame the husband, or others to refrain from excessive emotional outbursts if the husband agrees to come for the joint interview. Also, the worker has to brief both parties not to interrupt, and to avoid personal attacks. For instance, one male social worker reported that, in cases believed to have high emotional reactivity, he would talk with both parties in individual sessions first and say: "If I ask you to remain silent or take 'time out' for a while in some situations, can you support me?"

Sometimes, a woman may take up a blaming stance in the first joint interview. Being blamed and feeling shamed in a discussion on marital discord in front of a female social worker, the husband would not come for second interview. Hence, one male focus group member reported: "The establishment of ground rules such as asking both parties to remain silent for a while if the worker requested this for both to regain composure, or to take turns to listen and to talk, can be very important."

Enhancing Positive Exchanges in First Joint Interview

To establish a conducive and constructive atmosphere, it is helpful for the couple to have some positive experiences during the joint interview. Hence, the worker could ask questions about the history of their romance, to foster the positive memory in both parties. Questions such as the following could help trigger their positive feelings towards each other: What are the things that you enjoy doing together? What did you like about each other when you first met?

Factors Helpful to Maintaining Participation

The focus groups observed that men were more likely to give up working on their marriage. However, as marital work would have a better outcome if both parties were involved, the intervention process has to incorporate strategies to keep the couple in counselling or workshop programmes so that they can work on their difficulties together.

Reframing the Marital Issue from Individual Defects to Relationship Difficulties

The spouse who initiates counselling may attribute blame for the problem to the other partner, without seeing her or his own contribution to the conflict. Exploration of their developmental history and family-of-origin experiences could enable them to address their complaints in the wider context. One participant suggested changing the frame to a relationship issue rather than attributing the problem to the partner's personality. She referred to a couple that was exploring family-of-origin and developmental issues, which enabled the wife to become more tolerant of her husband's "insensitivity". She became aware that, as an orphan, he was raised in a family with no siblings. Whereas she was used to being cared for by others, he was not accustomed to being taken care of and showing concern for others.

Understanding the Underlying Good Intentions of the Partner

The social workers can help the parties involved in counselling to reframe their complaints in order to take into account the needs, wants or yearnings underlying the relationship. Eliciting and making explicit the "good intentions" behind the behaviour of each person, and helping the couple to appreciate each other's hopes, dreams and vulnerabilities could help to keep both parties working on areas of tensions. The worker has to avoid being positioned as a judge to establish who is right or wrong. Rather, the task is to elicit acceptance of themselves and of the partners, and to instill hope through mutual understanding.

Validation of Men's Strength and Contribution in Marriage

The social workers observed that men would tend to stay in counselling services if they received validation in two areas. First, the men would feel less shamed if the worker validated their strength. Second, the men would stay in counselling if the social worker recognized their contribution to the marriage.

Topics of Mutual Concern to Promote Interest

Generally, it was not easy to interest men in attending marital enrichment programmes. However, some social workers found that men would have higher motivation to join marital enrichment programmes if these were packaged to cover topics such as stress management and enhancement of family relationships. For instance, one social worker reported: "It was observed that some couples were interested in coming for a talk on financial rearrangement after debt". The men would be involved more easily if the problem was not pinpointed to an individual but to the problems commonly encountered by couples or due to gender differences. They were interested and would be willing to discuss gender differences and how these differences affected their relationships.

Balance of Attention

Workers have to be extremely sensitive in handling the amount of time attending individually to the husband and the wife. Sometimes, after a joint interview, the wife may seek additional time to see the worker separately for a short session. It is advisable not to agree to this, to avoid giving the husband the impression that the worker is biased towards the wife and that he is being excluded. Rather, the worker could contact her later, and a similar amount of time could be spent with the husband in a separate interview.

Enhancing Understanding of Vulnerabilities

When a spouse, who may be the wife, is experiencing a sense of injury inflicted by the partner, she is able to cope with the situation better if she realizes that the hurt may not be intentional. Rather, the husband's behaviour reflects his dilemmas and vulnerabilities. If the other partner can appreciate the effects of his vulnerabilities on his responses, it is likely to help to improve the relationship.

Non-helpful Factors for the Couple to Stay Involved

Avoidance of Marital Issues

Some women are afraid to allow the worker to contact their husbands about difficulties in the marriage. Hence, they invite their husbands to attend counselling to discuss issues on parenting. The husbands are unlikely to come for second interview because they believe the concern is a parenting problem, which they consider to be the wife's responsibility. One participant quoted an incident in which the wife invited the husband for an interview to serve as volunteer in the family service centre. As stated by the participant: "They had a happy conversation and the husband was willing to be a volunteer. But he refused to come again for joint interview for other reasons". The social worker opined that it was better to address the marital problem directly rather than to focus on marginal issues.

Loss of Neutrality

One participant reported an incident in which the wife dropped out of counseling, as she thought the worker had paid more attention to the husband and over-identified with him. Hence, neutrality and having mutual engagement with both parties are essential.

Other Findings

Couple Resources That Enhanced Marital Improvement

Overall, the focus groups noted that couples that had strong beliefs about the importance of marriage had a higher chance of withstanding marital crisis. Hence, couples that had high expectations of marriage and a belief in marriage as a commitment would not forsake the relationship when facing stress. Also, this commitment was enhanced if they were helped to see the negative impact of marital conflict on children. Hence, it was observed that couples having extramarital affairs could rebuild their marriage if they could rekindle their commitment to the relationship. Of particular relevance in this regard is Rusbult's study on commitment (1993). His research suggests that greater commitment is associated with more constructive, accommodative responses to negative behaviour from a partner (Rusbult et al. 1991, 1998). This phenomenon confirms some of the observations of the focus group.

Positive changes occurred if the partners were able to acknowledge the limitations and constraints of the partner, without contempt. Acceptance of the negative side of partners and changes of perception of the character and personality of partners are crucial for marital improvement. The use of family-of-origin work and an understanding of the underlying needs and concerns behind the partner's behaviour are important in facilitating an increase of tolerance and acceptance.

Observations on Gender Differences in Handling Conflicts

One focus group observed that, when couples were in conflict, the women tended to use nagging and complaining to express their dissatisfaction. The men tended to remain silent, as they had difficulty in articulating their dissatisfaction and their emotions. Whereas the men would try to give reasons for or defend their behaviour, the women would resort to more verbal defences and arguments to justify their dissatisfaction. If the women found that they could not argue with the husbands, they would resort to crying or temper outbursts. Men would use avoidance strategies such as retreating or staying silent like a Buddha. If all these strategies failed, the men tended to have outbursts such as throwing things or even resorting to physical action to stop the women from nagging.

It was observed that women valued more understanding and concern from partners, whereas men valued more recognition and respect from the women. The couples would resolve conflicts more easily if one party was willing to express his or her vulnerability rather than using power to coerce the other side into changing. One of the negative responses observed was that, if one partner used divorce as a threat, the other party would consider this to be a lack of commitment to the marriage or believe that the other party was trying to overwhelm him or her with threats. Another negative response was contempt between couples. The partner would feel angry and hurt if the partner used contempt in dealing with the conflicts between them.

Discussion

Questioning Emphasis on Communication Skills Training

The participants in the focus groups found that communication skills training was not a critical factor in helping the couples to make changes. Rather, they observed that many couples had good communication skills, but they tended not to use these because of the strong emotional reactivity between them.

In our clinical training and consultation, we observe that communication skills training is a common strategy used by social workers and counsellors, particularly by newly trained social workers. This is reinforced by theory and research that emphasize communication skills training in marital enhancement, which suggests promoting "I" messages, reflective listening and enhancing positive exchanges (Jacobson & Margolin 1979).

The focus group participants considered that teaching communication skills alone would not be very helpful in improving marital relationships. It could be postulated that, as couples in conflict have negative attributions towards the motives and behaviour of one another, as well as patterns of negative responses, verbal communication training by itself could not tackle problems, due to a lack of positive interaction behaviour. In a Hong Kong study based on the Minnesota

Couples Communication Program, after four sessions of three hours' communication training, Pang (1998) found that there was no substantial improvement of communication skills among the couples.

The findings from the focus group identified one of the major mechanisms of change in marital counselling is to enhance acceptance and to change the negative perceptions of partners towards each other. We suggest that the initial focus of counselling and marital enrichment workshops for Chinese couples should not be focused only on skills training, on "I message", "listening" and "contingency reinforcement contract" or on "calming" emotions. Rather, enhancing acceptance and mutual empathy and negotiating issues of mutual concern are essential to sustain a marriage, as these contribute to *affirmation of affection for each other*. Couples who have learnt listening and expression skills may not utilize these competencies if they have negative attributions towards the behaviour and intention of their partners.

The second insight is that marital counselling and marital workshops could focus more on *self-affirmation*, which is taking care of one's self, through fostering self-belief and self-nurture. This also requires facing what one is potentially afraid of finding out about the negative aspects of the relationship, and searching for underlying personal needs and unfulfilled wants which may be holding back readiness to rectify problems. This perspective therefore provides belated recognition of the insight afforded by an early study by Birchler *et al.* (1975). These investigators showed that distressed spouses are not characterized by skill deficits so much as by failure to use the skills that are apparent in their transactions with strangers. Indeed, verbal skills in the context of marital discord may contribute to more rather than less dissatisfaction (Burleson & Denton 1997). Such considerations provide grounds for suspecting that aspects which most evidently differentiate between distressed and non-distressed marriages are the couple's attributions of each other's behaviour, expectations of marital improvement after counselling, and different assumptions about marriage.

Focus on Promoting Positive Interaction and Care Giving

Further, it is suggested that enhancing acceptance and intimacy between Chinese couples involves acknowledging the influence of their families of origin on their values and expectations in marriage. Law (1989), in a Hong Kong study, found a strong correlation between positive feedback and less negative feedback in couples with higher intimacy. In this study, positive feedback includes expressions of disagreement accompanied by an elaboration of one's personal feelings, as well as recognition of the partner's feelings, and allowing time for the other to elaborate his or her concerns. From the findings of the focus groups, we suggest that *mutual sharing of vulnerabilities behind strong emotions would enhance cohesion*. If the couple can share their vulnerabilities and *receive validation and support from the partner*, intimacy increases. Emotion is now recognized as motivational, a guide to adaptive behaviour, and a positive organizing force in human functioning (Damasio 1994; Johnson & Greenberg 1994). Much of marital counselling work involves helping couples to filter their negative interaction patterns by understanding underlying needs and vulnerabilities in order to facilitate acceptance of each other's expressions of strong emotions, such as anger and depression.

When one partner over-functions in relation to the other, so that responsibilities are unequally shared, the result is an accumulation of resentment and anger in the over-functioning partner (Napier 1999). Napier found that men are often unaware of the partner's anger, especially about inequalities in the sharing of tasks, until resentment is suddenly expressed at a later stage. This conflict becomes further intensified if the women have to go out to work. Hence, one focus group observed that, when women initiate complaints, it might be that they feel they have over-functioned in the relationship and have not been taken care of adequately. The mutual sense of being cared for serves to validate each spouse as being special and important in the relationship.

Gender of the Social Worker

While considering gender issues in offering services, surely the gender of the social workers could be a significant factor in affecting the involvement of the male party. As the majority of the social workers rendering marital counselling services are female, some men may find it difficult to talk about their marital difficulties and sexual problems in front of a female worker. However, they might also feel hesitant about talking with a male worker, if their wives seemed to be understood more by a stranger than by the husband. When a male worker engages the husband after the wife has initiated counselling, it would be helpful if the worker is perceived as a comrade who shows deep understanding of men's suffering and difficulties in marriage. The female focus group suggested that it would be better if the female worker contacted the husband for his assistance in helping his wife. Her approach could be that she was enlisting his views as the husband of her client, so that he could provide valuable information to help his wife. In most agencies, male workers tend to be assigned marital cases with males as the applicant of services. Generally, the women will respond if they are asked to come as resource persons.

Conclusion

The present article reports on the major findings of a limited focus group study undertaken among experienced social workers involved in marital counselling and marital enrichment.

To meet the needs of couples participating in counselling or enrichment programmes, the consensus arising from the focus groups is that activating a positive stance in enhancing acceptance and care-giving is most helpful in developing cohesion and a sense of well-being in marital relationships. When couples receive validation and support from each other, they could feel safe about sharing their vulnerabilities and yearnings. The spouses would be more able to share anxieties over their "feared selves" if they are confident that this behaviour will not activate attack and counter-attack. Often, through reviewing their conceptions of marriage and affirming their commitment, counselling could facilitate couples staying together in facing stress and crises. It is also essential to enable couples to develop positive alternative responses apart from complaining, avoidance, physical action or contempt in dealing with conflicts. Instead of attributing the problem to character faults or defects in the partner, they could work together to search for resources within the relationship to cope with the dilemmas and demands of their marriage.

Perhaps the most interesting finding from this study is that promoting a constant flow of positive interaction between the spouses is more conducive to marital well-being than emphasizing skills in verbal communication or conflict resolution. Gottman upholds this perspective. Further, he recommends working with couples to developing a robust emotional bank account of mutuality, intimacy, goodwill and respect (Gottman 1999).

This discussion is a small step forward in tapping into the practice experience of frontline practitioners working with couples. Further research on the viewpoints of clients who have received counselling services or participated in enrichment workshops would be helpful in providing other insights in working with couples.

References

Bernard J. (1982). *The future of marriage*. (Revised Edition) New Haven, CT: Yale University Press.

Birchler G.R., Weiss R.L. and Vincent J.P. (1975). Multimethod analysis of social reinforcement exchange between martially distressed and non-distressed spouse and stranger dyads. *Journal of Personality and Social Psychology. 31*: 349–60.

Bloom B., Asher S. and White S. (1978). Marital disruption as a stressor: A review and analysis. *Psychological Bulletin 85:* 867–94.

Burleson B.R. and Denton W.H. (1997). The relationship between communication skill and marital satisfaction: Some moderating effects. *Journal of Marriage and Families 59:* 884–902

Burman B. and Margolin G. (1992). Analysis of the association between marital relationships and health problems: An interactional perspective. *Psychological Bulletin 112*: 39–63.

Census and Statistics Department (2003). *Demographic trends in Hong Kong 1981–2001*. Retrieved September 11, 2003 from Hong Kong Government Web site: http://www.info.gov.hk/gia/general/200212/23/atablee.htm

Chan Ko Ling (1998). *An evaluation report on group therapy for the male perpetrators, the battered women and the children witnessing the domestic violence* (Research report). Hong Kong: Hong Kong Family Welfare Society.

Damasio A.R. (1994). *Descartes' error: Emotion, reason and the human brain*. New York: Putnam.

Doherty W.J. and Simmons D.S. (1996). Clinical practice patterns of marriage and family therapists: A national survey of therapists and their clients. *Journal of Marital and Family Therapy 22*: 9–25.

Ewart C.K., Taylor C.B., Kraemer H.C and Agras W.S. (1991). High blood pressure and marital discord: Not being nasty matters more than being nice. *Health Psychology 103:* 155–63.

Fincham F.D., Beach S.R.H., Harold G.T. and Osborne L.N. (1997). Marital satisfaction and depression: Different causal relationships for men and women? *Psychological Science 8:* 251–357.

Fern E.F. (2001). *Advanced focus group research*. Thousand Oaks, CA: Sage.

Garfinkel I., McLanahan S., Meyer D. and Seltzer J. (Eds.) (1998). *Fathers under fire: The revolution in child support enforcement*. New York: Russell Sage Foundation.

Gottman J.M. (1999). *The marriage clinic: A scientifically based marital therapy*. New York: W.W. Norton.

Gottman J.M. (1998). Towards a process model of men in marriage and families. In A. Booth and A. Crouter (Eds.) *Men in families: When do they get involved? What differences does it make?* Mahwah, NJ: Lawrence Erlbaum.

Gottman J.M. (1994). *Why marriages succeed or fail.* New York: Simon and Schuster.

Gottman J.M. and Krokoff L.J. (1989). Marital interaction and satisfaction: A longitudinal view. *Journal of Consulting and Clinical Psychology 57:* 47–52

Gottman J.M. and Levenson R.W. (1992). Marital processes predictive of later dissolution: Behavior, physiology, and health. *Journal of Personality and Social Psychology 63:* 221–33

Hong Kong Family Welfare Society (2002). *Survey on conflict resolution of married people.* Hong Kong: Hong Kong Family Welfare Society.

Hong Kong Government (2000). *Hong Kong annual digest of statistics.* Hong Kong: Census and Statistics Department.

House J.S., Landis K.R. and Umberson D. (1988). Social relationships and health. *Science 241:* 540–5.

Jacobson N.S. and Margolin G. (1979). *Marital therapy: Strategies based on social learning and behavior exchange principles.* New York: Brunner/Mazel.

Johnson S.M. and Greenberg L.S. (1994). *The heart of the matter: Perspectives on emotion in marital therapy.* New York: Brunner/Mazel.

Kiecolt-Glaser J.K., Fisher L.D., Ogrocki P., Stout J.C. and Speicher C.E. (1987). Marital quality, marital disruptions and immune function. *Psychosomatic Medicine 49:* 13–34.

Kiecolt-Glaser J.K., Kennedy S., Malkoff S., Fisher L., Speicher C.E. *et al.* (1988). Marital discord and immunity in males. *Psychosomatic Medicine 50:* 213–29.

Kiecolt-Glaser J.K., Malarkey W.B., Chee M., Newton T., Cacioppo J.T. *et al.* (1993). Negative behavior during marital conflict is associated with immunological down-regulation. *Psychosomatic Medicine 55:* 395–409.

Kiecolt-Glaser J.K., Newton T., Cacioppo J.T., MacCallum R.C., Glaser R. *et al.* (1996). Marital conflict and endocrine function: Are men really more physiologically affected than women? *Journal of Consulting and Clinical. Psychology 64:* 324–32.

Kiecolt-Glaser J.K., Glaser R., Cacioppo J.T., MacCullum R.C., Snydersmith M. *et al.* (1997). Marital conflict in older adults: Endocrine and immunological correlates. *Psychosomatic Medicine 59:* 339–49.

Law C.K., Chan C.L.W., Young K., Ko G., Wong Y.C., Mehram T., Chang K.C. and Li L. (1995). *Contemporary Hong Kong families in transition.* Hong Kong Women's' Foundation and Department of Social Work and Social Administration, University of Hong Kong, Monograph Series No. 21.

Law M.S. (1989). *An exploratory study of the communication pattern and level of intimacy among married couples.* Unpublished Master's Thesis, Department of Social Work and Social Administration, University of Hong Kong.

Li C.L.S.D. (1999). *Face orientation and self-disclosure of ability and morality: Does gender make a difference?* Unpublished Doctoral Dissertation, Department of Social Work and Social Administration, University of Hong Kong.

Nadler A., Maler S. and Friedman A. (1984). Effects of helper's sex, subjects' androgyny, and self-evaluation on males' and females' willingness to seek and receive help. *Sex Roles, 10,* 327–39.

Napier A.Y. (1999). Experiential approaches to creating the intimate marriage. In J. Carlson and L. Sperry (Eds.). *The intimate couple.* Philadelphia, PA: Brunner/Mazel.

Pang Hang-hang (1998). *An outcome study of couples communication training group.* Unpublished Master's Thesis, Department of Social Work and Social Administration, University of Hong Kong.

Rhyne D. (1981). Bases of marital satisfaction among men and women. *Journal of Marriage and the Family 43(4): 941–55.*

Rusbult C.E. (1993). Understanding responses to dissatisfaction in close relationships: The exit-voice-loyalty-neglect model. In S. Worchel and J.A. Simpson (Eds.) *Conflict between people and groups: Causes, processes, and resolution.* Chicago, IL: Nelson-Hall.

Rusbult C.E., Bissonnette V.I., Arriaga X.B. and Cox C.L. (1998). Accommodation processes across the early years of marriage. In T.N Bradbury (Ed.) *The developmental course of marital dysfunction.* New York: Cambridge University. Press.

Rusbult C.E., Verette J., Whitney G.A., Slovik L.F. and Lipkus I. (1991). Accommodation processes in close relationships: theory and preliminary empirical evidence. *Journal of Personality and Social Psychology 60:* 53–78.

Simmons D.S. and Doherty W.J. (1995). Defining who we are and what we do: Clinical practice patterns of marriage and family therapists in Minnesota. *Journal of Marital and Family Therapy 21:* 3–16.

Smith D.A., Vivian D. and O'Leary K.D. (1990). Longitudinal predictors of marital discord from premarital expressions of affect. *Journal of Consulting and Clinical Psychology 58:* 790–98.

Stets J.E. and Hammons S.A. (2002). Gender, control and marital commitment. *Journal of family issues 23(1):* 3–25.

Wan Yee-nui (1996). *A study of marital satisfaction and stability of China wives and Hong Kong husbands.* Unpublished Master's Thesis, Department of Social Work and Social Administration, University of Hong Kong.

Whisman M.A., Dixon A.E. and Johnson B. (1997). Therapists' perspectives of couple problems and treatment issues in couple therapy. *Journal of Family Psychology 11:* 361–6.

Wong Yu Cheung (1995). Gender issues in marital satisfaction. Unpublished Master's Thesis, Department of Social Work and Social Administration, University of Hong Kong.

Yeung C. and Kwong Wai Man (1998). A study of the attitudes of pre-marital couples toward marriage in Hong Kong. *Hong Kong Journal of Social Work, 32(1):* 71–84.

Young K. (1995). *Understanding marriage: A Hong Kong case study.* Hong Kong: Hong Kong University Press.

Young K. (1993). *Marriages under stress: A report on marriage counselling cases at the Hong Kong Family Welfare Society and the Hong Kong Catholic Marriage Advisory Council.* Resource Paper Series No. 20 Hong Kong: Department of Social Work and Social Administration, The University of Hong Kong.

Young K. and Kwan R. (1995). The men speak out over their extramarital activities in China. *Hong Kong Journal of Social Work 29(1):* 47–59.

陳高凌 (2001).〈義與面子在華人家庭暴力裡的運作及對治療之啟示〉。(The operation mechanism and implications of Yi and the concept of face in family violence of Chinese families)《本土心理學研究》第十五期,第63–111頁。

Appendix 1: Guidelines for Focus Group

Introduction

In your experience, which partner, husband or wife, initiated attending counselling services/marital enrichment (ME) workshops?
Generally, what were the responses from the partner being invited?
According to your observation, what motivated the partner to initiate the contact? What made the other party agree to be involved/not involved?

Counselling Process

What were the couples' expectations towards self + the partner in receiving counselling services/marital enrichment workshops?
What were the helpful factors/non-helpful factors that helped couples to improve the marital relationship in the counselling process/marital enrichment workshops?

Conflicts

From your experiences, what are the differences between male and female partners in solving conflict?

Promotion Strategies

If we have to encourage people who are resistant to receiving counselling services/marital enrichment programmes, what are your suggestions for social workers to encourage them to join such programmes?
How could partners encourage their spouses to be involved in marital enrichment workshops/counselling services?

11

The Changing Nature and Ideology of Marriage in Hong Kong

C.W. LAM., W.M. LAM, TIMOTHY Y.K. LEUNG

Marriage is normally assumed to be heterosexual and monogamous, and embedded with enduring love and companionship as its ideal purposes. This model of marriage, however, is facing serious challenges in many countries, as illustrated by an increase in the divorce rate and the proportion of single parent families. In contemporary Hong Kong society, the meaning and function of marriage has also been challenged.

In this chapter, we first present a general picture of the contemporary scene in regard to family and marriage systems in Hong Kong. Then, we discuss how we should respond to changes and what social welfare professionals could do in the face of the challenges posed by the changing marriage system.

The Changing Nature and Ideology of Marriage

A marriage is a legally recognized union between a man and a woman in which they are united sexually; cooperate economically; and may give birth to, adopt, or raise children (Strong *et al.* 2001). In most countries, marriage is also normally assumed to be heterosexual and monogamous, and embedded with enduring love and companionship as its ideal purposes. This model of marriage, however, is facing serious challenges, as illustrated by several phenomena. The divorce rate and the proportion of single parent families are growing. The birth rate and the marriage rate are in decline, and alternative family types, such as stepfamilies, cohabitation and poly-relations, are becoming popular.

To take the United States as an example, during the last half of the twentieth century, divorce replaced death as the most common end point of marriage, for the first time in human history. In fact, from 2000 to 2002, the divorce rate remained at the high rate of four per 1000 population (National Center for Health Statistics 2003a), and thirty-three percent of all births in the US in 1998 were to unmarried women (Nelson and Moore 2001: 9). Hence, it is no surprise that families with children headed by a single parent grew from twenty-four percent to twenty-eight percent of all households from 1990 to 2000 (Annie E. Casey Foundation 2003). What is more depressing is that people who still believe in the marital relationship and get married for a second time also often end up separated or divorced from their spouse, the failure rate being twenty-three percent after five years of marriage and thirty-nine percent after ten years (National Center for Health Statistics 2002). Coincidentally, from 1990 to 1999, there was a nine percent decline in the birth rate, from 6. 78 million to 6.28 million per year (National Center for Health Statistics 2003b).

As traditional marriage declines, alternative dyadic relationships such as cohabitation have emerged. "Non-marital co-parenting" has risen in the US, as many couples see cohabitation as an alternative to marriage while being committed as parents of their children (Pinsof 2002). The percentage of children born to unmarried women increased from six percent in 1960 to thirty-two percent in 2000 (Markman, Stanley, and Blumberg 2001). In the US, cohabiting, marriage and childbearing, which used to go together in adult life, are now three different events that people can choose separately. The National Center for Health Statistics (2002) reports that three-quarters of women in the US have been married and about half have cohabited outside of marriage by the age of 30. It seems that cohabitation serves as an alternative marriage, or as a halfway house, allowing people to get to know their partners before getting married. However, as Brown and Booth (1996) state, some research shows that premarital cohabitation is positively associated with unstable marriages. Couples that cohabit before marriage have more marital conflict and a higher chance of divorcing than do couples that do not. These findings, though indicative rather than conclusive, seem to suggest that the traditional marriage is still the safest model of pair bonding.

In contemporary Hong Kong society, the meaning and function of marriage has been challenged, but there has been relatively little public discussion of the issue, and there is a shortage of locally conducted research into what people really think about marriage. As far as the academic field is concerned, this is a picture that is not in any way commensurate with the importance that is attached to marriage by our society. Nevertheless, based on the limited research available, we first present a general picture of the contemporary scene in regard to family and marriage systems in Hong Kong. Then, we discuss how we should respond to changes and what social welfare professionals could do in the face of the challenges posed by the changing marriage system.

Changes in the Family Structure in Hong Kong

As a result of socio-economic changes that occurred in the previous century, the family structure in Hong Kong has been changing. Although there was a dearth of research on the evolution of the family system in Hong Kong before World War II, some researchers postulated that the family structure in the territory at that time was mostly of the extended type with incomplete membership composition. The reason was that, after the colonization of Hong Kong in 1841, a large number of Chinese emigrated from the Mainland to the colony because of better job opportunities. Temporarily, most of them stayed with families of relatives in Hong Kong (Maranell and Heckmann 1975). With the rapid socio-economic expansion and population growth of the colony after World War II, the immigrants put down roots and formed their own families. As a result, the stem family system became the major type of family system in Hong Kong, taking the form of a single-track, three-generation family on the paternal side, and consisting of the parents and usually one married son with his family (Maranell and Heckmann 1975). During the 1960s, when Hong Kong became industrialized, the small nuclear family consisting of two parents and their children had become the norm. This conjugal type of family was the general pattern that most middle-class Chinese families in Hong Kong had adopted by the 1970s (Wong 1972).

Accompanying the increase in the number of small nuclear families was the improvement of the status of women in Hong Kong that began during the 1970s. The setting up of the social security system in 1971 protected women from economic hardship after separating from their husbands. The introduction of the no-fault divorce policy in 1972 also made women's position in marriage less disadvantageous. The industrialization of Hong Kong during the 1960s provided thousands of job opportunities for young women. Together with the expanding job market, universal education enacted in the early 1970s provided young women with greater opportunities to work in society before marriage. As a result of these changes, women became less financially dependent on their maternal families and husbands than they had been in the past. With more opportunities to engage in social activities, women began to demand more autonomy in marriage as well as respect from their husbands.

However, even though the nuclear family has been the dominant type of family since 1970, some studies suggest that the Hong Kong family system has not been completely replaced by isolated conjugal families (Lee 1991), as children and their nuclear families still maintain a close relationship with parents and siblings. This type of "modified extended family", a term coined by sociologists, appears to be one of the main types of families in Hong Kong (Podmore and Chaney 1974; Lee 1991).

The changes in the family structure and the rise of women's status in the past three decades are the two major factors contributing to the drastic increase of divorce decrees in Hong Kong. The number rose from 354 cases in 1972, to 2,062 cases in 1981, and further to 13,453 in 2001 (Figure 1). In the same period, the crude marriage rate (the number of marriages per 1000 population) recorded a decrease of more than thirty percent. However, recent figures released by the government suggest that there has been a very significant increase in the number of people in Hong Kong delaying marriage. The median age for men to get married was twenty-seven in 1981 but increased to thirty in 2000. For women, the median age increased significantly from 23.9 in 1981 to 27.3 in 2000 (Table 1).

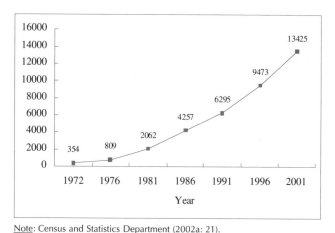

Note: Census and Statistics Department (2002a: 21).

Figure 1.   Number of divorce decrees (1972–2001)

Table 1.   Crude marriage rates (number of marriages per 1,000 population) and
median age at first marriage by sex

		1971	1976	1981	1986	1991	1996	2001
Crude marriage rate by sex	F	11.5	16.3	17.5	14.0	14.1	11.0	9.5
	M	11.1	15.6	16.1	13.2	13.6	11.0	9.9
Median age at first marriage by sex	F	22.9	23.4	23.9	25.3	26.2	26.9	27.5
	M	27.8	26.8	27.0	28.0	29.1	30.0	30.2

Note: Census and Statistics Department (1983, 2002a: 20–3)

Challenges to the Marriage System

One local study on marital quality and the well-being of married adults found that women are not satisfied with marriage and that their dissatisfaction gets stronger the longer they have been married. Married women also show more psychiatric symptoms and midlife crisis problems. However, men were found to be generally satisfied with marriage, increasingly so the longer they have been married (Shek 1995). Another study that sought to examine the pattern of marital power distribution between couples reported that, although fifty-seven percent of the respondents shared the marital decision power equally with their partners, twenty-eight percent of them were dominated by their husbands or wives. The study also found that women who are in husband-dominated relationships experience the highest rates of both verbal and physical martial aggression and the lowest level of marital satisfaction (Tang 1999). Although these studies are not conclusive in regard to the issue of the quality of marriage in Hong Kong, they have cast doubt on the resilience of the marriage system in Hong Kong.

In fact, the marriage system in the territory was seriously affected by some significant political events in the last decade. The political uncertainty generated by the return of Hong Kong to China brought about large-scale migration (Law et al. 1995: 7). A new type of family has emerged, the so-called "astronaut family", which is a family that has immigrated to another country but in which the husband comes back to Hong Kong alone to work. One study that conducted in-depth interviews with twenty-four wives from Hong Kong and Taiwan suggested that the physical absence of husbands has a significant effect upon family relationships and individual experiences. Women reported boredom, loneliness and fear because they lost the emotional support of the immediate and extended families and, more importantly, the daily support of the husband. Conflict between spouses was relatively common and, as a result of the long distance separating them, problems such as extramarital affairs had led to many families breaking up (Waters 2002).

   With the economic reform of China in the 1990s, an increasing number of Hong Kong residents began working across the border. According to Young (1994: 157), the typical Hong Kong male resident working in China is "a trained, skilled man highly motivated in his career at the prime of life, earning a high salary in a low salary environment, and living away from his family and home". Therefore, these men attract young women who seek constant financial support. The number of extramarital affairs between Hong Kong male residents and women in the Mainland has risen, as has the number of individuals seeking professional help because of affairs. For instance, the number of extramarital counselling cases at the Caritas Family Service, one of the major NGOs in Hong Kong, increased from 341 (forty-seven percent of all marital counselling cases) in 1993 to 527 (sixty-two percent of all marital counselling cases) in 1994 (Guo 1995: 17). The number further rose to 654 in 2002, and the enquiries about extramarital affairs through a hotline operated by the agency increased to a record of 180,272. Hotline callers whose partners had affairs while working in China constituted the second major source of enquiries (Caritas 2003: 8). The partners experienced depression, anger, anxiety, helplessness and conflicting emotions at discovery of the affairs (Young *et al.* 1995). The level of intimacy between partners and the trust relationship in the marriage are upset. Divorce is often the final outcome.

Diverse Family Types in Hong Kong

With the increase in the divorce rate, single-parent families are becoming more common in Hong Kong. The number of such families has increased at an average annual rate of 5.4% over the past decade, much higher than the rate of increase of 0.65% for dual-parent families (married persons living with children aged under eighteen). There were 58,460 single parents in 2001, many more than in 1991 (34,538) and 1996 (42,309). Consequently, the proportion of single parents to married persons living with children has risen from 2.3% in 1991 to 3.7% in 2001 (Census and Statistics Department 2002c). Although the number of single fathers has increased moderately from 1991 to 2001, single mothers far outnumber their male counterparts, having shown nearly a two-fold increase during this period (Table 2). The number of single parents who were divorced or separated increased from 18,700 in 1991 to 44,424 by 2001. In contrast, the number of single parents who were widowed dropped from 15,838 to 14,036 over the same period.

Table 2. The number of single parents and the distribution of the population by sex and marital status

		1991	1996	2001
Number of single parents[a]	F	23,059	30,402	45,072
	M	11,479	11,907	13,388
Number of single fathers per 1000 single mothers[a]		498	392	297
Never married (%)[b]	F	29.0	28.9	30.1
	M	36.5	34.2	33.9
Married (%)[b]	F	59.8	59.3	57.2
	M	60.2	62.0	61.7
Divorced/separated (%)[b]	F	1.4	2.2	3.3
	M	1.1	1.6	2.1
Widowed (%)[b]	F	9.8	9.6	9.4
	M	2.2	2.2	2.2

Note: Census and Statistics Department ([a]2002c: 17; [b]2002b: 17).

In spite of the subject's growing importance, studies on single parents in Hong Kong are limited. Two studies indicate that single parents are worse off financially than parents in two-parent families (Lee, Law, and Tam 1999; Law 1991). Having a lower level of education and being a single parent were found to be the main reasons why single parents have a lower household income. Moreover, the studies found that single parents in Hong Kong do not have adequate time for child care or recreational activities, and they have more difficulties in child care than do their married counterparts. In sum, these two studies show that life satisfaction is directly affected by single-parenthood. This may be a result of the stigma that is still attached to single parents. Some local studies have shown that stigmatization is negatively related to the psychological well-being of single parents in Hong Kong. In two surveys of public opinion of single-parent families, it was found that more than forty percent of the respondents had a negative view of single parents, and as many as thirty-four percent of the respondents agreed with the statement "a single-parent family is an abnormal family type" (Ngan et al. 1998; Rudowicz 2001).

Remarriage is a way out for divorced persons if they do not want to live as single parents. According to the Census and Statistics Department (2002e: 56), the number of registered marriages in which one party is marrying for the first time and the other party has been married before increased from 1,891 in 1981 to 4,689 in 1996. Local research on remarriage is limited. A study on a sample of single parents (with fewest available resources, such as recipients of Public Assistance or clients of family service agencies) in the early 1980s reported that sixty percent of the respondents did not consider the prospect of remarriage because they did not have faith in marriage, lacked self-confidence, had a low self-image or were worried about their children's welfare after remarrying (Young *et al.* 1985). Another recent study that looked at the remarriage considerations of single parents, however, suggests that those subjects with better education and a higher income, and who are more resourceful and capable in caring for themselves and others, are expected to have a high level of satisfaction in remarriage (Chiu and Kwan 1997). One qualitative study exploring the personal experiences of remarried persons with dependent children points out that remarried persons experience their family relationships as a triangle (Tai 1998). This self-spouse-child triangle forms the basic triangle of the stepfamily. Experiences of remarried persons are closely related to their extended families, their social networks and the socio-cultural context. As far as these external factors are concerned, the study found that most of the respondents believed that the social attitude towards remarriage in Hong Kong has become more liberal. Some of the respondents felt accepted by the spouse's extended family or by society.

Nevertheless, people in Hong Kong still seem to attach a stigma to cohabitation. Although research on cohabitation as an alternative form of a dyadic relationship is rare in Hong Kong, a study of the attitudes of 284 premarital couples (who were participants in marriage preparation programmes run by a Catholic agency) found that 88.7% of the respondents explicitly rejected cohabitation. The main reason for the minority (about one-tenth of all respondents) that considered cohabitation as an alternative to legal marriage was that they felt "there is very little difference between cohabitation and legal marriage so long as the partners are committed to each other". They also felt that "cohabitation allows me to test whether the relationship can work before committing myself further in a legal marriage" (Yeung and Kwong 1998: 75). This finding is consistent with a Western study that found that most cohabiting couples felt strongly that they were committed to the relationship and maintained that cohabitation and marriage were not essentially different (Jamieson *et al.* 2002). It seems that, for some people in Hong Kong, there is a lot of tension between the quest for a long-lasting relationship and the lack of faith in the sustainability of marriage. Yet, it is worth noting that another Western study on cohabitation found that couples who had cohabited before marriage had greater marital instability than couples who had not. This finding indicates that engaging in premarital cohabitation may lead to poorer communication after marriage and greater marital instability (Cohan and Kleinbaum 2002).

Although the popularity of different family types in Hong Kong has yet to be documented, the above-mentioned social trends point to the decline of the traditional form of family and marriage constituting a couple and a child (or children) in a long-lasting relationship. In fact, the crude birth rate in Hong Kong has steadily declined, from 16.8 live births per 1,000 people in 1981 to 7.2 in 2001 (Table 3). The number of households with no children has increased dramatically in the last two decades.

Table 3. Median age of women at first childbirth, and crude birth rate

	_1981_	_1986_	_1991_	_1996_	_2001_
Median age of women at first childbirth	25.1	26.6	28.1	28.8	29.3
Crude birth rate per 1000 population	16.8	13.0	12.0	9.9	7.2

Note: Census and Statistics Department (2002a: 17; 2002d: 17, 73).

A Review of the Changes in Marriage Values in Hong Kong

The struggle to change the outmoded marriage laws in Hong Kong has lasted over twenty years, from the post-war years to 1970, when the _Marriage Reform Bill_ (1971) was eventually passed (Lam 2004). Before the bill was enacted, the Chinese customary marriage[1] based on "Tsing Law" had been recognized by the British colonial government and had been legally valid in Hong Kong since 1843. The pertinent specifications allowed men to take concubines and _kim tiu_ marriages, which essentially permitted polygamous unions.[2] In 1972, Hong Kong adopted the _Matrimonial Causes Ordinance_, which defines the irretrievable breakdown of a marriage as the sole ground for divorce. Accordingly, petition for divorce could only be presented to the court if a couple had been married for at least three years, and with at least one of the following to have occurred as proof of the irretrievable breakdown of a marriage: "adultery", "unreasonable behaviour", "two-year desertion", "two-year separation with consent" and "five-year separation without consent" (Liu 1999; Chiu, Lee, and Lam 2002).[3]

In recent years, the number of divorces in Hong Kong has been increasing. One of the reasons for this is that the procedure for getting a divorce was simplified after the _Matrimonial Causes Ordinance_ was amended by the government in 1996. In accordance with the Hong Kong Law Reform Commission's recommendations, firstly, the three-year bar to present a petition for divorce was lifted. Moreover, in addition to the five grounds for proof of the breakdown of a marriage, a "joint application" procedure was introduced, whereby an application for divorce could be made after just one year of marriage (Chiu, Lee, and Lam 2002; Liu 1999).[4]

The changes of law and in the divorce rate indicate that Hong Kong people's attitudes toward marriage have been constantly evolving in the past few decades, though the development still remains uncertain. For instance, using a convenient sample of young couples joining a premarital preparation programme (N=284), Yeung and Kwong (1998) found that the respondents treasured the virtue of traditional marriage values, such as a long-lasting marital relationship. Most of the respondents (ninety-eight to ninety-nine percent) in this study agreed that "sharing of love and care", "mutual help, support and encouragement", and "marriage as companionship" are the three major reasons for getting married. This shows that a "companionship marriage model" has gained widespread acceptance in Hong Kong. Moreover, the young couples in the study still strongly supported marriage, 74.6% believing that extramarital affairs were unacceptable. Furthermore, 36.8% of people surveyed in 2001 considered divorce unacceptable (Hong Kong Federation of Youth Groups 2002). A study found that most young people believe that one should not be engaged in more than one relationship at a time. "Courtship followed by marriage" was considered the proper order of things among the respondents. A majority of the respondents considered getting married to be their goal in life. A relatively high number of the respondents had a positive attitude, saying that they were confident they could sustain a marriage forever (Social Sciences Research Center 2003). Hence, it appears that there is still a strong view of marriage as a lifelong commitment, in the younger generation (aged from twenty to thirty) in Hong Kong.

Notwithstanding the uncertain development of people's attitude towards marriage, the decline of traditional marriage in Hong Kong is still evident (refer to Figure 1 for statistics). Moreover, it is not a process that has already ended and can now be reviewed. Rather, it is an ongoing development, and its effect can be felt in our daily lives.

Is the so-called breakdown of the institution of marriage a sign of impending social change? Will people necessarily suffer from this change? Can we prepare ourselves, harness this change and take full advantage of it? In answering these questions, we found that we again reached the limits of the social sciences. It is at least the case in Hong Kong that not enough rigorous empirical research has been conducted to support fruitful discussion of marriage. Nevertheless, such a discussion will still be useful insofar as it is able to enlighten us and help us to develop a reflective practice.

How Should We Respond to Changes into the Future?

Advances in technology have had a significant impact on social institutions, human behaviours, norms and values. Marriage, as an important institution of human society, is instilled with elements of change and adaptation. In fact, the signs of change in marital relationships today indicate the adaptation and experimentation of the system in order to survive and cope with the overwhelming confusion in the values and ideology of the pair relationship in present-day societies.

As mentioned, there are many alternatives to marriage, varying from abolition to continuance. The discourse on marriage and its values is neither static nor homogenous but has been interwoven with different streams of thought. In the process, participants have been enriching this intellectual pursuit by drawing from different traditions of their cultures. Different traditions in a common culture sometimes become conflicting ideologies; the picture is in no way a unified one. Given the changes in the social context in which the marriage system functions, the values may need to be constantly reviewed or reconstructed.

Hong Kong's *Marriage Reform Bill* and *Matrimonial Causes Ordinance*, and much of the current discussion on values of marriage reflect an ethnocentric preference for a Judeo-Christian tradition of a companionate partnership in sharing and complementarities. This point of view incorporates the perspective of an intimate relationship that promotes growth for individuals who are autonomous and actualizing, to develop their potentials. Yet, it cannot be assumed that this particular value is still viable in different cultural contexts. In other cultures, the ideal individual may be conceived of in different ways. For instance, the individual may be seen in a more relational sense, so that the self is partly constructed by the relationship with his or her family, as individual autonomy and actualization sometimes give way to the interdependence among family members. In that case, individual identity is not expressed by the individual; rather, it may be expressed in relation to the extended family or community (Allen 1993: 46–7).

To sum up, at the present stage of discourse on marriage and its values, rather than following some specific tenets, we need general principles that can be interpreted on our own cultural basis, while drawing on assistance from a moral commonwealth. To prevent a slide into an anarchic state of morals, however, the first thing needed is a consensus or base line of principles. Although it is very dangerous to have no values at all, it is equally dangerous to follow every moral principle available. What follows is a discussion of certain basic principles that, we believe, will contribute to a more active and reflective debate on marriage and its values in Hong Kong.

The decline of traditional marriage brings in two more fundamental questions: What are our ultimate expectations of marriage? Should we indeed have any expectations of this institution? Three principles are worth considering before answering these questions. The first principle is "continuity". The development of human society cannot be dissociated from its existing basis. This means that the type of system or social institution that can obtain popular consensus and application is usually what follows historical trends.

"Feasibility" constitutes the second concern. Marriage is a two-edged sword, as is the family. Although the functions of these institutions are said to be decreasing, they are still the main sources of support for many people and perform various social functions such as socialization and the provision of daily care[5]. So, we have to accept modified forms of marriage and the family, unless we are prepared to have the worst situation of a disintegrated society, or we are ready to choose different establishments that can continue to perform the existing functions of marriage and family.

Compatibility of the forms of marriage and family with the core values of society is the third concern. We should be clear about what we expect, from a variety of possible options to conventional marriage. It is worth noting that some aspects of conventional marriage are criticized for violating what we consider to be valuable. But what is valuable to us: freedom of choice, personal dignity and self-respect, self-actualization, a sense of well-being? These values point only towards an end; that is, what are our conceptions of the good life? Indeed, our discussion of the marriage system cannot be dissociated from a reconstruction of our expectations of life, interpersonal relationships, society and social institutions.

The above three principles shed light on our discussion of how to respond to the challenges faced by the family and how to assess the evolutionary changes to marriage in the millennium. The principle of *continuity* illustrates the importance of re-examining the general acceptance of the conventional pair relationship if changes to marriage have to be built upon it. Statistics show that, even though marriage is in grave difficulty and is said by some to be dying, it is still popular. In places like Hong Kong, where a form of traditional (Chinese) culture prevails, the marriage rate is still higher than the divorce rate. For instance, the crude marriage rate (number of registered marriages per 1,000 population) in 2002 was 4.7, compared with the crude divorce rate (number of divorce decrees per 1,000 population), which was only 1.91 (Census and Statistics Department 2003: 18; also refer to Figure 1 and Table 1). Many people enter marriage with the hope of achieving personal happiness or self-actualization. Also, many divorced people re-enter marriage with the same hope. This is vivid proof that marriage, as part of human beings' developmental tasks, is deeply rooted in human civilization. It has long been popular and its merits appear to be very much alive. In fact, the existing institution of marriage and the practice of it express and entrench modern people's sense of what they want, what they believe in and what they would like to maintain.

These observations lead us to questions related to the second principle of choosing an alternative to marriage: *feasibility*. How functional is the conventional marriage? It has to be admitted up front that the functions of marriage are on the decline. For example, care and attention can be purchased from psychiatrists, nurses and many other caring agents. Sexual desire can be satisfied by buying and selling activities (such as prostitution or pornography). In short, many needs that used mainly to be met within a marital relationship may now be settled by market activities. However, in other respects, marriage seems irreplaceable. Waite (1995) has found that couples live longer, have a healthier life and report fewer symptoms of mental illnesses such as depression or anxiety. Similarly, Waite and Gallagher (2000) have found that being in a long-term and exclusive marital relationship will result in a more satisfying life. Furthermore, numerous studies have documented the importance of a "complete" family for children (e.g., Wallerstein, Lewis, and Blakeslee 2000), and that children from families with single-parent mothers are more likely to fail at school, to have poor marital relationships and to become welfare dependants (Garfinkel and McLanahan 1986). Children will develop better if they can maintain enduring relationships with *both* parents (Popenoe 1996). Also, the infant mortality rate among children born to unmarried mothers is twice as high as that of children born in wedlock (Mathews, Curtin, and MacDorman 2000, cited in Nelson and Moore 2001).

Although some feminists may query the political correctness of the above findings, it cannot be denied that society today is highly competitive, individualistic and production-oriented. Marriage is the tiny inner world in which we can make good the shortcomings of the greater outer one. Although we can indeed purchase care and attention, the human need for security, permanence, intimacy and deep connectedness with other human beings cannot really be satisfied by buying services in the market. Undeniably, a successful marriage can be our principal source of life satisfaction (Whitehead 1998). We are personally rewarded, and affectionately and sexually gratified in a marital relationship, and it provides us with emotional sustenance. Marriage and the family form a significant and irreplaceable security base for many people today (e.g., as summarized by Hawkins *et al.* 2002). Importantly, recent research has found that marriage does not always end in failure. Couples that have high expectations of, and feel strongly committed to, marriage are able to maintain a better marriage in the long run, as they are more committed to staying in the marriage and initiating changes to improve the relationship with the spouse (e.g., Rosier and Feld 2000).

Clearly, then, marriage still has many merits. However, does the institution embody our overall conception of the good life? What ideals of human development should we expect from changes to the nature and ideology of marriage? These questions lead us to consider the issues surrounding the third principle: *compatibility of the forms of marriage and family with the core values of society.*

Although the question of what constitutes the good life appears to be a matter of *value choice*, it is still possible to make sense of it by asking what makes us human. Both the supporters and the opponents of marriage would agree on one point: that one of the purposes of human relationships is to help individuals to actualize and transcend themselves. Whereas supporters of marriage would defend the institution for its function of gratifying the human need for connectedness (which in turn helps the individuals involved in a relationship to move on to a higher goal of life), opponents demand the institution's abolition due to its tendency to hinder personal growth. Thus, self-actualization and self-transcendence are perhaps values that both parties consider should be found in a marital relationship. If this is true, then self-actualization and self-transcendence are two of the constituents of the good life, and a good society is one that helps an individual to develop his or her capabilities in these areas. Hence, the objective of marriage or its modifications is to provide both an atmosphere and the substance of love, caring and adventure, as this would make human growth, self-actualization and self-transcendence possible. Any "marital" system should be a kind of social arrangement conducive to nurturing each person within a society. Individual freedom within a marriage is not an end but an instrumental value that facilitates room for personal development and generating creativity.

Based on the above principles, a marriage should be a social institution that contributes to the growth of individuals. A desirable marriage should be a relationship in which the partners are committed to their own and to each other's growth. If they decide to have children, the marriage provides a secure base for the nurturing and development of children. It should aim to create a supportive and caring relationship, and increase the security of individuals' identities. It should encourage the sharing of the rewards of one's growth with one's partner, thus facilitating the growth of both oneself and one's partner. Further, this relationship should be flexible enough to allow for change. It should be constantly renegotiated in the light of the changing needs of individuals, and it should seek consensus in decision-making, tolerance of individual growth and openness to new possibilities for growth. The two partners in a marriage should be able to achieve more personal and interpersonal growth together, without losing their individual identities.

A desirable marriage incorporates many facets, including realistic expectations, trust, commitment, mutual affirmation, role flexibility, open and honest communication, and companionate sharing. In sum, marriage will stay with us, but it needs to be flexibly responsive to changing circumstances, for in this age of worldwide and quick exchange of information and ideology, many movements are affecting the transformation of the marriage system. The most prominent are the feminist movement, the marriage movement, the human potentials movement, the gay movement, as well as technological advances in birth control and birth promotion. Hence, the current emphasis should be on the process of discussion of prime values and structures. Through a process of fuller communication, different ideas should be under constant review and examination from people of different cultural and religious backgrounds, thus stimulating innovation. As Rhodes argues: "Dialogue is central to ethics" (1986: 19). Our choices of marriage and family forms need to be flexible enough to accommodate changing life demands and diversity in lifestyle possibilities, including a single life for those who wish to remain unmarried.

This paper has thus tried to open up a thought-provoking area for intellectual and political reflection. The first stage should involve a reassessment of the final goal and the values of marriage, and discussion of how to tailor the system for different cultures as well the consideration of possible new marriage paradigms.

Implications for Social Work Practice and Social Work Education

With regard to social work practice, it has to be noted that the divorce rate has soared over the past two decades (refer to Figure 1) and more people are facing marital stress. Divorce is a difficult experience for the involved parties, as it causes emotional turmoil, economic damage and great psychological adjustment. Many divorcées suffer depression, their children experience stress and adjustment difficulties, and services catering for their needs in Hong Kong are inadequate (Lau 2003a, 2003b). As social workers committed to promoting the well-being of individuals and families, it is important that we be aware that people subscribe to different marriage models. A social worker who is oriented towards a contract model will tend to suggest that a couple consider divorce if they find that the relationship is unable to meet their needs. However, such a social worker may have difficulty understanding the ambivalence of couples who have severe complaints but who are reluctant to proceed with a divorce because the marital model they endorse may be different from that of the social worker. For a client who subscribes to the conventional marriage model, who believes that the purpose of marriage is not to satisfy individual desires and who is committed to raising children in a two-parent family, divorce will always be an extremely difficult, if not impossible, path to choose. Hence, the saying that "to understand others, you need to understand yourself first" is particularly true for social workers providing marital counselling services. When appropriate, it is important for social workers to reveal their values to clients, to let them understand their assumptions and values, in order to facilitate a genuine dialogue and build a worker-client relationship that is based on trust.

Second, social workers must help a couple to clarify the values and assumptions they hold about marriage, as each party may subscribe to a different model of marriage. This is equally important for clients who have begun divorce proceedings, so that the one who has decided to leave can provide an explanation to the partner who is reluctant to have the marriage dissolved.

Couples today have high expectations of marriage and of their partner's ability to satisfy their needs for intimacy, affiliation and economic support. Conflict and disappointment in marriage is common. A recent survey by the Hong Kong Family Welfare Society (2002) found that as many as twenty-five percent of couples in the sample had considered divorce after experiencing marital conflict. Hence, it is important to provide more couple enrichment programmes and help couples to bring about conflict resolution. Social workers have also to be innovative in devising creative strategies to encourage couples to seek help when their marital problems are still in the early stages. In our experience, it is common for couples to only seek professional help when their marital relationship has deteriorated beyond recovery. Also, how to maintain the marital relationship should be an important part of family life education[6], which has to be provided more extensively. For instance, it is important to help couples understand that having a child brings a tremendous amount of stress and demands to the relationship, even for those who have hitherto had a good marriage. Couple groups offer a promising means of service for married persons because, through them, clients feel that they are not alone but have the support of other members of the group. Moreover, modelling and vicarious learning can occur in groups. Such experiences are important for clients who may feel too ashamed to seek help from their relatives or friends in solving their marital problems.

Nevertheless, it has to be noted that, when a growing number of people explore and experiment with alternative forms of dyadic relationships, and diverse family types in Hong Kong gradually emerge, it is likely that the focus and scope of marital counselling would need to change. In the future, we may need to expand the scope of marital counselling to a kind of relationship counselling, to incorporate the counselling services for various forms of intimate relationships.

In regard to social work education, more training in the skills and ethics of social work is needed to equip practitioners to successfully render marital counselling. One goal that could receive more focus is to involve men in counselling services, because they rarely initiate or use such services in Hong Kong. Also, in research and development we need to maintain an evidence-based practice in the martial enrichment programmes. Both academics and practitioners should be sensitive to gender and culture issues. Social work education has to equip social workers with the perspective that our culture needs to be sensitive to gender issues and to the stereotyped roles assigned to men and women within each society.

We are not proposing an uncritical endorsement of marriage as an institution that needs to be preserved at all costs. Social work education has to teach students how to help clients whose marriage is beyond repair to separate in a peaceful manner, especially in order to minimize harm to children. Hence, social work students need to be trained to provide such services as marriage preparation workshops, marital enrichment workshops, and stress management for couples, couple counselling and group counselling, as well as post-crisis therapeutic groups for couples that have experienced extramarital affairs. Knowledge of divorce mediation for couples and family-rebuilding groups for children could also be developed and made available as appropriate.

Social work educators need to be conscious of the fact that, although inequality in marriage is oppressive for both men and women, marriage is a social institution that provides important interpersonal caring and support in our society. If the purpose of social work education is not just to instill practical skills in students, then educators could conduct more study on moral and political issues related to marriage. For those who still believe that marriage is a desirable life choice but find traditional familism restricting, the possibilities of critical familism put forward by Wall and McLemore are worth investigating further:

> Critical familism works toward equality between family members and commitment to the communication needed to implement it, seeing self-giving as important but subordinate to mutuality. It requires an analysis of power relations that block equal regard and a restructuring of the ecology of supports for equal regard families. Finally, critical familism recognizes situations in which family dissolution is necessary and offers support for single parents, stepparents, single adults, and gays and lesbians raising children (Wall and McLemore 2002: 261).

A final point to make is that social workers should advocate a family social policy in Hong Kong that would involve deliberate government action. Family policy should not be just a remedial social policy aimed at resolving family problems (family break-up, welfare dependency etc.) but a constellation of family-related programmes and services to promote family well-being. This could include programmes and policies designed to achieve specified, explicit goals regarding the family, such as child welfare, family counselling, and some housing policies. At a higher level, it could also include endeavours that will strengthen the family system in the six domains of social welfare: health, education, human resources and employment, social services, income maintenance and housing (Kamerman and Kahn 1978; Zimmerman 1995). Hence, as Chow (1996) argues, family policy in Hong Kong should be developed as a coherent plan of action that provides assistance to all kinds of families, so that the family could be preserved as a cohesive unit for the provision of comfort and security, care and welfare to its members.

In its ideal form, family policy should recognize the continuing resilient familism that exists in Hong Kong and draw upon the cultural and social resources of Chinese families. At the same time, family policy should recognize the growing diversity of family forms and be flexible enough to respond to changing needs and problems.

Notes

1   Under Chinese customary law, there were seven ground rules for husbands to divorce their wives: failing to bear sons (not daughters), having a fatal disease, being jealous, failing to obey and serve the parents-in-law, being too garrulous, committing adultery, failing to obey the husband and bringing down the family fortune after marrying into the family. To make the divorce effective, the husband could simply make an announcement in the presence of family members. But women did not have the same right to end a marriage (Lang 1968; Leung 2001).

2   *Kim tiu* (兼桃) marriages mean "a recognized arrangement whereby under exceptional and strictly regulated circumstances a man may formally marry more than one Principal Wife and maintain a separate household in respect to each of them" (Ridehalgh & McDouall 1960: 33; also Committee on Chinese Law and Custom in Hong Kong 1950: 16–7, 201–3). Divorce under Tsing Law refers only to divorcing a wife, as there is no corresponding term for divorcing a husband. Further, women are not entitled to inheritance rights. Indeed, an important endeavour of the postwar women's movement in Hong Kong was to eradicate these various themes of Tsing Law from application in the territory.

3   Adultery means consensual sexual intercourse between a married person and a person of the opposite sex, not the other spouse, during the marriage. Unreasonable behaviour refers to a married person's behaving in such a way that the other spouse cannot reasonably be expected to live with him or her. Desertion refers to a separation that is against the will of one spouse, such as one party abandoning the other or leaving the home with the intention of permanent separation. A married person must be deserted by his or her spouse for a continuous period of at least two years before he or she can file for a divorce. A two-year separation with consent refers to a situation in which a married couple has lived apart for a continuous period of at least two years before filing the petition, and the other spouse agrees to a divorce. A five-year separation without consent refers to a situation in which a married couple has lived apart for a continuous period of at least five years before filing the petition; the other spouse's consent to the divorce is not required.

4   In a joint application, a married couple must prove to the court that the marriage has irretrievably broken down because the couple has lived apart

for a continuous period of at least one year before the application. A written notice signed by both parties one year prior to making the application to the court is also acceptable (Liu 1999). As a result of this new measure, application for divorce has become much simpler and easier.

5   For instance, it was found in 1982 in the US that about 2.2 million Americans were providing assistance to their elderly relatives, and the majority of these caregivers (eighty percent) provided an average of four hours of care daily to their relatives each week. Moreover, people prefer to seek "advice, assistance, or encouragement" from family members when faced with critical problems (quoted in Gilbert, Specht, & Terrell 1993: 4).

6   Family Life Education (FLE) in Hong Kong is a form of community education, both preventive and developmental in nature. It aims at enhancing family functioning and strengthening family relationships by equipping individuals with the knowledge and skills required to cope with changing roles and demands in life. The programmes cover knowledge and skills for improving the quality of family life, promoting interpersonal relationships and preventing family problems. Promotional and educational strategies are commonly used in the delivery of FLE services in Hong Kong. Currently, there are nine family life education service operating agencies providing thirty-eight family life units in Hong Kong (Family Life Education Resource Center 2003b; Social Welfare Department 2003; Lam 1990). The FLE has been integrated into the newly established Integrated Family Service Center as a result of a proposal by a consultancy study of family service conducted in 2000. In recent years, large-scale public education campaigns have also been organized annually to increase public awareness of the importance of harmonious family relationships (Family Life Education Resource Center 2003a).

References

Allen J. (1993). "The Constructivist paradigm: Values and ethics". *Journal of Teaching in Social Work*, 8(1/2), 31–54.

Annie E. Casey Foundation (2003). KIDS COUNT online (www.aecf.org, July 22, 2003).

Brown S.L. and Booth A. (1996). Cohabitation versus marriage: A comparison of relationship quality, *Journal of Marriage and the Family*, 58, 668–78.

Caritas, Hong Kong (2003). *The group facilitators' manual for counseling groups on extramarital affairs* (螢火耀同途，活出我精彩：婚外情輔導小組導師手冊). Hong Kong: Caritas. (In Chinese)

Census and Statistics Department (1983). *Demographic trends in Hong Kong 1971–82*. Hong Kong: the Government Printer: The Government Printer.

Census and Statistics Department (2002a). *Women and men in Hong Kong: Key statistics* (2002 edition). Hong Kong: The Government Printer.

———— (2002b). *2001 Population census thematic report: Women and men.* Hong Kong: The Government Printer.

———— (2002c). *2001 Population census thematic report: Single parents.* Hong Kong: The Government Printer.

———— (2002d). *2001 Population census main report* (Volume 1). Hong Kong: The Government Printer.

———— (2002e). *Demographic trends in Hong Kong 1981–2001.* Hong Kong: The Government Printer.

———— (2003). *A graphic guide on Hong Kong's development (1967–2002).* Hong Kong: The Government Printer.

Chiu H. and Kwan R. (1997). *Decision on remarriage: Research report on a preliminary study of remarried families and remarriage considerations of single parents in Hong Kong.* Hong Kong: Hong Kong Christian Family Service Center.

Chiu M.C., Lee S.W. and Lam M.H. (趙文宗，李秀華，林滿馨). (2002). *Hong Kong laws and practices* (香港法律與實務：中國內地/香港婚姻法實務). Hong Kong: Joint Publishing Co. (In Chinese)

Chow N.W.S. (1996). The Chinese society and family policy for Hong Kong. *Marriage and Family Review,* 22, 55–72.

Cohan C. and Kleinbaum S. (2002). Toward a greater understanding of the cohabitation effect: Premarital cohabitation and marital communication. *Journal of Marriage and the Family,* 64(1), 180–92.

Committee on Chinese Law and Custom in Hong Kong (1950). *Report of the Committee on Chinese Law and Custom in Hong Kong,* Hong Kong: The Government Printer.

Family Life Education Resources Center (2003a). Hong Kong: Social Welfare Department. (http://flerc.swd.gov.hk/lm_io/lm_io_main.asp, October 24, 2003).

Family Life Education Resources Center (2003b). Hong Kong: Social Welfare Department. (http://www.family-land.org, October 24, 2003).

Garfinkel I. and McLanahan S.S. (1986). *Single mothers and their children.* Washington, DC: The Urban Institute (pp. 1–2).

Gilbert N., Specht H. and Terrell P. (1993) *Dimensions of social welfare policy* (3rd edition). Englewood Cliffs, NJ: Prentice Hall.

Guo Zhi-ying (郭志英) (1995). *How to avoid and tackle the problems of extramarital affairs* (婚內婚外：預防及處理婚外情問題). Hong Kong: Caritas Family Service. (In Chinese)

Hawkins A.J., Nock S.L., Wilson J.C., Sanchez L. and Wright J.D. (2002). Attitudes about covenant marriage and divorce: Policy implications from a three-state comparison. *Family Relations,* 51(2), 166–75.

Hong Kong Family Welfare Society (2002). *Survey on conflict resolution of married people.* Hong Kong: Hong Kong Family Welfare Society.

Hong Kong Federation of Youth Groups (2001). *Youth trends in Hong Kong 2001.* Hong Kong: Hong Kong Federation of Youth Groups.

Jamieson L., Anderson M., McCrone D., Bechofer F., Stewart R. and Li Y. (2002). Cohabitation and commitment: partnership plans of young men and women. *Sociological Review,* 50(3), 356–78.

Kamerman S.B. and Kahn A.J. (Eds.) (1978). *Family policy.* New York: Columbia University Press.

Lam Kwai Lan (1990). *An exploratory study of the issues related to the diffusion of innovation in human services — The case of HKCSS's evaluation guideline for FLE programs.* Unpublished MSW dissertation. Hong Kong: University of Hong Kong.

Lam Wai-man (2004). *Understanding the political culture of Hong Kong: The paradox of activism and depoliticization.* New York: M.E. Sharpe.

Lang O. (1968). *Chinese family and society.* Hamden, CN: Archon Books.

Lau Y.K. (2003a). A critical review on social work practice with post-divorce families in Hong Kong, *Hong Kong Journal of Social Work,* 37(1), 73–84.

Lau Y.K. (2003b). Social welfare services for single parent families in Hong Kong: A paradox. *Child and Family Social Work,* 8(1), 47–52.

Law C.K., Chan L.W.C., Young K., Ko L.P.C., Wong Y.C., Mehrani T., Cheng K.C. and Li W.L. (1995). *Contemporary Hong Kong families in transition.* Hong Kong: Hong Kong Women's Foundation, and Department of Social Work and Social Administration, The University of Hong Kong, Monograph Series No.21.

Law C.K. (1991). *Needs on single parent families: A comparative study.* Hong Kong: Hong Kong Family Welfare Society.

Lee Ming-kwan (1991). The organization and change of Hong Kong families (香港家庭的組織和變遷). In Qiao, J. (Ed.) *Chinese families and their changes* (中國家庭及其變遷). Hong Kong: Faculty of Social Sciences, The Chinese University of Hong Kong (pp. 161–70). (In Chinese)

Lee M.Y., Law C.K. and Tam K.K. (1999). Parenthood and life satisfaction: A comparison of single and dual parent families in Hong Kong. *International Social Work,* 42, 139–62.

Leung E. (2001). Speech by Secretary for Justice at the World Women Lawyers' Conference organized by the International Bar Association in London. (/general/200103/01" www.info.gov.hk/gia/general/200103/01, October 23, 2003).

Liu A.N.C. (1999). *Family law for the Hong Kong SAR.* Hong Kong: Hong Kong University Press.

Maranell G.M. and Heckmann F.W. (1975). Dimensions of family bonding: A comparative example. *Journal of Marriage and the Family,* 37, 985–1000.

Markman H.J., Stanley S.M. and Blumberg S.L. (2001). *Fighting for your marriage.* San Francisco, CA: Jossey-Bass.

Mathews T.J., Curtin S.C. and MacDorman M.F. (2000). Infant mortality statistics from the 1998 period linked birth/infant death data set. *National Vital*

Statistics Reports, 48(12). Hyattsville, MD: National Center for Health Statistics.

National Center for Health Statistics (2002). Cohabitation, marriage, divorce, and remarriage in the United States. *Series Report, 23(22)*, 103–6. (www.cdc.gov/nchs/release /02news /div_mar_cohab, July 24, 2002).

National Center for Health Statistics (2003a). Births, marriages, divorces, and deaths: Provisional data for October–December 2002. National Vital Statistics Report, 51(10). (www.cdc.gov/nchs/data/nvsr/nvsr51, June 17, 2003).

——— (2003b). U.S. pregnancy rate down from peak; births and abortions on the decline. (www.cdc.gov/nchs/releases/03facts, October 31, 2003).

Nelson D.W. and Moore K.A. (2001). *The right start state trends, child trends and KIDS COUNT special report.* Baltimore, MD: The Annie E. Casey Foundation Child Trends.

Ngan R., Rudowicz E., Chan W.T. and Au E. (1998). *The psychosocial adjustment and needs of single parent families in Hong Kong.* Hong Kong: Department of Applied Social Studies, City University of Hong Kong.

Pinsof W.M. (2002). The death of "till death us do part": The transformation of pair bonding in the 20th century. *Family Process*, 41(2), 135–57.

Podmore D. and Chaney D. (1974). Family norms in a rapidly industrializing society: Hong Kong. *Journal of Marriage and the Family*, 400–7.

Popenoe D. (1996). *Life without father: Compelling new evidence that fatherhood and marriage are indispensable for the good of children and society.* New York: The Free Press.

Rhodes M.L. (1986). *Ethical dilemmas in social work practice.* London: Routledge & Kegan Paul.

Ridehalgh A. and McDouall J.C. (1960). *Chinese marriages in Hong Kong.* Hong Kong: Government Printer.

Rosier K.B. and Feld S.L. (2000). Covenant marriage: A new alternative for traditional families. *Journal of Comparative Family Studies*, 31(3), 385–94.

Rudowicz E. (2001). Stigmatization as a predictor of psychological well-being of Hong Kong single mothers. *Marriage & Family Review*, 33, 63–83.

Shek D.T.K. (1995). Gender differences in marital quality and well-being in Chinese married adults. *Sex Roles*, 32, 669–715.

Social Sciences Research Center, University of Hong Kong (2003). *Youth in Hong Kong: A statistical profile 2002.* Hong Kong: Commission on Youth.

Social Welfare Department (2003). (http://www.info.gov.hk/swd, October 28, 2003).

Strong B., DeVault C., Sayad B.W. and Cohen T. F. (2001). *The marriage and family experience: Intimate relationships in a changing society* (8th edition). Belmont, CA, USA: Wadsworth/Thomson Learning.

Tai L.Y.Y. (1998). *A study of the experiences of remarried persons in Hong Kong.* Unpublished M.Soc.Sc. Thesis. Hong Kong: Department of Social Work and Social Administration, University of Hong Kong.

Tang C.S.K. (1999). Marital power and aggression in a community sample of Hong Kong Chinese family. *Journal of Interpersonal Violence*, 14(6), 586–602.

Waite L.J. (1995). Does marriage matter? *Demography*, 32, 483–507.

Waite L.J. and Gallagher M.(2000). *The case for marriage*. New York: Doubleday.

Wall J. and Miller-McLemore B. (2002). Marital therapy caught between person and public: Christian traditions on marriage. *Pastoral Psychology*, 50(4), 259–300.

Wallerstein J., Lewis J. and Blakeslee S. (2000). *The unexpected legacy of divorce: A 25-year landmark study*. New York: Hyperion.

Waters J.L. (2002). Flexible families? 'Astronaut' households and the experiences of lone mothers in Vancouver, British Columbia. *Social & Cultural Geography*, 3(2), 117–34.

Whitehead B.D. (1998). *The divorce culture: Rethinking our commitments to marriage and family*. New York: Vintage Books.

Wong F.W. (1972). Modern ideology, industrialization, and conjugalism: The case of Hong Kong. *International Journal of Sociology of the Family*, 2, 139–50.

Yeung C.S.T. and Kwong W.M. (1998). A study of the attitudes of pre-marital couples toward marriage in Hong Kong, *Hong Kong Journal of Social Work*, 32(1), 71–84.

Young K.P.H., Chau B., Li C.K., Tai L.Y.Y., Yim V.P.L. and Wong Y.C. (1995). *Study on marriages affected by extramarital affairs*. Hong Kong: Caritas Family Service, and Department of Social Work and Social Administration, The University of Hong Kong.

Young K.P.H. (1994). Maintaining connections in long-distance marriages: The Hong Kong-China interface. In Rhind, N. (Ed.) *Empowering families: A collection of concepts and methods*. Hong Kong: The Hong Kong Family Welfare Society (pp. 155–73).

Young K.P.H., Li C.K., Cheung M. and Law L. (1985). *A report on single parent families in Hong Kong*. Hong Kong: Department of Social Work, University of Hong Kong.

Zimmerman S.L. (1995). *Understanding family policy: Theories & applications*. Thousand Oaks, CA: Sage Publications.

12

Reconstruction of Traitional Values for Culturally Sensitive Practice

Julia Tao Lai Po-Wah

This chapter examines the challenge posed by social change and professional values to some of the traditional norms and moral imperatives deeply embedded in the Chinese culture. Drawing on the various case studies in this volume, it analyzes the dilemmas confronted by local social workers in trying to reconcile these deeply held cultural norms, such as respect for family obligations, social harmony and the common good, with the goals of supporting individuality, expanding the boundary of personal freedom, promoting fairness and upholding equal respect and concern in their work with married couples or distressed families. As a response to the challenge, this chapter proposes a reconstruction of Chinese traditional notions of the self, family obligation and harmony, through a critical re-examination and reinterpretation of these concepts in the classical Confucian moral tradition as expounded by the early founders Confucius — Mencius and Xunzi. Such a critical reconstruction is useful for avoiding blind conformity and for preventing the fossilization of traditions, by making them more responsive to contemporary concerns while remaining both sensitive to and vigilant of the stabilizing as well as oppressive tendencies of our highly valued cultural norms and practices.

Culture and Practice

Each author in this volume has, in his or her own way, tried to address challenging questions posed by the tension between professional values and the cultural imperatives of the Chinese tradition that still constitutes the bedrock of Hong Kong society. The challenges are further sharpened and rendered more poignant both by social changes emerging from within Hong Kong society and by social movements in the wider international community, bringing about a gradual shift in traditional perspectives and conventional understandings of the meanings of marriage and the values of the family.

Two such social movements are of particular significance to the profession of social work in their practice in relation to marriage and family intervention: the feminist movement and the gay movement in the second half of the last century. These movements have accelerated social change in many contemporary societies, and Hong Kong is no exception. On the one hand, they have successfully drawn attention to victims of oppression, marginalization and domination in society under the existing systems of patriarchy and hierarchy that constitute the basic structure of our society. Importantly, also they have championed the victimized and the powerless, defending their rights to justice, equal respect and autonomy. On the other hand, these movements and changes and the paradigm shifts that they imply, are making both the institution of marriage and of the family increasingly unstable. In particular, the family as an institution is under a great deal of attack from the feminist perspective, because it is considered the site of oppression for women, and marriage is regarded as the source of women's vulnerability. Both institutions are increasingly associated with violence, abuse, exploitation, injustice and betrayal of trust rather than being the locus of love, caring, intimacy, fairness and trust. The feminist critique calls for the serious attention and response of those who continue to support marriage as one of the most fulfilling human relationships, and the family as the ideal context in which the human person can best be nurtured through learning about love, caring, intimacy, fairness and trust.

The need to respond is particularly urgent in the Chinese society of Hong Kong, where there is a strong cultural imperative to value the family and family relationships, paralleled by an equally strong self-critical awareness in society to re-examine and re-evaluate traditional norms and values to avoid fossilization and blind conformity to traditions. Given the emphasis placed by Chinese Confucian moral tradition on filial piety, common good, social harmony, and personal virtues, social workers in the local context are often confronted by difficulties in trying to reconcile these deeply held cultural norms with the goals of promoting individuality and expanding the boundary of personal freedom, as well as promoting fairness and upholding equal respect and concern in their work with married couples or distressed families to facilitate growth and maturation. The dilemmas are both complex and challenging. How do we sustain a sense of individuality without undermining harmony? How do we support a sense of personal choice without eroding trust and connectedness? How do we uphold a sense of fairness without sacrificing intimacy?

At one level, each author in this volume is writing about his or her individual practice experience in helping clients to cope with the different problems which they are faced with in their respective life circumstances. In this sense, each essay is an individual narrative. At another level, they are writing collectively about some common themes highly pertinent to Hong Kong Chinese society as a whole, which is at the meeting point between the East and the West, and between the traditional and the post-modern, both in value orientations and social practices. In this sense, each entry forms an integral part of a collective voice as well as an ongoing dialogue that seeks to articulate and to address these common themes from diverse perspectives. They are driven by the common search for a plurality of resolution approaches, and joined by the shared objective to create new space to enable differences and individuality, trust and freedom, intimacy and harmony to be balanced and to flourish, even within the context of increasing pluralism and diversity in our basic human institutions. In many instances, as they draw on traditional Chinese culture and values for intellectual resources to underpin their practice, they simultaneously bestow new meanings on that culture and its values. Through reinterpretation and reinvention, they give better support to the life and aspirations of their clients.

Creative Tensions in Practice

Forgiveness in Marriage: Balancing Harmony and Fairness

As the author of this paper points out, Confucian teaching of benevolence as the cornerstone of a harmonious society provides the cultural root of "forgiveness" in marriage. But at the same time, it has been pointed out that "in maintaining harmony, the interpersonal boundary is blurred, and fairness is forsaken". This raises interesting and important questions: What should be the proper relation between maintaining harmony and upholding fairness in the family context? How should one prevent the loss of individuality if interpersonal boundaries are indeed blurred or even cease to exist within the context of intimate family relationships? Is forgiveness really incompatible with the pursuit of fairness in relationships? How do we respond to the feminist charge that forsaking the principle of fairness in family relationships will leave the oppression, exploitation and domination of women in the domestic sphere even more likely to go unnoticed and even less likely to be resisted or prevented? More important still, how do we respond to the larger feminist challenge that cultural traditions and values, including both the dominant Western as well as the Chinese Confucian moral tradition, are highly gendered and are an integral part of the patriarchal system which they also serve to justify?

These questions set the stage for a set of deep reflections on the nature and goals of social work interventions as well as the role of traditional values and cultures in shaping options, constraining choices and guiding intervention in our work with families and married couples.

Rediscovery of the Self for Divorced Chinese Women: Balancing Social Roles and Self-Identity

This paper acknowledges the devastating effects of divorce and its damage to the attendant sense of "self-identity" for Chinese women because of the traditional understanding of woman's identity largely through her roles as mother, daughter-in-law and wife. Hence, the loss of these social roles inevitably implies the loss of identity or a sense of selfhood for women. It lays stress on the reconstruction of identity in divorce intervention aimed at enabling the divorced women to discover that there is an "inner" self, an internal life, and a subjective consciousness which underpins the social roles they play and which supports a continuous sense of "personhood" within, notwithstanding changes in the social roles we play in the external world.

From such a perspective, practice intervention, although remaining critically aware of the cultural and social context of the divorced couples, did not abandon culture and tradition altogether as irrelevant or unhelpful considerations. Instead, it was able to draw on relevant cultural resources to empower the divorced women who participated in the workshop meetings. The workshop meetings, organized around a set of holistic health concepts borrowed from Chinese medicine, were able to help the participants to become liberated from oppressive traditional norms of patriarchy on Chinese women and to attain an appropriate sense of balance and harmony in their re-established self-identity as divorced women.

Long-Term After-effects of Childhood Sexual Abuse on Married Life: Balancing Individuality and Intimacy

This paper highlights the problems of (1) impairment of trust, (2) deficiencies in communication, (3) fear of intimacy, and (4) sexual dysfunction as some of the major after-effects of childhood sexual abuse on married life. The goal of practice intervention seeks to rebuild the sense of self of the survivors on the understanding that only when one is in possession of a strong and integrated sense of self will one be able to engage in trust, communication, intimacy and sex with another human being in a meaningful and fulfilling way. Intervention strategies are sharply focused on enabling survivors to break away from the downward spiral of self-negating, self-degrading and self-blaming kind of thinking and behaviours. Cultivating a new perspective is the first step in an empowering process to enable the survivors to see themselves as the victimized and oppressed rather than as the guilty and shameful. Facilitating the discovery of new strengths and potentials is the second step in the process to create distance between the oppressed self of the past and the more competent and mature self of the present. Supporting the construction of a different self-identity is the third step in the empowering process through engagement in activities that offer opportunities for realizing potentials and developing talents.

What is underscored is the need for constructing a strong self that can participate in relationships of trust and intimacy. In the absence of an established sense of individuality, there is no way to establish connectedness and bonding with other individuals in a deep and significant manner. In this sense, achieving a strong sense of individuality is a pre-condition to being able to engage in relationships of trust and intimacy. In other words, trust and intimacy require and support a strong sense of individuality rather than being a threat to or being incompatible with a strong sense of self. But for survivors of childhood sexual abuse, rebuilding a strong self-identity and re-engaging in relationships of intimacy are a real challenge.

Ambivalent Exit and Ambiguous Entry: Balancing Moral Norms and Social Practice

This paper points to the increasing vulnerability of marriage and family institutions in Hong Kong. It examines the experience of divorced men and their perceptions about their former spousal relationships. It acknowledges that there is an obvious gender difference in the home-

and family-building experience between males and females in our culture. "The Chinese male is socialized to achieve outside the home, with little emphasis on his role at home besides being the wage earner and disciplinarian. In marriage he encounters his wife as an expert with the emotional and practical aspects of creating a home, because the Chinese female is traditionally groomed to be the caregiver in the family". They are heavily dependent on women for building a family, looking after the children, and maintaining a nurturing home environment. This explains why, at the point of divorce, they have to surrender custody of their children to their ex-wives, despite their affective bond with the children and the cultural imperative to maintain family continuity. Their perceived fairness of the divorce settlement is another major factor in affecting their remarriage decision.

This paper underscores the theme that a strong sense of self is essential to the possibility of making any real commitment, on the part of both female and male partners, to fulfil the nurturing role in family relationships. A self that has developed largely on the basis of cultural stereotypes and that lacks the support of equal worth and respect from society will be a distorted self with impaired capacity for making deep commitments and shouldering caring relationships of a nurturing kind. It also echoes the point that a sense of fairness in distributional arrangements is related to the fulfillment or non-fulfillment of obligations and commitments within the Chinese family context. All in all, a sense of fairness and a sense of equal worth and respect appear to be essential to relationships in order for commitment to be sustained and for its nurturing role to be fulfilled. Building a strong sense of self in this case entails breaking away from cultural stereotypes and gendered social norms to uphold the moral norms of fairness and equal respect based upon a self-awareness of equal moral worth of oneself and of the other person.

Dilemma in Marital Infidelity: Balancing Relational Autonomy and Individualistic Autonomy

The issue of choice and responsibility as the basis of self-respect is highlighted in this paper on decision counselling in marital infidelity. The therapist recognized that there is, on the one hand, the need for being self-focused, for protecting secrecy, for creating personal space and for non-disclosure of "hidden decisions", and on the other, that there are different levels of the self which make up the personal identity of the client. A recognition of the psychological, relational and moral levels of the individual offers valuable insights into the multiple dimensions of the self, which constitute the deep structure of the individual's personhood and which go beyond the external social roles occupied by the individual self. Personal growth implies not only an emphasis on the internal life of the self beyond the social roles it assumes. It also has to have the capacity to move away from an individualistic ethos or an individualistic understanding of the self to incorporate a "relational" understanding of the self if genuine growth is to be achieved. The ultimate objective is to acquire a notion of "relational" autonomy to replace the notion of "individualistic" autonomy in the process of self-reconstruction during the marital review. The outcome is the emergence of a more robust and deeper self-identity, from which can emerge principled decisions to take into due account the requirement of balancing self-respect and fairness in complex relationships.

The Making of a Second Spring: Balancing Individuality and Connectedness

This paper explores how, instead of being held back by the negative stereotype that our culture brings, it was possible for remarried persons to experience a rebirth in a positive light in the new relationship. But they had first of all to resist negative cultural stereotypes that tend to reduce women to mere objects for exchange in the market, and divorced women as "worn shoes" with degraded value. The paper argues that "learning to respect the other as an individual" and "accepting individual differences" can lead to a more mature way of handling intimate relationships. It was further observed that, although it is true that the mandate to get married be given by one's parents no long applies in contemporary Hong Kong society, parental approval of one's marriage is still considered essential. The influence of one's extended family is very significant, even after one reaches adulthood. In-law relationships have a significant influence on one's marriage and family relationships. A continuous process of "self-evaluation and self-searching" is required to achieve the right balance between rejecting traditional stereotypes or breaking away completely from cultural norms, and preserving a sense of connectedness and maintaining continuity with the culture and extended family relations into which one is born. The process of marriage, divorce and remarriage, as pointed out by the author, can be seen as an opportunity for engaging in such kind of searching, yearning and growth in many creative ways.

Reaching the Point of No Return: Balancing Risk and Continuity

This paper explores and analyzes how and why Chinese women make divorce decisions. The experiences of the Chinese wives in this study indicate divorce to be a psychological process of disenchantment rather than a process of weighing cost and benefit. "When the reappraisal of the marriage resulted in a subjective sense of violation of core beliefs, values, life themes and self-identity, requiring a new reconstruction of the self and one's world view, these wives considered they had reached the threshold of the decision to divorce". The study shows that it was "a subjective sense of violation of core beliefs, values, principles, life themes and self-identity" which was experienced as so devastating that it motivated dissatisfied Chinese women to reach a decision to divorce in order to acquire a new reconstruction of self identity and world view. They were no longer willing to put up with a relationship that was not compatible with their personal values. Neither were they willing to compromise their principles or to tolerate violation of core beliefs for the sake of fulfilling traditional role obligations and preserving cultural norms into which they had been socialized. They were fully capable of making a critical review of their core values to make decisions for their future lives, even though these decisions might involve great risk-taking and much uncertainty. Thus, although in one sense the decision to divorce might seem to be irrational, in another sense it was a rational decision to opt out of the existing marital relationship in order to build a new self-identity for preserving one's core values and beliefs even in the face of risks and uncertainties. The courage to take risks and to face uncertainties, instead of accepting conformity, is in itself a sign of a "rational" self trying to take charge of its own life and to fulfill dearly held values. Here, professional intervention has to find space for the emerging identity to engage in risking-taking while at the same time preserving core values to ensure continuity. Balancing risk and continuity, change and conformity are essential to the creation of new lives, new consciousness, and new identities.

Discovering the Spouse's Other-ness: Balancing Separateness and Difference

This paper describes the use of joint families-of-origin explorations to help couples develop an awareness of their spouses as separate and different persons who have unique histories of their own. The objective is to help them to see that their spouses are human beings-in-process;

that is, that they have been evolving from a past, and are in the process of transforming into persons-to-be. When they accept that their spouses are different and separate persons with their own dreams and struggles, and that they do not exist solely for the purpose of satisfying their needs, they will be more able to acknowledge and respect the differences that exist between them. They may even use these differences to enrich their lives together. In the process of sharing their different families-of-origin experiences, couples will also have a chance to listen to each other's wishes, desires, dreams, disappointments, and struggles. Professional intervention is directed at enabling them to find a new sense of resonance around their common humanity, while respecting their separateness and difference. The process strives to maintain a delicate balance between sustaining individuality and sustaining interconnectedness, which can be mutually enriching and growth-oriented.

Gender Consideration in Couple Work: Reflections from Social Workers Involved in Marital Counselling: Balancing Differentiation and Integration

This paper raises the issue of culturally assigned self-images and gender differences, pointing out how they can block the individual growth and development of married couples by preventing a healthy balance between differentiation and integration in marital relationships. More often than not, married men still need to see themselves as primarily providers whose sphere of activity lies exclusively outside the boundary of the home. Married women need to see themselves as fully integrated into the family network, because it is their primary responsibility to ensure "the well-being and emotional climate in the home". The differentiation of separate spheres and the distinction between "internal" and "external" functions tend to result in distorted developments in the marital relationship, because there is often only differentiation but no integration. In the end, they reinforce vulnerability, create distance, generate anger and inflict hurt, instead of conferring validation, promoting intimacy, enhancing cohesion and offering enrichment for the personal identities of the couples. Eventually, the couple becomes "feared selves" to each other. They try to take shelter in avoidance and disengagement instead of showing willingness to work together to achieve better mutual understanding, acceptance or adjustment. The resulting anger and fear generate another cycle of distortion and stereotyped behaviour in the relationship. The paper reports on the effectiveness of focusing counselling strategies to dispel tendencies to re-create negative cultural stereotypes and to foster positive engagement in order to achieve a proper balance between differentiation and integration in marital relationships. But more important is the high vigilance demanded of the professionals themselves, so that such cultural stereotypes are not unreflectively reinforced in the professional encounters with the married couples.

Three Overarching Themes

Three overarching themes have emerged from these papers which demand our critical analysis and response: tension between *justice* and *benevolence*, tension between *fairness* and *forgiveness*, and tension between *autonomy* and *harmony*. Intimacy, forgiveness and harmony are virtues critical to achieving and sustaining fundamental human relationships of the most intimate nature: family relationships involving parent and child, and husband and wife relationships. Justice, fairness and autonomy are foundational values important to our self-understanding and self-identity as human beings. Achieving a proper balance among these values is critical to establishing a strong self-identity and leading a flourishing life.

In the remaining part of this paper, I want to argue that we can draw on the ethical teachings in classical Confucianism to provide the moral and intellectual resources for a reconstruction of these key value concepts. In particular, I draw on the ideas of Confucius (551–479 BCE), Mencius (385–304 BCE), and Xunzi (298–238 BCE), who represent the classical pre-Qin Confucian tradition. Such a reconstruction will enable us to enrich our repertoire of responses to address these tensions through bringing about a more self-critical approach to practice and a more self-reflective understanding of the limit and value of our traditional culture in providing the background horizon of meanings to our professional intervention with the lives of our clients.

Realizing our Human Potentials: Confucian Notions of Autonomy and Dignity

A popular contemporary understanding of autonomy in Western moral tradition is self-determination. Immanuel Kant (1959) and John Stuart Mill (1962) are often cited as the philosophical source for a justification of this notion of autonomy. Although the central idea in Kant's concept is the autonomy of the will, contemporary interpretations tend to focus more narrowly on the Kantian notion of self-legislation to justify the claim of autonomy as self-determination. Mill, in contrast, claims that individuals should be free to shape their lives in accordance with their own views in order to actualize their individuality within the limits of harming others or harming one's own ability to make free choices.

Such a concept of autonomy places a high premium on rationality. The assumption is that all human beings have the capacity to think rationally. It is this rational capacity that allows a human being to have superior power over the rest of the creatures in the world. It is the basis of our human dignity. To recognize the humanity of a person is to recognize his or her rationality and to promote his or her autonomy. Autonomy is in this sense a primary value that stands at the heart of our humanity.

Confucian philosophy offers a different understanding of human dignity and its implication for the value of autonomy. From the Confucian ethical perspective, human beings are distinguished from other species by their potential for moral virtues. Morality rather than rationality or self-determination is emphasized as the distinguishing characteristic of humanity. The source of human dignity lies in our potential for moral virtue and for developing our moral character. Thus, it is virtue that stands at the heart of our humanity. In addition to focusing on autonomous choice and external independence, Confucian moral philosophy places a high premium on the inner self and the moral life of the human person as the realization of human dignity and the achievement of full personhood.

According to Mencius' thesis of human nature, human beings are born with four seeds or four potentials of moral virtues: *ren, yi, li, zhi* (仁、義、禮、智). They are also the "four beginnings" or "four moral possibilities" (四端) of the virtues of benevolence, humaneness, righteousness, propriety, and wisdom (*Mencius* 2A: 6, 孟子公孫丑句上 第六). When fully developed, these four seeds become the mind of compassion, the mind of shame, the mind of modesty, and the mind of right and wrong. Of these four virtues, *ren* is the highest. These four seeds of virtue are as much real and as much part of humans as their four limbs. Human beings should try to cultivate and develop these potential virtues in their life in the same way as we should try to exercise and develop our four limbs. But it is only through self-cultivation and self-development that we can avoid the life of someone with disabilities, both in the physical sense and in the moral sense, to attain the good life in which these distinctive qualities of human virtues can flourish.

It is said in *the Analects* 7:23:

"Heaven is the author of the virtue that is in me."

子曰：「天生德於予」

(論語／述而篇第七)

And it is said in *Mencius* (3A: 1) that everyone has the potential to become a sage or virtuous person:

"Shun and the Sage Kings and I are of the same kind."

「舜，何人也？予，何人也？有為者亦若是。」

(孟子／滕文公章句上 第一)

These moral potentials, endowed by nature, constitute the source of human dignity. However, human efforts in self-cultivation are necessary to ensure realization of our innate potentials. Although we are born with these potentials, we have to make choices and be provided with the right conditions and environment to develop into virtuous persons. Becoming a person, realizing our full moral potentials and attaining sagehood ultimately depend upon the deliberating, choosing, willing and acting of individual agents. It is human effort that accounts for different human achievements, although we are all born with the same potential as Yao and Shun. Thus, although "By nature, humans are nearly alike, By practice, they become very different" 「子曰：性相近也，習相遠也。」 (*The Analects* 17:2, 論語陽貨篇第十七). But Mencius himself also emphasized that there can be different paths to becoming a sage, although the goal of *ren* as a cardinal virtue is the same for all alike (*Mencius* 6B: 6).

In this regard, the Confucian thesis of inner dignity and equal moral worth can offer an important moral resource to support counselling work directed at supporting victims and survivors of various kinds of offences to restore a sense of self-respect, to open up a new way of positive self-understanding and to discover a new perspective on internal strength which can be drawn upon for gradual self-transformation to achieve a new identity. On this understanding, the Confucian account of human nature can also offer a lot of space for developing the autonomy, freedom, and inner life of individual human persons, including women, to lead flourishing and much richer lives. Its important insight is to see self-development as an "open-ended, other-directed", and "self-responsible" process, one that the individual is both free and responsible to take charge of. The human agent in this view is not passive but active, not determined but self-responsible, not static but changing, and not narrowly self-interested but capable of having regard for others as well.

Relational Autonomy and Individualist Autonomy: Confucian Notion of Benevolence

The Confucian cardinal virtue of *ren* is often expressed as the obligation to care for others in the Chinese culture. Mencius characterizes *ren* as love (*Mencius* 4A: 4, 4B: 28, 7A: 45, 7A: 46, 7B: 1). For example: 子曰：「愛人」 (孟子顏淵篇第十二樊遲問仁). *Ren* as love starts from filial love and extends to all other people (*Mencius* 4A: 27, 7A: 15, 7A: 45). Rooted in the feeling of not being able to bear the suffering of others (*Mencius* 7B: 31), it provides a basis for altruistic behaviour to others. Confucius himself urged that a person practising *ren* should start with parents and siblings and then extend *ren* to other people. The family is the moral starting point of our self-cultivation, for the learning, practice, and experience of *ren* as a primary virtue. This explains why Confucius considers filial piety to be the root of *ren*. The goal is to extend our altruistic concern and regard gradually from those who are close to us to those who are unrelated and to all spheres of life eventually, including the non-human sphere. In this understanding, the Confucian self is always a relational self, which presupposes connectedness rather than separateness of persons as the essence of human existence.

But, instead of seeing self-identity as no more than the sum of social role performance or understanding self-development as the unreflective conformity to external norms and conventions, the Confucian thesis offers a vision of the self that is socially oriented but not socially constituted in its self-understanding (Roetz 2001). According to Mencius, human beings possess an inner dignity because of their capacity to follow morality. They are able to hold onto their principles and virtues without bending to power and authority, and without being corrupted when confronted by wealth or dire poverty.

Genuine self-development requires critical reflection on one's external conduct, and independent judgement to evaluate what is appropriate and inappropriate in accordance with the ideal of *ren*, instead of acting merely according to social norms or individual desires or preferences.

The Confucian self is therefore both autonomous and other-regarding in seeking self-fulfillment. This implies that, under the cardinal ideal of *ren*, the Confucian self is neither just concerned with narrow uncritical self-interest nor entirely under the dictate of social roles and conventions. The autonomy favoured by the Confucians is a kind of "relational" autonomy instead of "individualistic" autonomy (Tao 2003). The human dignity advocated by the Confucians is grounded in the development of the inner life and internal well-being rather than focused on external behaviours or role performance.

Such an understanding of human virtues and relational autonomy can lend support to "a recognition of the psychological, the relational and the moral levels of the individual" by offering valuable insights into the multiple dimensions of the self, which go beyond the external social roles occupied by the individual self. This will have special relevance for counsellors and social workers who are assisting in the reconstruction of identity in divorce intervention aimed at enabling divorced women to discover that there is an "inner" self, an internal life, and a subjective consciousness inside which underpins the social roles they play and which supports a continuous sense of "personhood" within, notwithstanding changes in the social roles they play in the external world. At the same time, it can provide women in general with more space to develop their self-identity and to expand the boundary of personal freedom. It can also be drawn upon to facilitate the personal growth of married couples to move away from an individualistic ethos to develop mutual caring and intimacy. It can provide a counterpoint to the dominant individualistic understanding of the self by emphasizing its relational insight to support the building of a more robust and deeper self-identity for our clients.

Balancing Differentiation and Integration: Confucian Notion of Harmony

Contrary to popular belief, Confucian emphasis on harmony is not opposed to individuality or autonomy. Harmony is an important value in the Confucian system because it is the celebration of individuality or difference. It is a state in which new forms are unfolded, new patterns are constructed and new things are created. Instead of signifying stagnation and changelessness, harmony as a state presupposes fluidity, difference, change and creativity. This explains why, in *The Analects*, Confucius himself emphasizes the important distinction between "harmony" and "conformity" in this way:

> "The moral person *ho* (harmonizes) but not *tung* (conforms);
> the mean person *tung* (conforms) but not *ho* (harmonizes)."
>
> (*The Analects* 13: 23)

> 子曰：「君子和而不同，小人同而不和。」
>
> (論語／子路篇第十三)

It is important to recognize that harmony in the Confucian understanding is not the same as homogenization or conformity.

Harmony is valued as an important imperative, not because it promotes uniformity or that it suppresses differences. Harmony or *ho* (和) is valued over homogeneity or *tung* (同):

> Harmony gives rise to new things. Homogeneity will lead to stagnation. To balance one thing by another is called harmony, which will lead to enrichment.
>
> (*Guo-yu*, chapter 16, "Zheng-yu")
>
> 夫和實生物同則不繼。以他平他謂之和故能長而物歸之
>
> (國語／卷十六《鄭語》)

It is very clear that, from the Confucian perspective, harmony or *ho* does not mean the suppression of individuality or the maintenance of a static state. Harmony or *ho* is to be pursued because it gives rise to new things, new patterns, new forms, and new possibilities. It suggests a state of balance between differentiation and integration. *Tung*, which suggests conformity or sameness, is to be rejected because it leads to stagnation.

In this understanding, professional intervention or counselling directed at creating harmony in the life and fundamental relationships of our clients is not to be equated with encouraging conformity, suppressing individuality, or promoting stagnation. Neither does it mean promoting self-negation, self-denial and self-subjugation. The goal of counselling should aim to support individuality, encourage creativity or promote diversity, to achieve harmony. Such harmony is an important source of mutual enrichment and an integral part of the good life sought by human beings.

The Confucian notion of harmony emphasizes the "balancing" but not the "suppression" of individuality, the "celebration" but not the "devaluation" of differences. It can provide a philosophical grounding for professional intervention to build a strong notion of the self in couples work to support greater autonomy and innovations in self-expression to realize strengths and talents.

Interconnectedness and Interdependency: Confucian Notions of Fairness and Reciprocity

Reciprocity, not equality, is the central principle that structures interaction and interpersonal relationships. Fairness requires the realization of reciprocity rather than equality of treatment in human relationships. The notion of reciprocity has many interpretations. One approach is to conceive of it as a give-and-take relationship emphasizing a simple tit-for-tat notion, referring to direct and exact return in kind. In the Confucian account, reciprocity is not conceived of as a kind of transaction like an exchange of gifts or goods. Neither is it to repay a debt or to fulfil contractual obligations necessary for maintaining membership in some mutually beneficial exchange scheme. What reciprocity in Confucian ethics prescribes is to return good for good.

Such a notion of reciprocity is expressed in the often-cited Chinese proverbs: "An earlier generation plants trees under which later generations find shelter and repose"「樹欲靜而風不止，子欲養兒親不在」 and "As you drink the water, think of the fountainhead from which the water sprouts"「飲水思源」. Moreover, Confucian reciprocity is a notion of generalized reciprocity, as the two proverbs exemplify. Adopting a Confucian notion of reciprocity can enable us to recognize our non-voluntary obligations: the obligations we acquire to both humans and non-humans in the course of our life, "but acquire without regard to our invitation, consent or acceptance". The major normative task for such a self is not to protect individual rights or to maximize individual preferences and desires but to maintain interdependence with others and with nature in a reciprocal relationship of harmony based on a respect for connectedness and difference. Reciprocity emphasizes mutual recognition and appreciation; it can support harmony and differentiation in human cooperation better than equality that tends to emphasize sameness. Reciprocity emphasizes interconnectedness and interdependency; it can sustain intimacy and trust better than equality that tends to focus on separateness and independence.

The Western ideal of justice in the sense of distributional equality or giving everyone his or her due (see, for example John Rawls, *A Theory of Justice* 1971) is absent in the Confucian moral tradition. The highest ideal is to become a person of *ren*. Humans are under a moral imperative to develop their potential to become a moral person and attain full humanity or *ren*. To be a person of *ren* requires that one can be benevolent to people in general, regardless of their relationship to oneself. Confucian *ren* or benevolence does not require that one should love all humans equally or similarly. The Confucian notion of justice is encompassed in the moral imperatives to develop benevolence to extend caring to all, to nurture reciprocity to achieve fairness for all, and to nourish harmony to sustain the individuality of all.

Restoration of Relationships: Forgiveness and the Golden Rule in Confucian Ethics

Another important aspect of the Confucian notion of reciprocity in human relations is the virtue of *shu* 恕, often translated as "forgiveness". It is expressed as the Golden Rule: "Do not do unto others what you do not want done unto you" 「己所不欲，勿施於人。」 (*The Analects* 12: 2, 論語顏淵篇十二). This is a general rule that applies to all. But what does it mean in practice? Does it imply not seeking any recompense or any apologies even though one has been made the victim of injury or wrongdoing by another party? Does it require returning the injury and the wrongdoing with benevolence and kindness? Or, does it mean simply waiving the right to revenge? How do we balance fairness with forgiveness to achieve reciprocity?

According to Bishop Joseph Butler's 1726 sermon, "On Forgiveness of Injuries", forgiveness is a moral virtue (a virtue of character) that is essentially a matter of the heart, the inner self ... It is the overcoming of vindictive passions, the passions of anger, resentment, and even hatred that are occasioned when one has been deeply wronged by another. In this sense, forgiveness can be seen as a healing virtue that brings with it great blessings — chief among them the capacity to free us from being consumed by our anger, the capacity to check our tendencies toward cruelty, and the capacity (in some cases) to open the door to the restoration of those relationships in our lives that are worthy of restoration. Because all of us will sometimes wrong the people who mean the most to us, there will be times when we will want to be forgiven by those whom we have wronged. For this reason, no rational person would desire to live in a world where forgiveness was not seen as a healing virtue. The important question is how are we to reap the blessings of forgiveness without sacrificing our self-respect and our respect for the moral order in the process?

The Confucian insight on this question is recorded in *The Analects* 14: 34, when someone asked Confucius: "What do you say concerning the principle that injury should be recompensed with kindness?" 「以德報怨，何如？」 Confucius' reply was: "Recompense injury with straightness, and recompense virtue with virtue" 子曰：「何以報德？，以直報怨，以德報德」 (論語憲問篇第十四). The insistence on straightness to recompense injury is regarded as necessary by Confucius for keeping up an element of *fairness* within the virtue of *shu* or *forgiveness*. It does not endorse self-denial or self-sacrifice but insists on upholding fairness for the injured self. In this sense, the Confucian notion of reciprocity lends support to the virtue of fairness by endorsing not only the return of good for good but also the return of "straightness" for "injury". At the same time, it can also support the virtue of forgiveness by establishing a reciprocal link with the other person as a human being like me, reminding us that there will be times when we will want to be forgiven by those whom we have wronged.

In counselling victims of wrongdoings, social work or counselling professionals are justified, from the Confucian perspective, to support their clients to seek recompense, to ask for apology, or even to withdraw kindness or caring in order to uphold fairness. But equally important are efforts to facilitate their clients' cultivation of the healing virtue of forgiveness as an integral part of a new identity, the internal strength for starting a new life.

Controversies over Confucian Teachings

It is true that Confucianism has meant many things over the centuries in China. Among other questions is its relevance in contemporary life. Some people say that it sacrificed individuals for the sake of families and was particularly oppressive to women.

Debate on Contemporary Relevance

The repudiation of Confucianism was at its most stringent towards the end of the nineteenth century, on exposure to Western liberal thinking, further intensified in the twentieth century with the influence of Marxist-Leninist thought. Confucian tradition was held responsible for the backwardness of the Chinese people and for obstructing modernization, serving as a justification for the major political movements of the twentieth century: in 1911, the May Fourth Movement, and the 1949 revolution through to the Cultural Revolution of the 1960s. However, in recent decades, the sheer dynamism and the economic expansion of East Asian economies such as Japan, South Korea, Taiwan, Hong Kong and Singapore with their Confucian heritage, has highlighted the fact that Confucianism together with nationalism has offered a modernizing force for economic growth, social stability, individual strivings, and collective endeavours (Rozman 1991).

In 1986, the International Forum on Chinese Cultural History in the People's Republic of China reported a "cultural fever", prompting a rethinking of Confucian traditional culture and the prospects it offers to provide the roots of industrial development with an Eastern orientation. It was suggested that Confucian thinking could serve as the foundation for modern needs such as patriotism, self-cultivation, and renovation of the family and management of society. It could counter Western self-centeredness with a humanistic tradition of mutual respect and affinity with the family and the state (Wong He, Dec. 1986). As we step into the twenty-first century, dramatic expansions of our technological capacities through newly available chemical and biological means have made us even more aware of the need to search for a new understanding of the relation between humankind and nature on the one hand, and between self and society on the other. The need to respond is becoming urgent.

Among the many different attempts to respond, in January 2004, an international conference was held in Beijing on bioethics, focusing on genetic engineering, cloning, and use of human subjects in research, genetic screening, and informed consent in medical practice. It brought together academics, medical doctors, consultants of WHO, scientists, philosophers, and social scientists. No fewer than ten of the papers engaged in discussions on Confucian ethics and its relevance to contemporary bioethical issues. More than half of the papers came from Mainland and Taiwanese Chinese scholars.

Historical trends show that, in the last century, the Confucian tradition has gone through periods of decline and revival, yet its persistence in affecting various spheres of living in Chinese societies reflects and confirms its amenability to reinterpretation and reconstruction.

Sacrificing the Individual for the Family

A possible starting point is the concept of filial piety or *xiao* (孝), which has been understood as the paragon of Chinese ethics. Max Weber calls it "the one basic social duty", "the absolutely primary virtue", which "in case of conflict preceded all other virtues" (1951, 57). It is often regarded as responsible for suppressing the self of the individual by advocating a "morality of submission" in Chinese society. It was greatly vilified by young intellectuals in the May Fourth Movement. They rebelled against the value of high regard for filial obligation, considering this as submerging the individual to the family, perfecting the self to better serve others. This was again graphically reactivated during the Cultural Revolution when "awakened" youth rebelled against the restraints of the family.

But it is actually possible to have a different understanding of filial piety or *xiao* based upon a more careful analysis of the concept as revealed in the classical texts of *The Analects*, *Mencius* and *Xunzi*. It is a far more complex concept than mere submission or deference to the old or to authority. It is true that both Confucius and Mencius emphasize the careful treatment of parents by respectful sons and daughters (*The Analects* 2: 7). But Mencius also made it very clear that filial obedience must be rooted in the self-respect of the individual: "I have never heard of anyone who, having lost his self was able to serve his parents" (*Mencius* 4A: 20). He therefore reminds us: "There are many duties one should discharge, but the fulfillment of one's duty towards one's parents is the most basic. There are many things one should watch over, but watching over one's character is the most basic" (*Mencius* 4A: 19).

> 孟子曰：「事，孰為大？事親為大；守，孰為大？守身為大，
> 不失其身而能事其親者，吾聞之事；失其身而能事其親者，吾
> 未之聞也 … 孰不為事？事親，事之本也；孰不為守？守身，
> 守之本也。」
>
> (孟子／離章句上第十九，廿)

Discharging filial obligation and obedience to parents are important duties, but so is the duty to watch over one's moral character. And, in the opening passage of the chapter on *Zi dao* in *Xunxi*, we are further reminded that there are three levels of human conduct that can be distinguished, and filial piety is the lowest of the three:

> To practice filial piety at home and respect the elder in public, this is the *minor* conduct of man. To be compliant towards one's superiors and exert one's energies towards one's subordinates, this is the *medium* conduct of man. To follow the *Dao* and not the ruler, to follow justice and not the father, this is the *great* conduct of man. (*Xunzi, Zidao,* Ch. 29)

> 「入孝出弟，人之小行也。上順下篤，人之中行也；從道不
> 從君，從義不從父，人之大行也。」
>
> (荀子／子道篇第二十九，廿)

What is clearly asserted is the superiority of virtue over authority. Xunzi further points out that disobeying parental order is in fact the morally right thing to do under three conditions: (1) when obeying will create danger instead of security to parent, (2) when obeying will bring disgrace rather than honour to parent, and (3) when obeying will imply animosity instead of embellishment to parent (*Xunzi, Zidao*, Ch. 29). Again, what is asserted is that role obligation should be suspended if this is necessary for upholding the *Dao* or more foundational moral ideals.

「孝子所不從命有三：從命則親危，不從命則親安，孝子不從命乃衷；從命則親辱，不從命則親榮，孝子不從命乃義；從命則禽獸，不從命則脩飾，孝子不從命乃敬。」

(*荀子／子道篇第二十九*)

In this sense, filial piety presupposes a strong moral character capable of constant self-vigilance to watch over one's inner life rather than a "characterless" person or a "selfless" individual who is only capable of submission and conformity. Contrary to common belief, Confucian filial piety requires a strong and autonomous self capable of maintaining self-respect, self-direction and self-improvement through reciprocal relationships with others under the moral ideal of *ren*. A reconstruction of the Confucian concept of filial piety is highly important for transcending the "self-other" dichotomy and for empowering the individual to assert himself or herself and to maintain self-respect.

Gender and Confucian Teachings

The place of women in the Confucian tradition has always been a subject of great controversy between those who hold the view that women are barred by the tradition from self-cultivation and those who argue that Confucius never considered women incapable of moral self-cultivation or that they are only capable of the caring virtues of model wife and mother. Surveys of early Confucian canon by contemporary scholars indicate that the original Confucian canon attributes to women the same moral and intellectual capacities, and makes caring a moral virtue for both men and women and the foundation of Confucian ethics of *ren* (see, for example, Li 1999, 115–38; Goldin 2000, 133–63; Raphals 2000, 223–48). Although gender segregation in the Confucian tradition started early in its long history, it is not obvious that the founders, Confucius and Mencius, had an oppressive attitude toward women. Importantly, also, in the Confucian moral tradition, *ren* is a non-gendered virtue, which is accessible to men and women, mothers and fathers, sons and daughters. Under the ideal of filial morality, both Confucius and Mencius accorded the mother equal status with the father in relation to children. They were not barred by Confucius and Mencius from participation in social and moral functions in society.

Even among scholars who are very critical of Confucianism there is agreement that evidence from *The Analects* through to the "Table of Ancient and Modern Persons" in the *Han History* shows that at least "in Warring States and Han narratives, women were represented as possessing the same virtues valued in men: moral integrity, intellectual judgement, the ability to admonish a superior, courage and chastity" (see, for example, Raphals 2000, 236). In the *Han History*, the "Table of Ancient and Modern Persons" includes women in the named designations of "Benevolent Persons" and "Wise Persons". It presents a nine-fold classification of 1,955 individuals from legendary times to the Qin Dynasty, classified under four named categories: "Sage Persons," "Benevolent Persons," "Wise Persons" and "Stupid (or morally slow) Persons (*Han Shu* 20). This evidence seems to show that gendered virtue ethics is not inherent in Chinese culture, nor are women portrayed as of necessarily inferior moral and intellectual status, incapable of becoming sages in Confucian ethics.

Without wanting to dismiss the connection between the gender system in China and Confucianism, what this essay attempts to argue is that the Confucian oppression of women is not a necessary implication of its general philosophy, and that women in Confucian China were able to participate in social and moral functions in society.

Granting in a general way that Chinese society was sexist, and accepting that we still have to confront the issue of the connection between the gender system and Confucianism, I am reminded in writing this essay of recent observations made by the historian, Patricia Erbrey (2000, xi): "clearly it is time to discard the exaggerated stereotypes generated by the rhetoric of the New Culture Movement" in China at the beginning of this century. Erbrey also points out that other historians over the years have produced increasing evidence that, in virtually every period of Chinese history, there were women who had enough leeway to create productive and meaningful lives. But she is certainly right in urging that the relationship between women's low status and Confucianism as the dominant social and political doctrine in China is in need of proper analysis and explanation.

It is also true that Confucian literature pleads for the social differentiation of gender. This doubtlessly left more than enough scope for patriarchalism. A reconstructed Confucian ethics, based upon a reinterpretation and expansion of its principles and values, can be useful for refuting traditional stereotypes of women and for supporting expansion and recognition of women's participation in social and moral functions as beings with equal moral worth and dignity in contemporary Chinese society.

All these discussions suggest that the evolution of feminism in China should not stop in our attempts to explore, analyze and evaluate what aspects of the Chinese culture can account for both the obstacles and the resources that lie in the way of Chinese women in their struggle to achieve and to be recognized in their achievements as moral persons. One way is to continue to examine the philosophical aspect of Confucianism and to assess whether conceptually Confucianism can find room to accommodate women's equality and autonomy.

Adopting a Reflective Stance

As participants of a culture, we all draw meaning from our culture, but at the same time, we also bestow and confer meanings on our culture. We all have to respond to the givens in our culture, but we are also free to reconstruct and reinvent the givens in our culture. A self-reflective approach can enable us to step outside the belief systems given by our culture to assume the critical stance of an impartial spectator, to question, adjust or reject these givens in our culture. Although we cannot question all our beliefs and principles at once, it is important to acknowledge that no belief is immune from criticism. If, however, we have examined our beliefs and found them satisfactory, there are good grounds for placing our confidence in them, and there are good reasons for putting them to use to give them shape and substance.

Acknowledgement

I wish to express appreciation to the City University of Hong Kong for funding the Research Project 7000133 "A Study of the Ethical Issues in Social Work Practice and Social Welfare Administration", which has provided the framework for philosophical reflection for this chapter.

References

Ebrey P. (2000). Foreword. In Li, Chenyang (Ed.) *The Sage and the second sex: Confucianism, ethics, and gender* (pp. ix–xiii). Chicago and La Salle, IL: Open Court.

Goldin P.R. (2000). The view of women in early Confucianism. In Li, Chenyang (Ed.) *The Sage and the second sex: Confucianism, ethics, and gender* (pp. 133–62). Chicago and La Salle, IL: Open Court.

Kant I. (1959). *Foundations of the metaphysics of morals* (L.W. Beck, Trans.) Indianapolis, IN: Bobbs-Merill.

Li Chenyang (1999). *The Tao encounters the West*. Albany, NY: State University of New York Press.

Mill J.S. (1962). *Utilitarianism, On liberty, Essay on Bentham. Together with selected writings of Jeremy Bentham and John Austin.* Edited with an introduction by Mary Warnock. London: Fontana.

Raphals L. (1998). *Sharing the light: Representations of women and virtue in early China.* Albany New York: State University of New York Press.

Rawls J. (1971). *A theory of justice.* Cambridge, MA: Harvard University Press.

Roetz H. (1993). *Confucian ethics of the Axial age: A reconstruction under the aspect of the breakthrough toward postconventional thinking.* Albany, NY: State University of New York Press.

Rozman G. (Ed) (1991). *Confucian heritage and its modern adaptation.* New Jersey: Princeton University Press.

Tao J. and Brennan A. (2003). Confucian and liberal ethics for public policy: Holistic or atomistic? *Journal of Social Philosophy,* 34 (4), 572–89.

Tao J. (1990). The Chinese moral ethos and the concept of individual rights. *Journal of Applied Philosophy,* 7 (2), 119–127.

Weber M. (1951). *The religion of China: Confucianism and Taoism.* (H.H. Gerth, Ed. & Trans.) New York: Free Press. (Original work published 1922).

Wong He (1986) Traditional culture and modernization. A review of the general situation of cultural studies in China in recent years. *Social Science in China,* Vol.7, No.4, 9–30.

Chinese Classics Cited

Ban Gu (1962). *Han shu.* Beijing: Zhonghus Shuju.

Confucius (1983). *The Analects.* (D.C. Lau, Trans.) Hong Kong: Chinese University Press.

Guo-yu (1937). [Conversations of the States] (a historical text) Shanghai: Shangwu yinshuguan, (a national history of eight states in the Spring and Autumn Period, allegedly written by Zuo Qiu-ming, who is also the alleged author of *Zho Chuan* or *Zuo's Commentary on the Spring and Autumn Annuals*), Chapter 16, "Zheng-yu".

Mencius (1984). *Mencius.* (D.C. Lau, Trans.) Hong Kong: Chinese University Press.

Xunzi (1999). *Xunzi.* (J. Knoblock, Trans.) Changsha: Hunan renmin chu ban she.

Index

and becoming free 109–10, 158–9
blocks to letting go 97
Life
journey reflection 72
life events 135
life theme violation 134
Living the good life 10, 256, 281

Marital
breakdown 131
crisis of infidelity 67, 71
withstanding crisis 232
distress zone 127, 132
enrichment programme 228–31
rebuilding 80–1
reconciliation factors that affect 90
relationship change after family-of-
origin exploration 38–40
relationship well-being 236
marital review 74–9
marital tensions contextual
background 77
Marriage
definition 243
discourse on marriage 10, 14, 257
in traditional Chinese society 192,
222
facets of desirable marriage 256–
7
merits of marriage 255–7
men's perceptions of marriage 178
Marriage laws
Marriage Reform Ordinance/Bill,
(1971) 1, 251
Matrimonial Causes Ordinance
(1972, 1996) 251, 253, 261–2
Marriage Law of the People's
Republic of China (1950) 1
Tsing Law 251, 261
Marriage models
companionship model 1, 222
contact and conventional marriage
models 258

Marriage values
alternatives, see Principles for
choosing alternatives to marriage
attitudes and values of the young
2, 252
change and adaptation 268
institution of marriage 253, 257,
260, 268
Meaning
construction and exploration 3
construction in dyadic interaction
121, 130,132
from culture 12–3, 289
of experiences for survivors of Child
sexual abuse 52–4
of life for Chinese women 144
new meaning of life 11, 154–5,
160, 164–5
and perception of hurt 96, 99,
113–4
of threats to relationship in divorce
121
reappraisal/reconstruction 128
of significant events 128–30, 132,
135, 137–8
socially constructed 13
Moral values 93
and virtues (Mencius) 277–8
Mutual
concern 230
help 165, see also Volunteering

Negative
behaviours 98
characterization of partner 130–1
stereotype of remarriage 193–4
negative labels suffering from
spouse's disloyalty and blame
82
Neutrality 232
No return
point of no return 127, 133
Normalization 157, 163